THE
BUNCH ATTACK

Using Compressed, Clustered Formations in the Passing Game

Andrew Coverdale
Dan Robinson

ISBN: 1-57167-044-0

Book Layout: Antonio J. Perez
Book Design: Andrea Garrett
Cover Design: Laura Griswold

Coaches Choice Books is an imprint of: Sagamore Publishing, Inc.
P.O. Box 647
Champaign, IL 61824-0647
(217) 359-5940
Fax: (217) 359-5975
Web Site: http//www.sagamorepub.com

DEDICATION

This book is dedicated to my wife, Elizabeth, who daily provides me with new inspiration to live; to my parents, Ed and Jessie, whose relentless generosity has allowed me to pursue my dreams; my sister, Betsy, the family's best athlete; and to my brother, Brad, my lifelong friend.

-A.C.

This book is dedicated to my wife, Delight, who during 23 years of being a coach's wife has, too often, had to be both a father and a mother at the same time, yet still fills my life with love; to my son, Scott, whom I have enjoyed coaching both in high school and college, and who has been able to express this offense on the field as no other quarterback; and to my daughter, Kelly, who has grown into a beautiful young woman right before my eyes.

-D.R.

ACKNOWLEDGMENTS

Football is more than any other thing, a game that belongs to the **players**, and **players** are what make us successful. We would like to acknowledge the long list of players we have had the good fortune to come in contact with in our programs. Their ingenuity, resourcefulness, creativity, and dedication have all been factors in our success. Clearly, we could have no success throwing the football without their collective talents. We would specifically like to acknowledge the superior quarterbacks and receivers we have worked with who gave life to the concepts expressed within this book.

While too many people have contributed, either directly or indirectly, to what has been assembled here to be fully credited, we would specifically like to acknowledge two men whose influence is evident throughout the book. Ed Zaunbrecher, now head coach at Northeast Louisiana, and Jerry Sullivan, receivers coach with the San Diego Chargers, assembled a pass offense at L.S.U. that was ahead of its time. Not only are their tactical ideas owed a great debt by this manual, but their understanding of and attention to technique and detail as well.

As our careers unfold, we become increasingly aware of the impact that the good coaches around us have on our professional development. The camaraderie of a football staff and the relationships built at camps, through recruiting, sharing ideas, and during college visits, as well as the mutual respect opponents share both on and off the field, all serve to help define us as coaches, and impact and motivate us in positive ways. The list of coaches who have had a positive impact on us would be incomplete without the mention of the men below. They all have helped influence our careers, shared long hours with us, seen the highs and lows that football can bring, and have contributed to our development in many ways. Without our contacts with these coaches, and others too numerous to be individually mentioned, this book would not have become a reality. We both gratefully acknowledge our relationships with these men.

A. J. Rickard (Harrison H.S.)
Rod Ballart (East Central H.S.)
Jim Plummer (Western H.S.)
Dick Dullaghan (Ben Davis H.S.)
J.R. Bishop (Wheaton College)
Tom Kurth (Elkhart Central H.S.)
Red Faught (Franklin College)
Larry Edmonson (L.S.U.)

Dick McKinnis (Harrison H.S.)
Steve Hurst (Kokomo Mustangs)
Terry Siddell (Southwood H.S.)
Scott Mannering (Cass H.S.)
Wayne Perry (Hanover College)
Mike Emendorfer (Hanover College)
Pete Peterson (Oberlin College)
teve Buckley (L.S.U.)

Northwestern High School Football Staff:

Dean Criss	John Schieffer
Brad Lytle	Bob Baszner
Chris Muhlenkamp	Andy Baker
Jay C. Breisch	Al Remaly
Mike Daily	Todd Reel
Greg Warner	Harold Canady
Mark Hollingsworth	Scott Mills
Paul Hamilton	David Laudensculager
Bryan Scott	Eric Mills
Mark Jones	

Taylor University Football Staff:

Steve Wilt	Bud Badger
Joe Romine	Eric Hehman
Ron Korfmacher	Dan Teeter
Kirk Talley	Doug Bonura

Noblesville High School Football Staff

Kevin Wright	V.A Atkins
Paul Schneider	David Hipes
Jeff Purichia	

FOREWORD

The "Bunch" package presented in this material introduces a fun and imaginative way to add a new look to your multiple formation look.

Coach Coverdale and Robinson have compiled one of the most complete outlines of this principle that I have seen. Its detail and comprehensive approach will be an excellent guide for you to use in implementing these concepts into your offense.

We have used the "Bunch" offense a great deal the last four years with the Minnesota Vikings and feel it is a viable part of our complete offensive package.

Whether you use multiple sets in your offensive scheme or are just looking for something new to add as a change up to your normal offensive scheme, you will find "The Bunch Attack" a valuable part of your coaching library.

Brian Billick
Offensive Coordinator
Minnesota Vikings

Football is a game of passed-down knowledge, with each new generation of coaches adding their own refinements even as they are indebted to men before them. We are all takers, plagiarists in a sense, at the same time trying to add our own innovations and adjustments to give our players a better chance in our own situations. As a result, much of the passing game currently used in football at all levels can be traced back to innovations of men like Bill Walsh and Joe Gibbs (and certainly these are two of the men who did true pioneering work in the area of the compressed split, "Bunch" offense that every team in the NFL uses now). These renowned gridiron coaches, whose ideas can be traced back to offensive masterminds such as Don Coryell and Sid Gillman, also drew upon the innovative theories of such early football pioneers as Clark Shaughnessy and Pop Ivy. The list of individuals who have had an impact and input into The Bunch Attack is almost endless.

Throughout this manual, we have endeavored to give credit where credit is due where specific plays and route combinations were used to illustrate our utilization of The Bunch Attack. Many of the other ideas not specifically cited were adaptations of things that we have seen other teams do successfully that we were subsequently able to package and fit within the overall scope of what we do offensively. As it turned out, we were pursuing some ideas and concepts related to The Bunch Attack concurrently with others in our profession. Nevertheless, we believe that we've been able to make some original, worthwhile contributions of our own along the way to The Bunch Attack.

The Bunch Attack and its relevance to you and your players
We are convinced through extensive study and experience that the ideas and specifics of teaching that you will find in this book constitute some of the soundest, most advanced football that can be found anywhere. Furthermore, this text represents a line of thought that is currently on the cutting edge of offensive football. However, we present them with the thought in mind that they are developed for the maximization of **players** and that without those **players**, the ideas would have no real life of their own. It is for that reason that we have tried to avoid some of the exaggerations and superlatives that litter some football books. Such books typically glorify the concepts rather than the people who make them work. Phrases like "unstoppable," "most explosive and powerful ever," and "too devastating to possibly defend against" are not found in the pages of this book.

On the other hand, if you are not looking for a quick fix or magic formula, but rather a tightly packaged, game-proven, teachable set of principles that you can naturally incorporate into what **you** do to improve **your** players, you have chosen a valuable resource. One of the key things to understand about the "Bunch" concept is that it is a *principle* as opposed to an entire offensive system. As a result, this book can be extremely useful to you, and specifically what you already do, regardless of your basic system and philosophy. The ideas in this book can be applied and taught to enhance the chances of players who are operating within most any fundamental offensive framework. Pro set, Wing-T, Run and Shoot, Single Back, Split-back Veer, "Ace" with two tight ends and two wide receivers, and Flexbone are among those offensive sets' general styles of attack that fit this bill. With this goal in mind, we introduce you to **The Bunch Attack.**

CONTENTS

CHAPTER 1

The "Bunch" Principle of Attack:
An Introduction

Ultimately, the objective of any offensive coach's work is to put his best athletes in positions and matchups that allow them to make positive things happen; being able to do this with the equal threat of run and pass obviously provides even greater chances of success. For many teams, establishing a consistent passing threat on a year-to-year basis poses problems, often because of deficiencies in ability or arm strength at the quarterback position, or limited speed and/or skill at wide receiver. A lack of balance can ensue which allows defenses to zero in on and thwart the running game. Sustaining drives in tough third down situations becomes difficult, as does coming from behind. Regardless of an individual coach's philosophy concerning the use of the forward pass, not having the ability to go to some sort of passing package with confidence and consistency at critical times will most often prove costly at some point during a season.

One concept that is increasingly becoming a part of the answer to some of these problems at all levels of football is the use of "Bunch," or "Cluster" type formations in the passing game. The idea of using severely tightened splits to create different types of problems for pass defenses began to take shape prominently in the offenses of the San Francisco 49ers and Washington Redskins during the 1980s, and has since grown in its use substantially. Currently, this type of Bunch attack is being employed on a wide scale in different forms throughout the NFL, and has steadily increased in influence at the collegiate and high school levels. Included among the teams that feature it the most are the 49ers, Detroit Lions, Minnesota Vikings, Pittsburgh Steelers, and Green Bay Packers professionally; Boston College, Southern California, and Wisconsin collegiately.

In our case, initially at the high school level, we found that the development of a Bunch package successfully addressed a lot of needs that we had: it equalized some of our voids in talent, enhanced the opportunities we had for our feature players, helped protection, gave us good answers in tough situations, caused real problems for defenses we faced, and most importantly, was easily incorporated into our system—as it could be most any system—with a minimal amount of new learning. The specifics of those and other benefits will be discussed and illustrated at length in the next chapter.

Defining "Bunch": Basic concept of expansion and compression of receiver splits

Fundamental to the passing game is the idea of varying receivers' splits to create better opportunities for specific routes. On a Slant or hooking pattern, for example, most teams widen the man running those routes to create a stretch of the defense horizontally and more operating room to the inside. Conversely, on out-breaking patterns, the split will be compressed to allow more room to the outside and shorten the throw and the amount of time the ball has to be in the air. A reduced split also provides the capacity to attack with routes across the field and to quickly assault the middle areas, where the weakest coverage people are often located. Diagrams 1-1 and 1-2 illustrate:

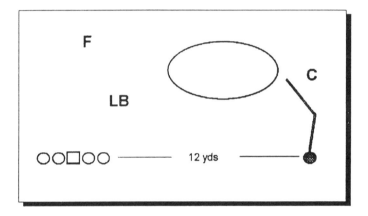

DIAGRAM 1-1
WIDENED SPLIT FOR AN INSIDE ROUTE

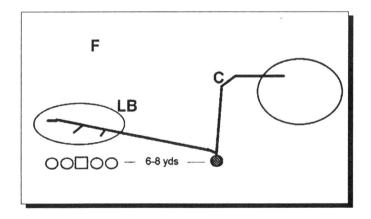

DIAGRAM 1-2
TIGHTENED SPLIT FOR AN OUTSIDE OR CROSSING ROUTE

"Bunch" then, in its most basic form, is just a continuation and extension of that principle. By compressing the splits of all receivers on a side, throws are shortened, opportunities are created with a lot of room outside, multiple people are in a position to attack the center of a pass defense or across the field, and in the process the additional benefits of natural picks and rub-offs are gained.

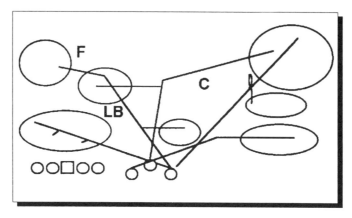

DIAGRAM 1-3
SOME FUNDAMENTAL ATTACK AREAS ACCESSIBLE WITH BUNCH

What does this book offer you?
Regardless of your basic offensive philosophy, you will likely find that "Bunch" principles can be incorporated in large or small measure into what you're doing right now, probably within the systematic and formational structure you already use, and they can help solve some specific problems that may hinder your offensive efficiency. Three of the misconceptions that we have encountered most in talking with other coaches are that Bunch is: a) a concept for only pass-happy coaches, b) only a specific trips formation used in one-back offenses, or c) something that is too elaborate and complicated for high schools to incorporate. None of these, in fact, are true!

Coaches who like to run the ball as a rule will find packages that can tie in nicely with their best run formations and can be employed using play action passes off their best run actions; they will also find that when teams try to shut down what they do best by putting eight or nine defenders close to the line of scrimmage and play man coverage, they'll have some solid possibilities to look at. On the other hand, if you would like to be able to throw more, but do not have consistently good athletes that can beat people outside one-on-one, or have trouble finding a capable thrower, there are elements within what will be discussed here that will provide you with some high percentage passes that are not difficult throws, and give you a chance to function by leveraging people open.

Those coaches who employ strictly two-back sets will see that because "Bunch" is a principle of attack rather than a specific formation, it can be employed just as effectively within the confines of the formations they already have.

Perhaps most importantly, the information offered here does not constitute a whole arena of difficult, new learning that would prove overwhelming at any level below college. Rather, it is a reapplication of routes that already exist within many offenses into a different environment that causes different kinds of problems for defenses, with new learning happening much more in terms of technique than assignments. Execution, then, can happen at an optimal level. Bunch, in our experience, has proven itself teachable and effective all the way down to the ninth grade level.

There are numerous other categories into which you may fall as a coach reading this book. Perhaps you are looking for ways to improve your success rate inside the opponents' 20 yard line, in the "Red Zone", or you may simply be interested in staying current with the "cutting edge" of offensive football, and in continuing to stay a step ahead of the defensive coaches you face. These are but two of many additional classifications of coaches who will profit in some way from the offerings of these pages.

CHAPTER 2

Theoretical Considerations: Understanding Bunch's Specific Benefits and Concerns

We have found through study and experience that the bunching of receivers provides us with many distinct benefits in various situations. The fact that we could point to these with such concrete specificity solidified our decision to use it on a larger scale within our offense.

Specific benefits and advantages associated with Bunch

1. By condensing the formation, space is created for receivers running outside routes. By squeezing people down, you can outrun people to a spot on deep throws, or shorten the throw and create running opportunities after the catch for short or intermediate throws. If you have one player who is a terrific athlete and playmaker, providing him with this kind of leverage to the outside is one of the best things you can do for him; give him field to run to and tell him to make a play.

2. Bunch formations in many of their forms create possibilities for instant, multiple, backside attack areas that are not available in normal spread sets (refer to diagram 1-3). This is beneficial in a number of ways. First, defensive structures that overload themselves to a formation's strength can easily be attacked where they are weakest. Secondly, active defenders who work hard to get underneath routes on their side usually open their hips that way, making it difficult for them to defend a route in their area coming from the other side. In this case, multiple receivers can get into his area. Thirdly, an offense instantly becomes harder to practice and defend against because the areas in which a defense can be attacked are diversified.

3. Taught properly, bunched sets can break man, and man under coverage, with different types of natural picks and bubbles for defenders to run through and around. Separation is the central key to having success against man coverages, and if your receiver is not superior athletically to the defender over him, he is not likely to get that separation unless some is created by design. Bunch brings with it numerous options that allow you to do that for all different types of throws, long, short, and intermediate. Diagrams 2-1 and 2-2 illustrate the difference in potential problems for a defender trying to cover a Flat route run from a standard set, and a Flat route run from a Bunch set.

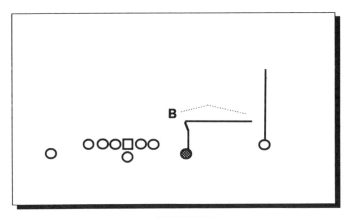

DIAGRAM 2-1
DEFENDER COVERING A FLAT ROUTE

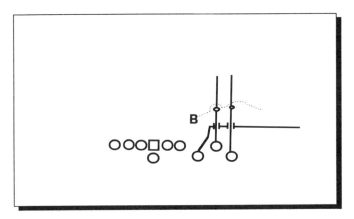

DIAGRAM 2-2
DEFENDER COVERING A FLAT ROUTE RUN FROM A NORMAL SET RUN FROM A BUNCHED SET

4.   Different types of problems are created for zones:
  •   Natural flood situations occur against teams which do not adjust to trips.

  •   "Trail" type routes create open "vacated zones." As you can imagine, much of the Bunch passing game relates to crossing receivers underneath; what often occurs, then, is underneath defenders looking for those routes and jumping them, leaving a late hole between where defenders have vacated. Diagram   2-3 illustrates a basic example of this.

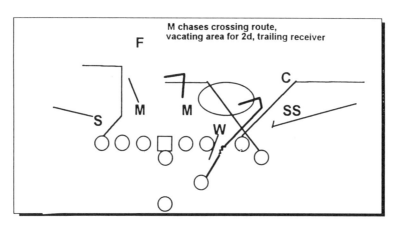

DIAGRAM 2-3
ILLUSTRATION OF A "TRAIL" CONCEPT ROUTE VS. ZONE DEFENSES

• It is harder for defenses who use pattern-read zone concepts to find receivers as they're dropping because so many things are happening in their immediate vicinity at once. As you'll see especially in the Mesh route, many of the routes and releases start out looking the same but branch off differently to attack different aspects of the defense. The thing that stops successful passing the most, whether against pattern-read defenses or not, is pattern recognition. The way we set up our route packages with tags and so forth, we systematically destroy pattern recognition and, in fact, use it against the defense. For that reason, Bunch is excellent against good, well-coached defenses, which is especially good because you're always looking to build your offense in a way that it can succeed against your best opponents. Because many of the throws are timed to spots in zones, full recognition and reaction in time to make a play is a more difficult prospect.

This idea of manipulating defensive recognition had a direct hand in the San Diego Chargers' divisional playoff win over the Miami Dolphins in 1995. Throughout the season, San Diego had experienced repeated success with a particular Bunch route in the Red Zone. With less than a minute to play, trailing by six, they had moved the ball to the Miami eight. The play they used gave every appearance of the route they had relied on during the year: same formation, motion, and backfield action. However, they changed the route of the motion man, bringing him through and across the formation instead of to the flat as they had previously, and he broke wide open for the winning touchdown. It was an excellent call at the perfect time, using the defense's preparation and programmed reaction against it.

- Frequently, zone defenders are coached to drop to spots on the field; Bunch formations change the whole frame of reference for the people who are dropping. Obviously their lateral footwork will not be as it normally is, among other things, and so we've changed the whole manner in which they're used to playing defense and reacting. Many of our adapted Bunch routes create width instantly, giving the offense a chance to hit a receiver outside immediately against defenders who are not prepared to get to that spot, either backing up or sitting and looking instead of working for width at the snap.

- Bunch naturally paves the way for additions to your offense that can attack overloaded defenses, such as: backside delay, swing, and frontside-to-backside crossing routes against teams which, either by alignment (e.g., 4-2 with the Will LB brought to the trips) or by drop, load up to the bunched trips.

5. It is an excellent answer for the blitz because it allows for seven man protection while lending itself to attacking blitz coverage naturally with rubs and timed throws off quick drops. It may even chase opponents out of blitz calls, because many defensive coordinators may not want to belly up man-to-man against a Bunch alignment.

6. Bunch naturally provides answers for several different types of difficult situational offense—some of these include Red Zone, Overtime, Two Point Play, 3d and 3, and 3d and 4-6. Appendix A is specifically devoted to this very thing.

7. A defense's best answer to a team with a strong running game and/or a team with no speed threat at wide receiver is to commit secondary people to fast run support and play man coverage. Bunch's natural picks are a way to gain separation and create throwing opportunities against these tactics even if you do not have a receiver with great speed. Being able to somehow break man coverage is crucial to keeping defenses from doing things such as bringing the free safety out of the middle to play eight and nine-man fronts. If you can get them out of such looks, your running game will function much better. In traditional offense, with average or less speed on the outside, this can be a real problem because you can't create the necessary separation; but if you can hit just one deep rub down the middle out of a bunch set vs. a blitz with no free safety, that may be enough to chase your opponent's defensive coordinator out of the types of fronts and blitzes that are smothering your running game.

8. Conversely, Bunch allows us to take a fast guy, a playmaker, and do two things for him: first, with our flexibility related to formations, we can create

about any matchup we want for him. With the exception of deeper routes, Bunch makes double teaming any one receiver effectively very difficult, especially on short outside routes. Secondly, the rubs, etc. give our playmaker an even greater advantage, even more separation, and an even better chance to make a big play.

9. Bunch creates short throws that are often right in front of the quarterback. Shallow crosses, Whips, Flats, and the like are routes that QBs with even the most limited tools can be schooled to see and complete with a high percentage. Hooking type patterns (e.g., a Deep Curl) oftentimes cause trouble for a below average quarterback because of the distance involved. Now such a pattern is much closer to him, often with a throwing lane that is clearer; you have the same good route concept and you've given your player a better chance to succeed.

10. Bunched formations allow an offense to attack the weakest pass defenders on the field. Many times, your wide receivers against another team's cornerbacks may not be great matchups because of athleticism. Tight ends and running backs, or even wideouts, working against linebackers and strong safeties underneath, however, gives you a much better chance. At lower levels especially, linebackers are schooled so hard in defending the run that they do not pass drop well at all. Bunch's natural attack areas exploit that (refer to Diagram 1-3).

11. It can aid the outside running game by shortening the edge around which you have to run and by creating crack angles. You can also utilize a full one back running game: zone, stretch, counter, trap, dive, speed option, toss, draws, etc., with any bunch formation. Again, if you have a burner in the backfield, you're creating leverage to outrun people to a spot, much like a Fade route in the passing game. Also, the attention given a trips bunch to one side by the defensive structure will often allow you terrific angles for a running game back the other way (Diagram 3-10).

12. Bunch is good to the wide field and the boundary, providing an attack for both. If you do a film study of the teams who successfully employ Bunch, you will see that the idea that you can't throw to multiple receivers into the boundary is a myth. Because you can Bunch into the boundary, it then becomes very difficult for teams to set their 3-deep coverage to the field. This in turn gives you some opportunities to a single receiver to the wide side away from the bunched trips. The free safety gets put in a jam as well, whether playing a Man Free type coverage 3-deep zone. Should he help over the top of a potential one-on-one mismatch to the wide field and neglect the trips side, or work the trips side and leave his corner singled? This quandary is depicted on the next page.

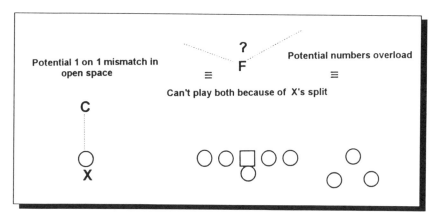

DIAGRAM 2-4
DILEMMA OF FREE SAFETY AGAINST A BUNCH INTO THE BOUNDARY

13. It creates an entirely unique problem for the defense that requires a special set of adjustments (especially from predominantly man coverage teams). It forces them to play adjustment defense (e.g., Banjos, Triangles, or other types of man adjustments in which defenders switch responsibilities based on the releases of receivers) with which their players may not be entirely comfortable or do well. This creates a greater likelihood of defensive breakdowns, unless a team is willing to spend an inordinate amount of time practicing against it, in which case they have lost valuable practice time against base offense. Having met with defensive coaches in meetings, it is obvious that nothing agitates them more than when they see something on film that is out of an offense's usual mode of operation for which they'll have to game plan, draw up cards, drill and do new teaching. Of course, we will also have built-in ways to handle the different types of adjustment defenses, the switches, robbers, disguises, and the like.

14. At the same time, we're not doing much new learning other than the technique details which will be discussed later. Bunch fits right in with our base offense and is, in fact, a natural extension of it. Because we were reapplying basic route structures and formations already in place, it did not entail a whole separate sphere of learning for our players. So we, in effect, painlessly added to our offense a potentially devastating dimension, for which any defense that plays us had better have answers, without diluting the overall focus of what we wanted to be doing.

15. Bunch provides an opportunity to dictate coverage and lock defenses in to the types of things you want to attack. For example, some defenses may check to purely zone coverages vs. a pre-snap Bunch look. You may have a quick route or a screen or a hooking pattern that you want to throw in a certain situation, but only against a zone because your matchups or the route structure isn't as

favorable against man. By lining up in a Bunch set, you'll get them into what you want. You can motion out, if need be, to get the set you need to run your play, because rarely will a defense check coverage twice.

Potential disadvantages and cautions

Part of being properly prepared to incorporate any new concept within an offense is understanding its potential weaknesses and problems that can occur and working toward minimizing them. While Bunch in our case was no burden to learning in the sense that basic route structures and responsibilities that players already knew were used, we were also fully aware of the fact that it brought with it the need for different technique and coaching points for it to be successful.

The area of technique we had to concern ourselves with the most was in the area of releases. Suffice it to say that if bunched receivers do not understand how to release, when to release, and perhaps most importantly what their purpose is within the route, you invite all sorts of problems by lining up people this close together. This part of the teaching is dealt with at length in Chapter 3.

The other concern you must address fully is the blitz. One of the first things most defensive coaches will do to thwart a new wrinkle in the passing game is to try and pressure it, as they should. It is important to build into your bunch teaching , as it is in any aspect of your pass offense, that your quarterback always has a quick developing route that he can get to if he feels immediate pressure, and that he knows right where that is. This is not a reference to a "hot" breakoff or adjustment system, but rather something that is built in to your basic route design.

Bunch on the whole should offer an exceptional answer for the blitz, because defenses who do blitz often have to commit themselves to man coverage, for which Bunch is tailor-made. The throws happen, most generally, in a quick, timely manner as well. The specific teaching against the blitz, though, is vital. One key thing is that you abolish the fear and bail out mentality players tend to have against the blitz; we sell our kids on the fact that blitzes are our opportunity to get big plays by being smart. We tell them to "recognize it, attack it, and defeat it."

CHAPTER 3

Bunch's Guiding Principles, Package Basics, and General Attack Concepts

Flexibility/Simplicity

These are buzz words you always hear in offensive and defensive clinic talks, but they are really applicable to the Bunch as we've organized it. We use flexible route packages already built into the offense. Many of our best Bunch routes come from our basic three step drop patterns. This flexibility is particularly valuable in the case of Bunch because defensive reactions to it are so unpredictable from week to week. A flexible, teachable structure allows you to make minor adjustments, with which your players are already familiar, to defeat those different reactions, rather than forcing them to deal with major overhauls or something completely new.

Give it different looks—Dress it up

If Bunch is going to be a substantial element of an offense, it needs to be dressed up with different alignments and motion to it and out of it. Why?

- If you have a feature player, this flexibility will allow him to line up in different spots to get him in the matchup running the route you want.
- Different types of motions can create leverage on man defenders for different types of routes and help beat the jam, which becomes a major key to success within a Bunch package.
- Motions complicate defensive recognition. For defenses with special game plan adjustments to Bunch, it gives them less time to get into those calls, if they get into them at all. If you line up to and then motion out of Bunch, you can create another problem altogether and certainly keep them from zeroing in on your approach. Again, all this is just window dressing. You as an offensive coach are still running your best basic plays.
- The fact that Bunch principles are applicable to so many different types of looks makes it something that can be incorporated as a portion, great or small, into most types of offensive structures. A Wing-T team, for example, will find that their basic Wing formation with the backs set Strong creates a form of Bunch. Two back, pro set offenses can do the same by placing a near back strong and bringing the Flanker in short motion.

Being very multiple in attacking defenses is a principle central to our whole offense, not just with Bunch. Our system of calling formations, as you will see in the next chapter, makes it very easy to move people wherever we want without being com-

plicated or excessively wordy. We have had the successful experience, at levels as low as 9th grade and Junior Varsity, of using 20-30 different sets a game, and have had very few problems. The entire system makes perfect sense to the players in a short amount of time. This system allows us to continually change formations, all the while using basic runs and quick passes applicable to all of them, until we find a concept to which the defense does not adjust soundly. It also puts defenders in a situation in which they never really get totally comfortable throughout a game. In other words, they're constantly having to concern themselves with lining up correctly, coverage checks, changing run support assignments, motion adjustments, everything except just lining up and reacting and playing aggressive defense. This keeps us on the offensive, because we're executing things that we're as confident and well rehearsed in as a standard I formation team is with an isolation play. The difference is that we're often doing so with exceptional leverage on the defensive structure, giving our athletes a great chance to make plays, because of the formations. This system is detailed in full in Chapter 4.*

Again, the NFL, and specifically a recent playoff game, provide a good illustration to draw upon. Trailing by four late, the offensive team used a sequence of 2-3 good solid Bunch routes consecutively deep in their opponent's territory, but they ran out of the exact same look each time. They had people open the first two times, but by the third play, the defense was comfortable in their adjustment and reacting aggressively to what was happening; they were able to instantly assess the set in front of them and understand how they could be attacked because the offense didn't change sets. As a result, the defense was able to effectively attack what the offense was trying to do.

Protection
In installing the passing game, we have always been PROTECTION FIRST coaches. Before we look seriously at implementing any new passing concept, we are asking, "How will we protect this?" This is the area in which we must be sound to function.

With Bunch, we almost exclusively rely on the same protections and checks we use throughout the rest of our offense: basic 90/190 quick set protection, and 50/150 cup/slide protection. We can also use 80/180 or 70/170, a reach and hinge, half-roll or sprint-out protection, to shorten the distance of the throw for certain routes. The specific concepts of how these protections are applied are discussed further in Chapter 5.

One of the particularly appealing benefits of Bunch is that the things you can do from it serve to help the protection aspect of your pass offense, in a number of different ways:

- The quick, timed nature of many of our throws from Bunch means that we don't have to protect as long. It also means that stunts and games are less effective because the ball is in the air before they can develop fully.

Even when we have a complete breakdown and/or the defense is unsound and blitzes to the extent that they leave a receiver uncovered, some of our routes can bail us out. Routes like Flats and Shallow Crosses can be completed before even a free rusher gets to the passer. It's like having a built-in hot system without having to teach sight adjustment and everything else.

In fact, within most any of our basic route structures, we will have one receiver with a short route designated as the "Q" receiver. It is not a hot breakoff, but rather the normal route within the package, except that he knows to look for the ball quickly out of his break. The quarterback has been taught this, too, and through his training he knows exactly where he can get the ball quickly if he gets any kind of immediate heat, from a blitz or otherwise. This element of the offense cuts down dramatically on sacks.

Important to all of this, though, is having instilled the overall discipline that any pass offense has to have to be successful. The elements of this include things like the offensive line communicating and protecting the middle first, receivers getting off the ball, escaping, and running consistent routes, the quarterback stepping up, feeling and/or ducking the rush when he needs to, seeing and throwing to uncovered receivers, with the footwork that enables him to deliver the ball quickly, and your whole offensive team using their time between the break of the huddle and the snap of the ball to see what's happening in front of them and know how they're going to attack. If you drill these things specifically throughout your passing game, you'll establish a foundation that allows the advantages Bunch provides on paper to come to life on game day.

- Contrary to conventional football wisdom, we are of the persuasion that our four receiver sets are an *asset* to pass protection; they limit the fronts the defense can use and define where blitzers can come from because, quite simply, at least four of their guys have to line up on our four guys to cover them.

From the early days of our summer practice, our QB is trained to look for the free safety coming out of the middle to cover man-to-man or blitz; when it happens, he knows that they can bring one more than we can block, so he systematically brings a receiver in to block the extra man. This is a constant throughout our offense that doesn't change in Bunch. A defense that does this against Bunch, however, could find itself in a lot of trouble. We can bring in our backside receiver, have a max protection, while maintaining a 3 man Bunch to our frontside working against man defenders. Now the defense has no deep help in the middle and is counting on getting to our passer, having no numerical advantage, while we're throwing off a quick drop to receivers quickly breaking free off multiple picks. If we have so much as one personnel mismatch, and many times even if we don't, we can make the defense pay a severe price for that formula. An example might look like this:

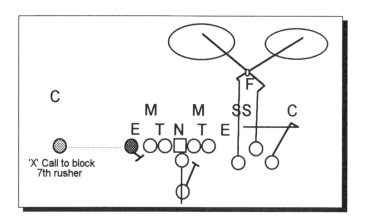

DIAGRAM 3-1
"SQUEEZE REX 6, 56 SWITCH" VS. A FULL BLITZ

It is harder for a Man defense to disguise, jump around and fake blitzes against Bunch, because a defender getting caught out of position has an even more difficult time than normal fighting through the rubs to cover his man. This is especially true with Man coverages employing special techniques—like a Banjo. They have to recognize what we're in, make their check, and immediately get where they have to be. If you add shifts, formations and motion problems to this, it becomes even harder for defenses to get adjusted.

- While you certainly won't deter a defensive coach whose basic philosophy and personality is to blitz, you may get much less blitzing from a team which only dabbles in the blitz, because they may be reluctant to get locked into Man coverage against Bunch.

Better yet, if you're playing a team who really likes to blitz, but checks to some vanilla form of zone when they see Bunch, you've taken them out of what they like to do. Once again, you're dictating.

One other special thing we have the capability of doing is to free release the fullback (who would normally be involved in protection) to get another receiver either frontside or backside in some form. We don't want a defense to ever be able to discount any of our five receivers as a potential threat. If we do this, he'll have a quick route which automatically becomes hot if his linebacker comes; more often than not, however, it will be used in situations where a zone with a four man rush is pretty certain and we can use him to create extra problems for zones. One example of this which you'll see in the diagram pages is motioning the Fullback to the Bunch side 8-12 yards outside the 3 receivers to create an extreme horizontal stretch and frustrate whatever special calls they're in (also a tremendous concept against Cover 2 Man). The motion allows us to see whether they're in man or zone, as well as whether we're going to have to throw hot to him.

Basic alignment rules and release mechanics
In a pure bunched trips alignment, we generally want the inside most receiver four yards outside the tackle on that side, with other receivers spaced one yard further outside each player inside. We can vary this if need be based on opponent, because we do want to make sure the formation is broken off enough to prevent widened ends from taking shots at our inside receiver on the way to his rush and disrupting the route's timing.

It is also often preferable to designate the middle receiver as the one on the ball, because often he's the one being used to release first and either clear out or rub for one of the other receivers who is off the ball. He is the player that we can most afford to get jammed, if anyone does, because often our primary receiver releases underneath that middle man, getting the ball quickly off the rub, and so a hard jam actually works to the defense's disadvantage.

A logical concern regarding Bunch, especially at the high school level, is the prospect of your receivers all banging in to each other, not getting away cleanly, and creating a confused, jumbled mess in a compressed area with no one left to throw to. For this reason, when you're installing and working routes in a Bunch environment, you want to be talking to your receivers about their purpose related to the route they're running, because that will dictate certain things they can do to help them function properly within the route. This is a good teaching principle for any pass, especially ones with crossing receivers, but becomes vital where Bunch passing is concerned. For example, quite often you'll have a receiver running a form of a clear out that can also serve as a deep man-beater if you get the right matchup, and the other two receivers have some sort of rub in relation to each other; one is designated "high," and the other "low." The receiver who is the clear-out/deep guy knows that he wants to get off the ball and into the pattern as quickly and cleanly as he can. If he's not aligned on the ball for some reason, he wants to align as close to the LOS as he can with out being on, and he'll come off the ball fast with a plan for escape if he sees a jam looming. The receiver with the "high" part of the rub knows that he wants to be, effectively, the second guy into the pattern, so if he's off the ball, he can release fairly hard underneath the man that's clearing and still get out cleanly; if he's on, he'll push up one step but then hesitate to allow the clear out man to get out ahead of him, whereupon he'll get into the pattern with acceleration underneath him. Often, as part of the assignment of being the High man, he has to look up the man covering the low man and release straight at him, mirroring him until he passes by underneath. If a receiver is the low man in a rub, he knows two things: first, he doesn't have to align especially close to the line of scrimmage, though he doesn't want to telegraph his intentions, and secondly, he knows that he should not be in any big hurry upfield; he's looking to let people clear and come off the line of scrimmage ahead of him (whether we actually have any receivers designated "low rub" man or not. In almost any Bunch route we have, one receiver or another will always operate this way off the ball, slowly and behind the others). He gets any upfield push (to keep defenders from squatting) from good, fundamental route technique—exaggerated arm drive, phony acceleration, weight over his toes, smooth stride, and eye contact—not with speed or initial acceleration.

Understanding and executing their purpose and role as well as their actual assignment naturally keeps receivers out of each other's way and helps your quarterback by developing the reads in a sequence which allows him to see where the holes happen and hit routes on time.

Important coaching point: Teaching the mechanics of rubs and picks

You can bet that as soon as you get into some of these looks and run Bunch routes in close proximity of each other, you'll have some maniacal defensive coordinator on the opposing sideline screaming to the official for offensive pass interference. Therefore, it is very important that you teach the mechanics of your rubs very meticulously. It may also be important that you tell the officials in your pre-game meeting that you have this in your offense and note the specifics of your legal technique. Interpretations and crew quality vary wildly at the high school level, and such a preemptive strike may be just what you need.

As you'll note by the language used throughout this book (e.g., "natural" picks), we start with the premise that by alignment and us rubbing close to each other much of the time, that a lot of positive things will spontaneously happen without us trying to force anything. A lot of times if you tell a high school receiver to go out and "pick" for someone, you'll get him zeroed in on a defender, pulling his arms in like a lineman, and decking some guy. This is exactly what you have to avoid, what you have to coach against, because as soon as an official sees your receiver's arms pulled in and him slowing to initiate contact, you'll get a flag for certain. We're constantly emphasizing that our receivers eyes stay upfield, and their arms drive through everything, including collisions if they happen.

With our basic premise, we start out by just running our routes and making certain receivers are executing their basic role and timing and technique correctly; part of this starts with running routes on air. We'll also start to correct errors like the ones just mentioned.

Only with that foundation laid will we begin to refine our techniques and angles to where we do a more efficient job of bottling defenders up and inducing them into collisions. They first have to be able to do the basic things as a habit before we can take the next step. Certainly some elements of this next phase will include things like releasing at the near shoulder of a defender over a receiver for whom we're picking, mirroring his lateral movements, and weaving right through him. Another technique would be using the middle receiver, on the ball, to engage a tight defender over him, working straight upfield; the next receiver inside or outside for whom we're picking will release right underneath him, and his defender will find a two-man collision that he has to run through or around. By the time he negotiates this, the ball is gone.

Installing flexibility through your teaching: Numbered receivers

We teach route assignments by numbering receivers related to the formation, not with rigid, specific assignments for specific positions. Generally, receivers are numbered from the outside in on either side of the ball (Diagram 3-2). Occasionally, they are numbered all the way across the formation, with #1 being the outside most receiver on the designated frontside (Diagram 3-3).

So, for example, when beginning to teach our "Mesh" route, we say that frontside #1 has a Whip Read, and is the high mesher, #2 has a Smash and is the clearing receiver, #3 runs a Flat and is the low mesh man and designated 'Q' receiver, and #1 backside runs a Post. As players learn this, we can plug any athlete into any position within a formation to get the guy we want running the route we think we can get from all kinds of different looks.

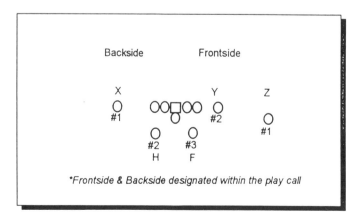

DIAGRAM 3-2
BASIC METHOD OF NUMBERING RECEIVERS

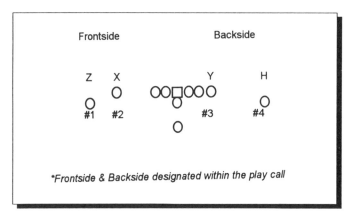

DIAGRAM 3-3
ALTERNATIVE METHOD OF NUMBERING RECEIVERS

Again using the Mesh as an example, let us say that your best receiver is your flanker, or "Z." One team you play might, because of the way they play zone defense, be vulnerable to the Whip Read portion of the Mesh route, so when you run it that week, you'll do it out of formations where your best player, Z, is the #1 (outside) receiver. Your next opponent might play Man coverage, and you know you can beat their strong safety deep on the Smash route. Because all your players have learned the whole structure from day one, you have no problem employing the Mesh out of sets where Z is #2 that week, running the Smash, and you have given your passing game its best chance of success.

We always say this in teaching: "It's not important <u>who</u> you are, but <u>where</u> you are." The formation section in Chapter 4 shows the receivers as they are numbered.

Highlighted routes used in attacking defenses
There are numerous individual cuts that can be and are employed within the Bunch concept, but because of the advantages implicit within them, there are six specific ones that are highlighted and utilized the most in attacking defenses. Each of these is a good, solid route in normal, spread sets, that has a chance for success against most any type of coverage we can see; using them with compressed splits and in bunched up sets enhances the strengths of each, which are illustrated and introduced below. In assaulting different types of defenses, these routes form a good nucleus from which to work. In fact, a high percentage of what we want to do from Bunch revolves around creating positive situations for one or more of these individual cuts.

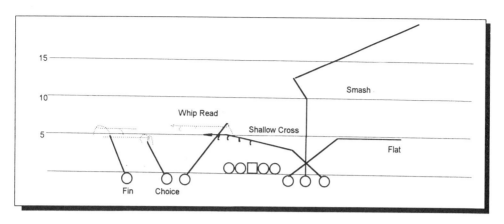

DIAGRAM 3-4
BASIC ILLUSTRATION OF FAVORED INDIVIDUAL BUNCH ROUTES

Smash. Terminology, of course, varies, but to us, "Smash" refers to a form of a "Corner" route by an inside receiver, with fine technique adjustments against different coverages. From normal sets, this route is generally completed at a higher percentage than other deep outside throws such as the Streak and the regular Post Corner simply because the added room to throw it allows the quarterback a larger margin of error and the receiver a greater chance to gain separation without running into the sideline. Man defenders, who largely play with some sort of inside leverage, have a difficult time getting their hips turned and accelerating over the top of the ball to make a play, especially since the additional room allows the quarterback to flatten the receiver directly away from him with his throw. Two deep safeties also have a difficult time getting the right angle over the top of a well-run Smash route, unless they run for width so fast that they make themselves vulnerable to the Seam route inside of them.

For these same reasons, it becomes even more potent when the receiver running it reduces his split even further into a Bunch set. Man defenders now have the additional problem of a potential rub to run around, as well as more space into which the receiver can accelerate away from him. Hash safeties have an even more difficult time defending it properly, again because the normal angles of drop and break that they have practiced do not hold up. Smash, then, will become a key way within a number of route packages to use the space Bunch has created, and generate higher percentage deep throw opportunities.

A detailed technique breakdown for this route can be found in the chapter on the "MESH" route, and other utilizations of are shown in the chapters on "Smash" and "FLOOD."

Shallow Cross. The Shallow Cross, both frontside and backside, is an integral part of our Bunch offense vs. both Man and Zone. There are several aspects of it that make it one of football's best routes:

- The Shallow Cross is very difficult for man coverage to defend tightly; separation is gained very quickly, and there is no break to slow the receiver down. He simply continues accelerating away, maintaining separation. It is particularly lethal against loose man coverage, where a defender may find himself running around numerous people to try and get a break on the ball, which is almost impossible to do in time.
- Properly taught, it gives receivers the flexibility to find holes anywhere along the plane of a zone defense, exposing any hole the defense may give you. This becomes vital at the high school level, because linebacker coverage can be so unpredictable. Instead of this defensive unpredictability being a disadvantage that scares you into staying away from the underneath passing game, a flexible system that coaches good non-verbal communication between quarterback and receiver can give the offense the distinct advantage.
- It is one of the easiest throws a quarterback could ever have to make.
- When underneath defenders work for depth, it becomes an especially potent weapon, because the receiver can get the ball quickly, while defenders are still backing up, and have a good opportunity to split defenders and make yards after the catch.
- Lastly, it can be used as an outlet option, giving the Shallow Cross the responsibility to get open in a hole and face the quarterback. It is a safe and efficient secondary route and a great drive sustainer because frequently defensive reaction to your primary route(s) leave it wide open, and, because the onus is placed on the receiver to get open between people, it is a throw that the QB can quickly get back to and easily throw because he knows he can throw it when he sees the receiver facing him.

The chapters on the CROSS and MESH route packages provide good examples of this principle being implemented.

Option-type Routes: Fin, Choice, Whip Read. Again, because of the unpredictability of defensive reactions to Bunch, Option-style routes that give flexibility to the receiver in finding openings prove valuable. They work especially well when the Option route is put in motion, allowing him to size up coverage as he moves, and also creating a good chance for man coverage to get picked off in the wash. Especially in a bunched environment, we try not to overcoach this to provide as much flexibility as possible, and to let athletes be athletes. The initial teaching may be as general as, "feel the defense, find an open spot, and face the quarterback, accelerate away if you're being chased", and then we'll begin to refine it against different coverages. This further helps us account for the variance and unpredicability of defensive reactions.

"MESH", " HINGE", "SMASH", and the "VERTICAL SWITCH" route packages all contain uses of these routes.

Flat. The Flat route provides an opportunity to strike quickly with a high-percentage route that can beat the blitz and get a good athlete running into open space with the football. Bunch's structure naturally lends itself to opening this route up off different types of rubs; it becomes the route that the defense must take away first. If they do that, the Flat then becomes the route that sets the table for others to get free behind it.

Specific examples of the Flat's use within the Bunch principle can be found in the "SLANT", "FADE"," MESH", and "FLOOD" route packages.

Multiple release combinations

One thing that we feel is very important to getting the maximum out of the plays we use in Bunch is to use different combinations of initial releases by the three bunched receivers. With practice, defenders can become fairly comfortable and adept at defending one or two types of releases, even in the tight confines of a compressed formation. For example, if the only release you use is to run #2 vertical and cross #1 and #3, defenses get a feel for locking those routes up and getting leverage, jamming, etc. But if, within a game or from week to week, they cannot with confidence know that an inside release by #1 will be followed by an outside release by #3, or that #2 will always release vertically, or whatever the case may be, Bunch becomes harder to practice against and feel confident defending. If you closely examine the basic packages we feature in later chapters, you will see that a wide variety of release combinations is used by #1, #2, and #3. We have instances where all three receivers in a Bunch release inside; we have instances where they all release outside, as well as just about every combination in between. In some cases we will use a "stacked release" concept, where our goal is to initially release them into the pattern with the appearance of one being behind another. Creating this uncertainty is an important idea within our attack, because the slightest moment of hesitation on a defender's part can enhance an already sound route concept immeasurably; it can turn what would have been a five yard catch into a five yard catch and a twenty yard run.

Attacking zones

Employing zone coverage would seem to negate some of Bunch's leverage offensively, but it is interesting to note that its expanded use in the NFL in the past two to three years has come about when offensive coordinators knew that they would see purely zone against it. There are reasons for this, many of which were outlined earlier. There are a few important common denominators to success against zones that have stayed constant as we've studied film of different teams running Bunch:

- Timing. Often the last receiver to release will be the zone beater. He's in no hurry at all, because he's seeing coverage develop in front of him, and he's seeing zone defenders turn their hips and commit to players that got into the pattern sooner. Natural voids develop that are easy to get into, and the quarterback sees it at the same time and gives the ball to the receiver well before the defenses can react. This is the thing that has made Bunch a real go-to package on 3rd and 4-6 situations, as well as a natural counter to the increasing amount of zone principles inside the 20. Conversely, this is the technique aspect lacking among teams who have had limited success with Bunch because they've just pasted it onto their offense without fully understanding and teaching it (note, for example, among NFL teams, the wide spectrum of success ratio among the 15 or so teams who employ Bunch; it's not all a result of defenses adjusting).

- Sit-down points. As was discussed in the section on the Shallow Cross and Option-type routes, teaching your receivers to feel where the dead spots are in zone coverages and throttle down in those voids, and training the quarterback to see those holes develop and throw to them on time are vital elements of defeating zones regardless of the formation. When you're operating out of Bunch and dealing with underneath defenders about whose reaction you may not totally be sure (because of the differences in talent, defensive concepts, and the fact that you've forced their people into a different coverage environment), it is important to know that your players have this flexibility and discipline to sit in the open spots as they find them. Obviously you want your route design to create and anticipate those holes as well. The timing of the releases and route development, as well as receivers understanding and carrying out their normal purpose is a major part of this.

  Another big part of it is the fact that we're always working to create reactions by defenders based on play recognition and releases which look the same, and then branch into the hole created by their reaction. The way the Mesh package is set up, as you'll see in a later chapter, is a good example of this.

- Developing routes behind short defenders. The next logical phase, then, is that defenses will become conscious of the ball-control game, and underneath defenders will tend to jump the Flat and Shallow Cross-type routes. Having the flexibility to take a man who releases as a clear out-type of receiver and sit him down behind all this in the 12-15 yard area gives zones another real problem, especially as defensive recognition develops. This is an especially important element at the high school level, where linebackers often take two to three steps up before recognizing pass, and where linebackers who get much depth in their drops are the exception. Play action marries up with this part of the Bunch offense beautifully. An illustration of this dynamic might look like this: (see the "Stem" variation of the MESH route for more specifics).

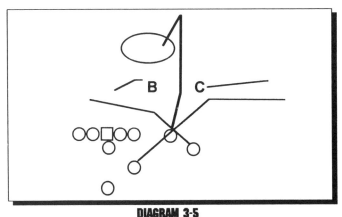

DIAGRAM 3-5
ATTACKING AT THE DEFENSE'S 2ND LEVEL WHEN SHORTER ROUTES ARE JUMPED

- Misdirection Push-Pull. Misdirection routes enable you to widen the holes of a zone and use a trail-type principle to get a man into that hole. Especially when defenders play Man techniques within a zone, often you'll turn their hip with your push, and be able to turn back into a now-widened hole. The quarterback, seeing it, will deliver the ball into that hole and have the receiver on his way before the defender can get fully readjusted. Timing is often vital. Diagram 2-3 makes reference to this idea, which is also illustrated by the following:

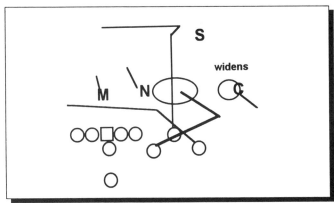

DIAGRAM 3-6
EXAMPLE OF A MISDIRECTION/"TRAIL" ROUTE CONCEPT

Attacking Banjo and switching man concepts

Again, misdirection routes in some form are the thrust of what we like to do against these defenses. We will, by release, give the defense something to which they can switch, and then break away from it (Arrow, Whip). A defender assigned the inside releaser is playing for a route which will go all the way inside, and thus anticipates maintaining leverage to the inside. If you release toward him, then, his hips will likely turn inside or he will at best be flat-footed in trying to react to a misdirected outside break. The reverse is true on outside-in breaks. "Whip" and "Arrow", discussed in greater detail in Chapter 6, are two specific individual routes that do this job:

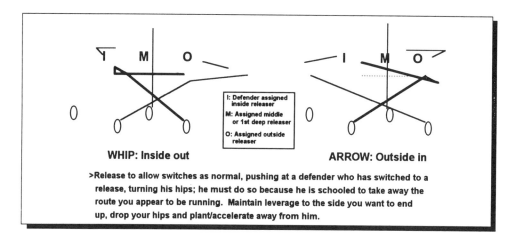

WHIP: Inside out   ARROW: Outside in

I: Defender assigned inside releaser
M: Assigned middle or 1st deep releaser
O: Assigned outside releaser

>Release to allow switches as normal, pushing at a defender who has switched to a release, turning his hips; he must do so because he is schooled to take away the route you appear to be running. Maintain leverage to the side you want to end up, drop your hips and plant/accelerate away from him.

DIAGRAM 3-7
MISDIRECTION ROUTES VS. BANJOS

Switching releases twice (which we would get to by either a "Wrap" or "Twist" tags, ideas illustrated in Appendix B) is a way to enhance this idea by rubbing off the man who has switched. This is an example of a Wrap technique used to free up a Smash route versus a Banjo concept:

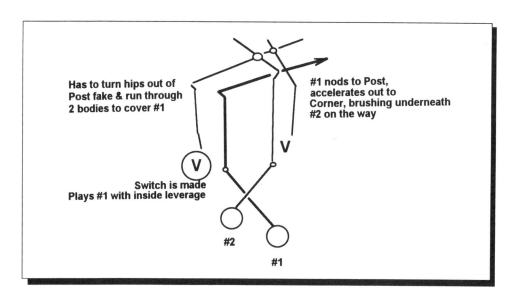

Has to turn hips out of Post fake & run through 2 bodies to cover #1

#1 nods to Post, accelerates out to Corner, brushing underneath #2 on the way

Switch is made
Plays #1 with inside leverage

#2

#1

DIAGRAM 3-8
EXAMPLE OF A DOUBLY-SWITCHED RELEASE TO CREATE A RUB VS. BANJO COVERAGE

The other idea to employ here is to release all the receivers in the same direction. Take as an example this time the outside defender in a Banjo. When the man over him releases inside, he can't step down inside very far initially, because the defensive call has anticipated someone from the inside coming out to him. Often you'll hear defensive coaches teach, "if your man goes in, someone else is coming out!" But if he gets no one releasing out to him, he's stuck with an outside receiver man to man who has gained initial leverage on him already. The reverse can also be done by releasing everybody outside initially, using what we refer to as a "Barrier" technique, illustrated below: This enables us to keep them from switching and still get a rub.

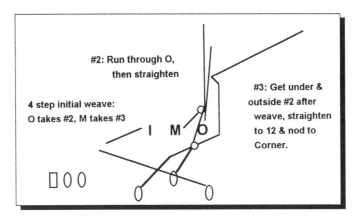

DIAGRAM 3-9
BARRIER TECHNIQUE VS. BANJO

Attacking overloaded frontsides
When a team overloads the structure of their defense to our trips, such as a 4-2 with the weakside linebacker or nickel back flopped to the three receiver side, there are five or six distinct ways that we have to answer that ploy, which our players will understand and we will have practiced regularly:

- Running game away from trips. A team that employs this type of tactic instantly gives you huge leverage to run back into the bubble they've created. You have angles to down block and an extra man for a zone blocking scheme. If they widen the weakside middle linebacker to compensate, you're all set up for a 1-2 hole Trap. We will have trained our quarterback to recognize this and give him the freedom, many times, to go right to a run check away from Bunch or any other Trips when we get this. An example of the leverage we're talking about might look like this:

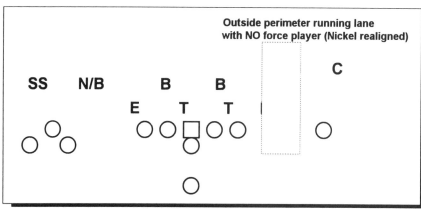

DIAGRAM 3-10
EXAMPLE OF RUNNING LANES VS. AN OVERLOADED DEFENSIVE STRUCTURE
SQUEEZE LEX 7 VS. 4-2 OVER

- Backside delay. By bringing a Shallow Cross all the way across the formation, perhaps swinging a Fullback on check release that way, and then delaying the Tight End behind the Cross, we can outnumber the underneath coverage on the backside. The timing gives the defense the opportunity to settle and react to their pattern recognition. We then bring an extra receiver out of nowhere into a huge hole that he's been watching develop for two seconds as he slow blocked; we teach the delaying receiver to be finding where he'll be going and to slide right into wherever the opening is after the Cross passes him. When the Delay is used in a timely fashion as a complementary part of a complete underneath passing attack, it can be one of the five or six best routes in football.

- Widened backside receiver. This is another way in which Bunch allows you to feature a player to whom you really want to get the ball; the formation structure gets them into an overload, and now you split out your best player 10-14 yards to the weakside, and you give him some space to make big plays; the next underneath defender has no chance of getting underneath a Slant, a Hitch, a Hook...you can choose whatever single routes your people execute best.

- Frontside to backside crosses. Because Bunch creates an immediate backside area as well as frontside, multiple crossing patterns at different levels that get people to the weak areas of overloaded defenses very quickly where there aren't people dropping is one of our best answers. What results is one defender to cover two receivers or two to cover three, and "triangles" that the quarterback can easily read. The OVER route package is a great example of this.

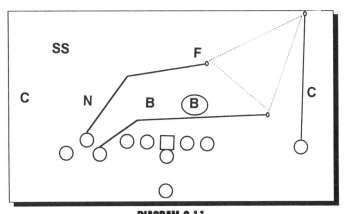

DIAGRAM 3-11
3 ON 2 TRIANGLE CREATED BY A MULTIPLE CROSSING CONCEPT VS. AN OVERLOADED STRUCTURE

• Post from the backside. Some overload structures keep their front and underneath structure intact, and make the adjustment by bringing the Free Safety over the Trips to help in coverage combinations. Other times, the Free Safety will just work hard in that direction out of a normal alignment. In either case, you must be able to execute the Post from a backside receiver into the vacated middle when this happens.

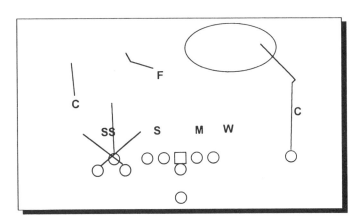

DIAGRAM 3-12
FREE SAFETY CREATING A HOLE FOR THE POST BY WORKING TO THE THREE RECEIVER SIDE

• Packaged sides. As our offense gets refined and more fully implemented throughout the season, we can begin to tag a single backside route or backside combination that the quarterback automatically knows he will go to if he gets an overloaded structure frontside. Chapter 18 illustrates some specific ways this might be used.

While all of these are sound and many have potential to do great damage, many times we do not want to lose the luxury of working our frontside routes just because a defense has decided to play something like a 4-2 Over. We still want to be able to dictate. So, we'll simply use formations to keep them out of these looks and still have our three man Bunch combination. This formation would be an example:

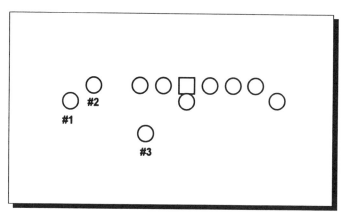

DIAGRAM 3-13
"SQUEEZE B LARRY 6"

The Tight End-Wing combination on the right should prevent any unusual adjustment to the left, and the offset back can function as #3 in the pattern. He can be hot, if need be, while we keep the backside Tight End in to block. This enables us to still have all of the combinations we want to the three receiver frontside, and the defense has been forced to balance up.

Attacking blitz man looks with no free safety
When you keep a tight end on the backside of your Bunch, you maintain the ability to Max protect, which is what you often have to do against full blitzes. Throwing quickly to your underneath rubs, especially in the flat, is always a sound answer, particularly if you have a great athlete whom you can spring outside to the wide field, allowing him to run and defeat defenders one at a time. We can also create rubs to get a guy deep down the middle quickly and take advantage of the void left when the free safety leaves to either blitz or cover a man.

It is worth noting that regardless of whether it is blitz coverage no one in the deep middle or regular man coverage with a free safety, we distinctly prefer some routes over others based on how tight the man coverage is. Shallow Crosses, for example, are fantastic against loose forms of man coverage; we can run the defender through traffic, hit the Cross quickly on the move, and the defensive back will never get there. While it can also be good against tighter man, you won't get as much sepa-ration, and often, it may be very tough to release beneath an extreme form of trail technique.

Those really tight forms of man, especially with the free safety out of the picture, give us the opportunity to work for our deep rubs, often using motion to help us. Certainly the specific routes depend on what your thrower and receivers can do, but it is important to know that there are differences in the way you want to at-tack the different forms and idiosyncrasies of man coverages.

Attacking "Wild Card" coverages

One of the things that makes coaching as a profession so stimulating is the chal-lenge of developing counters and adjustments to the other coaches' counters and adjustments to you. Defensive coordinators are capable of being every bit as inno-vative as offensive coaches, given the right resources. One thing that we always do that has helped us grow tremendously as a staff is to always try to develop de-fensive schemes and techniques to thwart our offensive concepts. It forces us to think through our offensive developments more thoroughly, and it helps us antici-pate adjustments we'll have to make. Further, we find it vital that we stay every bit as up to date on new coverage ideas as defensive coaches do. This type of de-velopment as a coach is critical to consistently giving your offense the best chance to succeed, regardless of what system is being employed.

The best general answer to the types of various adjustments you might see to Bunch that do not lie in the categories detailed above, is to be able, systematically, to disguise the same principle in different ways, and especially to shift and motion in and out of Bunch. In the latter case, sometimes you can get them into adjust-ment defense by initial Bunch alignment, then cause all sorts of havoc with motion out of it for which they a) may not have covered specific rules or b) have to check to a vanilla coverage and out of any special coverage technique, coordinated stunt, or blitz. In the former case, if the defense cannot recognize your look, or cannot recognize it quickly enough, they cannot get into tailor-made adjustments, which means that you'll likely be playing with leverage. One week your Bunch formation might be a straight-up, single back Trips Bunch with a backside Split End; the fol-lowing game you may line up in a bunched Twins set with a backside Tight End and motion your tailback to the split side to get into Bunch. Yet another week you might do it with conventional Split Backs, bringing the Flanker in short motion, and an-other you go back to the first form you started with, but shift to it; you may even use multiple forms of it within the same game as the season develops. We are for-tunate in our situation to have a system of calling formations that is versatile enough to allow us to do those types of things and more.

Of course we will have prepared specific ways to handle all the ways a defense can gear itself to shut down our best routes; 3 over 2 Triangle techniques, Robbers, Combinations, and so forth; often these types of coverages can be defeated by merely changing the route of one man within a basic route structure. The way our communication is geared and our system taught, it is very easy to make an adjustment with one man to beat what the defense has thrown new at us, and keep the rest of the route the same for everybody else. Even if we see something totally new during the course of the game, we don't have to grope for very long because we have a system structure that provides all the necessary tools. In this way build in a sense of being prepared for the unexpected which gives our players great confidence going into a game, while not diluting the focus of executing what we do best.

CHAPTER 4

Systematics: Creating a Versatile, Teachable Framework for Bunch

Formation terminology

To get the most out of all the different aspects of our offense, including Bunch concepts, we need a flexible formation and play-calling structure in order to create multiple formations, employ multiple motions, and create offensive matchups that give leverage to your system. There are many ways to approach this problem. Most multiple systems are built on the principle of small "building blocks" of information, each block used to communicate with a particular unit or person. The advantage of such a structure is that each player only need know those words or terms that apply to his position; yet by stringing together multiple blocks of information in different ways, a variety of ideas can be communicated.

As the coach sets his formation, he must place the tight end, wide receivers, and the backs in order to create different formations. If he is using an unbalanced line, then he must also devise a way to communicate with the linemen. We place personnel by stringing together building blocks of information in this general order:

Backs—Tight End/Recivers—H-Back—Motion

Backs are set in the first block of information to be communicated. There is a base set, or default, that is understood to be the set we will be in when no special call is given. For us the base 2-back set is an "I" set. When we use the "I" set, no back call is given. It is from this basic set that we build our adjustments.

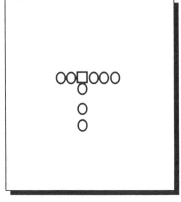

DIAGRAM 4-1
BASIC I FORMATION

If we want to create different backfield sets we do so with calls for the backs. "Split" sets the backs behind the tackles in a split backfield. "Strong" and "Weak" speak to the Fullback, adjusting him to a staggered alignment to or away from Y, respectively. Some years we use an offset "I", other years we keep the backs even. That is a personnel decision each year, or if needed we can create the additional needed calls to incorporate both ideas. "Blue" and "Brown" create offset backfields with the H-back to the call (Blue sets him left, Brown to the right).

In cases where a single back remains in the backfield, he is offset with an "A" (offset rigtht), or "B" (offset left) adjustment. Most of the time, the back learns to offset himself according to the job he's assigned (e.g., protect to a certain side, get into the route on a certain side) without the "A" or "B" call.

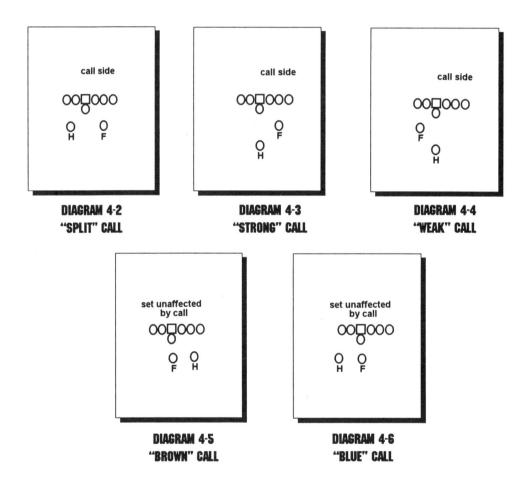

DIAGRAM 4-2
"SPLIT" CALL

DIAGRAM 4-3
"STRONG" CALL

DIAGRAM 4-4
"WEAK" CALL

DIAGRAM 4-5
"BROWN" CALL

DIAGRAM 4-6
"BLUE" CALL

The tight end, or "Y" receiver, is set into the formation by using words that correspond to his different alignments. Unless a call dictates otherwise, the "X" receiver aligns opposite the tight end, while the "Z" receiver aligns with him. Alignments to the right have boys' names assigned to them, those to the left have girls' names assigned. "Rip", "Rex" and "Ron" correspond to positions next to the tackle, halfway to the wide receiver, and outside the widest receiver, respectively. The corresponding positions to the left are "Liz", "Lex", and "Lou," respectively. Using the tight end as a wing is created with "R"and "L". The insertion of the word "Nasty" in front of the call creates the slightly flexed tight end position commonly referred to as a "nasty split" tight end.

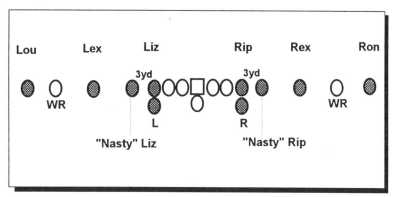

DIAGRAM 4-7
CALLS FOR THE TIGHT END, OR "Y" RECEIVER

The H-back is moved into positions out of the backfield into the formation by using a number code. Each position is numbered as an extension of our normal hole numbers: "6-8-10" to the right and "7-9-11" to the left. 6 and 7 put him just outside the tackle, 8 and 9 halfway between the tackle and widest receiver on his side, and 10 and 11 put him outside the widest receiver.

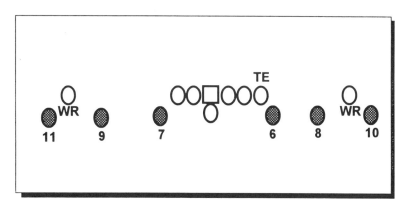

DIAGRAM 4-8
CALLS FOR THE H-BACK

By talking to the Y receiver with words and the H-back with numbers, we can use each block of information to create a very flexible system that is logical, and therefore easy to learn, for our players. The following diagrams illustrate the variety of formations easily created using this structure.

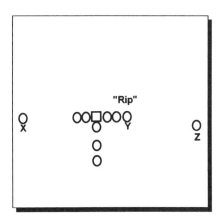

DIAGRAM 4-9
RIP FORMATION

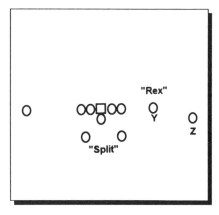

DIAGRAM 4-10
"SPLIT REX"

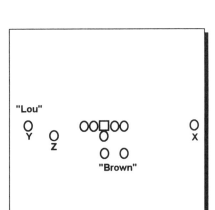

DIAGRAM 4-11
"BROWN LOU"

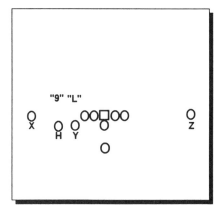

DIAGRAM 4-12
"L 9"

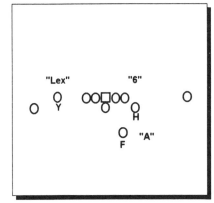

DIAGRAM 4-13
"A LEX 6"

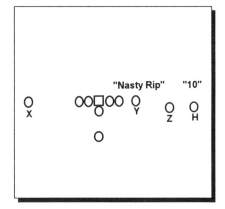

DIAGRAM 4-14
"NASTY RIP 10"

In each of the formations thus far, the wide receivers have simply aligned following their normal rule, that is: "Z with the tight end to the call, and X away from the call". There have been years we simply fixed both receivers with Z to the right and X to the left if we had two very similar receivers. If one receiver is clearly better, we usually place him at X so he is on the single receiver side. If he commands double coverage, then the two receiver side has gained an advantage. Also, in order to double him defenses may give up some strong side run support. A coach can define personnel and the base positions following what ever criteria his style of offense demands. When we want the wide receivers to align together on the same side of the formation we use the words "Ray" and "Larry". The "R" and "L" at the beginnings of those words tell the wide outs which side to align, while the Y on the end alerts the Y receiver to align as a Tight end opposite the call. "Ray" and "Larry" create standard slot sets to either side.

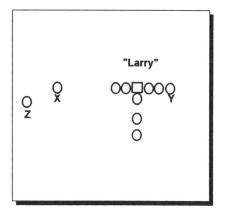

DIAGRAM 4-15
"LARRY" ADJUSTMENT

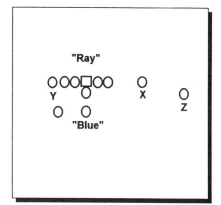

DIAGRAM 4-16
"BLUE RAY"

By employing the numbering system to place the H-back into the formation, we can create another set of formations that redistribute our receivers in different combinations.

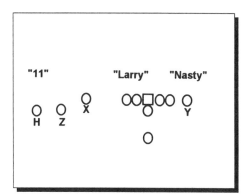

DIAGRAM 4-17
"NASTY LARRY 11"

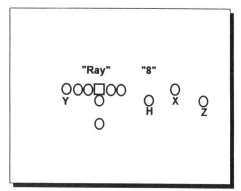

DIAGRAM 4-18
"RAY 8"

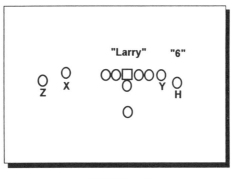

DIAGRAM 4-19
"LARRY 6"

We also use some other terms to speak to other people and create some specialized formations. The word "Slot" can also be used to set the H-back just inside tight end. "Rip Slot," "Liz Slot," "Ray Slot," and "Larry Slot" create very interesting single back formations.

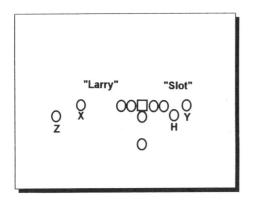

DIAGRAM 4-20
"LARRY SLOT"

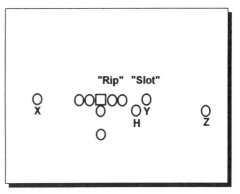

DIAGRAM 4-21
"RIP SLOT"

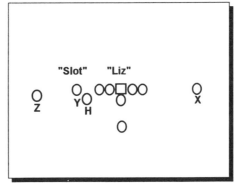

DIAGRAM 4-22
"LIZ SLOT"

The word "Wing" moves Z in to a standard 1 yard by 1 yard wing alignment. The word "Plus" moves Z inside of Y. "Tight" designates that the backside X receiver align himself inside as a tight end (usually "Tight" precedes the entire call).

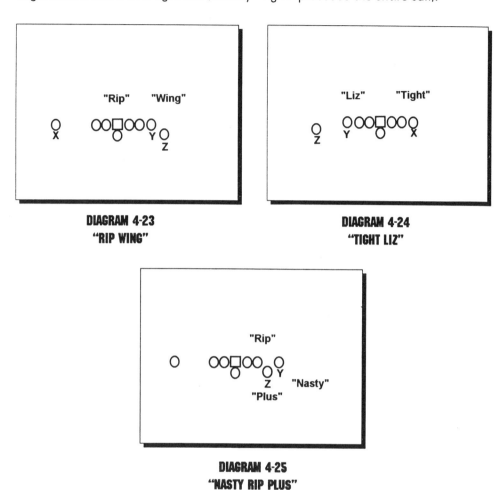

DIAGRAM 4-23
"RIP WING"

DIAGRAM 4-24
"TIGHT LIZ"

DIAGRAM 4-25
"NASTY RIP PLUS"

We can also move one of the wide receivers to an outside position opposite the side he would normally line up. This will be used for a number of purposes, one of which is to create a type of unbalanced set. This is done by calling "X Over", or "Z Over" at the end of a formation call to tell X or Z, respectively, to line up opposite and outside. Eventually, the "Over" gets dropped, and we just use "X" or "Z" to communicate this.

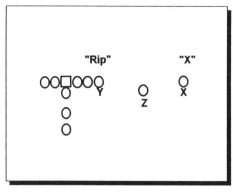

DIAGRAM 4-26
"RIP X"

Through the assembling of all these different building blocks, calling just about any type of alignment you could want is possible within this structure. We evolved to a point, however, that certain formation combinations with certain personnel groupings became basic to our offense. We then began to use abbreviated names for those two to three sets, and then package variations off of that base. For example, this set, using 4 wide receivers, became a fundamental one for us:

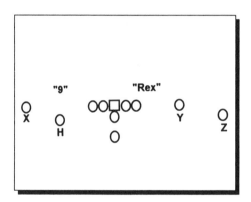

DIAGRAM 4-27
"REX 9", A.K.A. "FLEX"

Calling "Rex 9" could get us to this set in the normal structure, but we shortened it to just "Flex." With that in place, we began building in ways to make minor adjustments off of "Flex" that could create different matchups for our four wide receivers. "Flip", for example, exchanges the relative positions of the inside and outside receivers within the "Flex" package, while "Flop" tells receivers that would normally line up on the right in "Flex" to line up on the left. The variation of this theme that has the most relevance for the Bunch attack is a variation called "Twin," which tells both pairs of receivers to line up 4-5 yards wide of the tackle on their side, with the outside receiver 1 yard outside of the inside man.

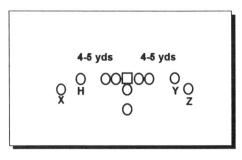

DIAGRAM 4-28
"TWIN" VARIATION OF "FLEX" FORMATION PACKAGE

The other major example of a set that became basic was a two-tight end, two-wide receiver, single back set.

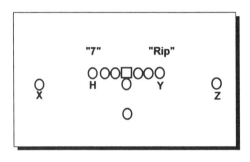

DIAGRAM 4-29
"RIP 7", A.K.A. "RAM"

In theory, we could call this "Rip 7", but we built a package around it, calling it "Ram," becuase it implies a different type of H to consistently block at a closed end position, and a different style of attack. "Liz 6," then, became known as "Lion." Again, Z goes to the call along with Y, and X goes opposite.

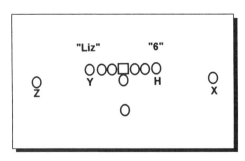

DIAGRAM 4-30
"LIZ 6", A.K.A. "LION"

The other basic structures of our formation calling and adjustment can then be applied to create different variations out of this two tight end package. "X" and "Z" calls move the called receiver to the opposite side, and "Slot" moves the H tight end inside Y.

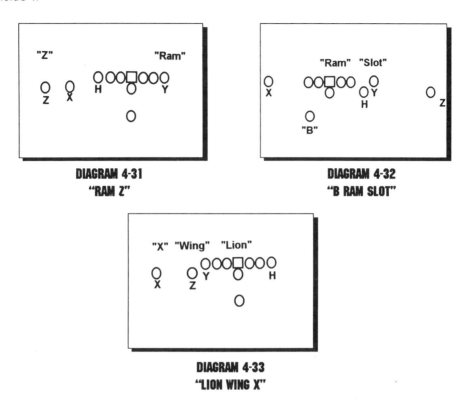

DIAGRAM 4-31
"RAM Z"

DIAGRAM 4-32
"B RAM SLOT"

DIAGRAM 4-33
"LION WING X"

Motion terminology
Once a basic formation structure has been established, creating a variety of versatile motions can be very helpful to any offense. There are many reasons to use motion within an offensive structure including:

- To decoy or disguise offensive intentions
- To give the same play or concept a new look
- To gain a blocker at the point of attack
- To force the pass coverage to declare man or zone
- To create coverage problems or checks
- To create personnel mismatches
- To force the coverage to bump, changing personnel and alignment

Regardless of these reasons, or many others, the single most important aspect of a motion system is the ability to communicate clearly *WHO* is performing *WHAT* type of motion, and *WHERE* does one want the ball snapped. Communicating the exact motion needed and the exact timing of the snap without a lot of memorizing for quarterback and receivers is essential. Many systems use words beginning with the receiver letter to employ different motions. These systems can be extensive depending on the differing types of motion one needs to employ. For example, the Z receiver could have to know such terms as ZIP, ZAP, ZORRO, ZOOM, ZING, etc., while Y and X would each have a different set of terms to know, and the quarterback would have to know them all. Then each play would need to have memorized the point at which the quarterback wants to have the ball snapped. After a while such a system may become cumbersome to your players, especially the quarterback or a receiver having to know several positions. If you can reduce this system or in any way simplify or clarify it then it can have advantages for your offense. In order to solve this problem for the players, yet keep the system versatile and flexible, another system has been devised.

When communicating motion to your players, two essential elements must be addressed:

- *WHO* do you want to go in motion?
- *WHERE* do you want them to go in motion to?

The best way to address this problem would be to individually address each player by name and specifically tell him where you wanted him to go. Clearly, if we could say, "Joe go in motion outside the right tight end", then both Joe and the quarterback would know exactly where to go and when the ball is to be snapped. We try to do exactly this by calling the position name X, Y, Z, H, or F and place him in motion to a specific spot using the standard hole numbering and formation numbers we employ in our base numbering system, that is 2-4-6-8-10 to the right and 1-3-5-7-9-11 to the left. Again, 6 and 7 take the motion man just outside the tackle as the insidemost receiver on that side; 8 and 9 take him halfway between the tackle and widest receiver, designating him the #2 receiver; 10 and 11 take him wider than the widest, and he becomes the #1 receiver. Such a system is similar to a map grid used on most standard maps to indicate the exact location of a specific city on the map.

For example, "Z9" alerts the Z receiver to go in motion to the 9 spot, regardless of where he has aligned within the formation. Z knows exactly WHO and WHERE to go and more importantly the quarterback also knows WHO and specifically WHEN to snap the ball. Most common motions can be easily communicated using this system and because of its simplicity it, can be easily taught and remembered. It serves as its own particular code, so it could be used in no huddle situations fairly easily. Illustrated below are examples of some ways we can use motion calls, in conjunction with some of our other building blocks.

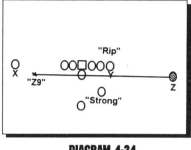

DIAGRAM 4-34
"STRONG RIP Z9"

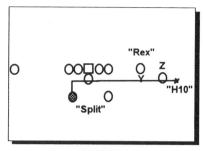

DIAGRAM 4-35
"SPLIT REX H10"

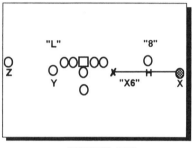

DIAGRAM 4-36
"L 8 X6"

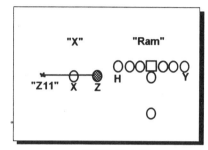

DIAGRAM 4-37
"RAM X Z11"

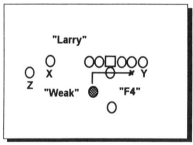

DIAGRAM 4-38
"WEAK LARRY F4"

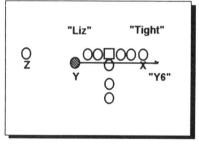

DIAGRAM 4-39
"TIGHT LIZ Y6"

Several of today's offenses have the need for more elaborate types of motions. By now adding a few simple motion words that apply to all the skill people, we can expand this system to incorporate many of the additional ideas we need.

IDIOT: motion to the opposite guard and back to the end man on the LOS
STUPID: motion outside the widest receiver and back to original position
CRAZY: motion to the opposite guard, return 1 man, and then continue on across to end man on LOS

RETURN: motion inside to the guard on your side and return to original position
Again, by designating who is to perform the motion, there is a simplified system
that requires little memorization. For example, "Z Idiot" clearly defines the Z receiver to motion to the opposite guard and back, as "H Return" also clearly defines
the motion required of the H-back.

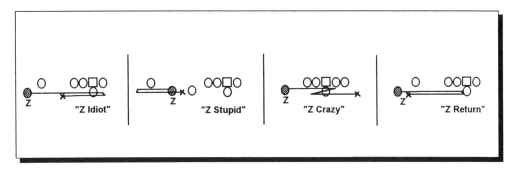

DIAGRAM 4-40
DEFINITIONS OF SPECIALTY MOTIONS

As you can see, this offensive structure offers multiple formations and motions creating a variety of packages that can be employed. The system structure can be
easily adapted year to year, with additions or deletions because of differing talent
or emphasis easily accomplished. With this structure the coach can adapt to changing personnel and abilities each year, but also to differing defenses week to week,
incorporating a variety of offensive looks and creating multiple matchup possibilities game to game or play to play.

Play-calling terminology
The basic play calling structure used in this offensive system is fairly simple. After
calling the formation and motion, runs or passes are called using series. The runs
can be put into series numbered 0-49 or simply called by their names. Either system can be created to meet the coach's needs. Passes can be packaged again by
series from 50-99 and 100-900, or if runs are all named, then passes can expand to
make use of the numbers from 10-49 as well. In this book, we will simply number
the runs for the sake of clarity. The run blocking system will not be discussed, but a
system of calls can easily be developed to meet any coach's needs.

The pass structure employs a two- or three-digit identification system. The first
digit identifies the protection call with the second digit identifying the route package. All two digit calls identify the frontside as right. By prefixing a "1" to the call
the frontside call is left. Therefore a pass call of "51" would indicate 50 protection
to the right, and the 1 route package and reads. Whereas a call of "151" makes the
frontside left, with protection left and the 1 route defined from the left.

When using 200 or 300 protection, the last two of the three digits are used to indicate which run is being faked prior to the pass. This, in turn, designates which is the frontside. In 200 protection, where a bootleg *away* from the fake side is being executed, an odd digit on the end dictates that the frontside be *right,* an even digit makes the frontside *left.* For example, "206" is a fake to the right with the quarterback bootlegging to a frontside that is on the left.

300 protection is defined as a run fake followed by a dropback set up between the guard and tackle to the fake side, therefore odd digits make the frontside *left,* even digits make the frontside to the *right.* "337", for example, would entail a fake to the left, which would also be the frontside for receivers.

The runs that we will use as the last two digits for the sake of this manual follow:

Running Play	Numbers Used
Inside Zone	06 (right) 07 (left)
Outside Zone	08 (right) 09 (left)
Blast/Isolation	36 (right) 37 (left)
Counter	26 (right) 27 (left)
Trap	40 (right) 41 (left)

Route Definitions. All route definitions are defined by receiver positioning rather than being individually defined. That is, the definition terminology uses playside, or frontside, receiver #1, receiver #2, receiver #3, counting from the outside most receiver positioned. The backside is numbered in a similar fashion, backside receiver #1, receiver #2, receiver #3 (see diagrams 3-2 and 3-3). As the coach changes the formation, different players may be doing different parts of the route, thus allowing the coach to create matchup problems and multiplicity in his offense. Let's use a basic route package as an example of how this might work. We define a basic three receiver "Flood "route as follows:

5 ROUTE PACKAGE	
Frontside receiver #1	GO
Frontside receiver #2	SAIL (12 yard breakout)
Frontside receiver #3	FLAT
Backside receiver #1	BACKSIDE RULE
Backside receiver #2	BACKSIDE RULE

If we look at this route from a basic "Brown Rip" formation, the definition would result in a play looking like this:

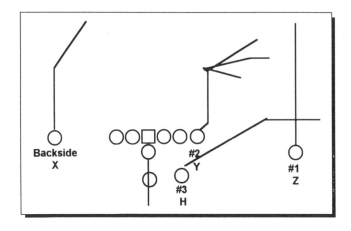

DIAGRAM 4-41
"BROWN RIP 55"

By changing the formation, we change which receiver is doing what routes. Observe the 55 route from a "Rex 6" formation (it has the same people as "Brown Rip" doing the route) and from a "Rip 8" formation (Y now has the Flat, H has the Sail).

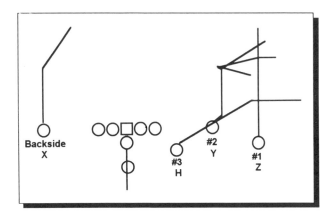

DIAGRAM 4-42
"REX 6 55"

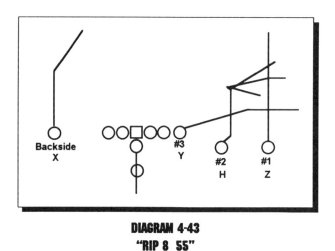

DIAGRAM 4-43
"RIP 8 55"

By using motion, we can again change who is doing what part of the route, yet the read and basic route structure remain the same for the quarterback. Observe RIP H10 and compare it to WEAK LEX Z8.

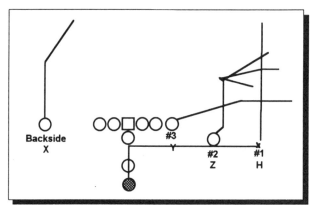

DIAGRAM 4-44
"RIP H10 55"

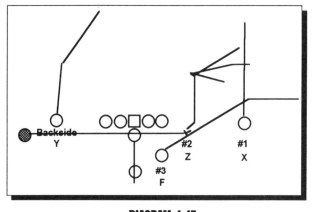

DIAGRAM 4-45
"WEAK LEX Z8 55"

As you can see, the basic formation system and our route definition allow the coach to dictate who will be matched verses the defenses' flat defender as an example. From the above examples the player running the #3 receiver's flat route could have been Y, H, F, or X. Without a lot of work, we could get Z in a #3 position to run the Flat route as in LIZ 8 Z6.

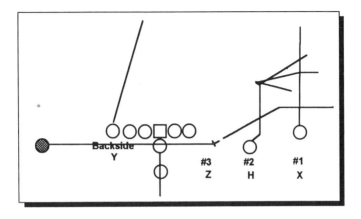

DIAGRAM 4-46
"LIZ 8 Z6 55"

Route tags. A basic route package can be simply altered by the use of specific tags that are clearly defined. We start by simply telling the receiver whose route we want to adjust, to run a different route as in "Joe run a drag" example "H Drag". This tag applied to any route would alert the H-back to run a drag route rather than his defined route in the package, regardless of where he is positioned in the formation. The QB is alerted to the tag and is taught that the tag has now become primary unless someone in the basic route came open early (never pass up one open receiver to wait for another to come open). For example, from the previous examples, we might want to change the way we attack from the 5 route package by giving the outside receiver a "Curl" route, or perhaps by giving the backside receiver a "Post Corner" to attack away from the frontside. Those tags are illustrated below.

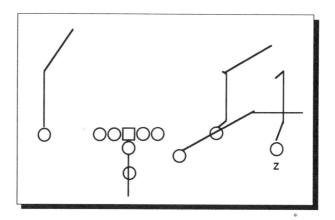

DIAGRAM 4-47
"REX 6 55 Z CURL"

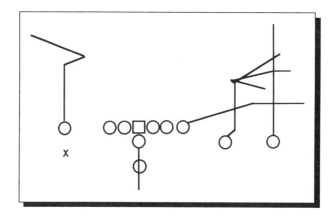

DIAGRAM 4-48
"RIP 8 55 X POST CORNER"

We also use *general* tags that alter the basic route design. An example is the *"Switch"* tag, which tells frontside (playside) receivers #2 and #3 to *switch* assigned routes. Regardless of who is in position #2 and #3 they are to switch the basic route definitions for receivers #2 and #3. A table of all these type of tags appears in appendix B. Observe our 5 route taking on different looks with the simple use of the "Switch" tag.

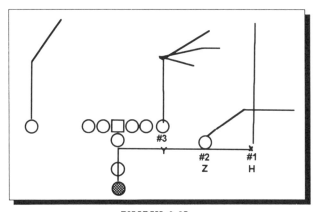

DIAGRAM 4-49
"RIP H10 55 SWITCH"

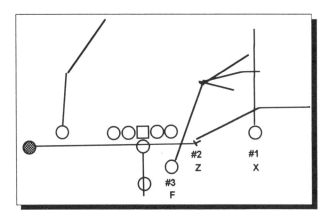

DIAGRAM 4-50
"WEAK LEX Z8 55 SWITCH"

Creating "Bunched" formations

Using this offensive system, we have an almost limitless amount of ways we can get to a "bunched" formation. Most any of our formation combinations can be made into a type of bunched situation by using one of three prefixes before the formation call. This prefix will tell any receivers who are split out within the formation called that they will all be lining up in very close proximity of each other at a particular width. This in turn alerts them that they will be using Bunch release mechanics and "traffic rules" (see Chapter 3) in getting out into the pattern.

We get to the various alignments for the bunched group of receivers by prefixing key code words indicating the width of our set. *"SQUEEZE"* fixes the inside receiver in the grouping 4 yards from the offensive tackle, with each succeeding receiver 1 yard from the next (if the inside receiver is a tight end or a back in the backfield, his alignment is unaffected). *"SNUG"* sets the inside receiver 8 yards from the offensive tackle. If the prefix *"CLUSTER"* is used, the grouping sets 12 yards off the offensive tackle but not closer than 6 yards from the sideline. Of course, game plan, personnel strengths, and situation can alter these basic definitions should the coach see fit. The set is determined by the normal formation call with the appropriate prefix simply indicating the change in relative alignment to each other and with respect to width away from the tackle.

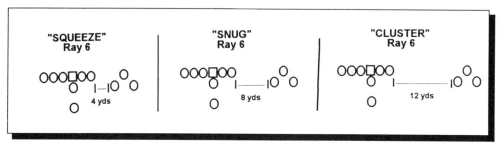

DIAGRAM 4-51

"RAY 6" FORMATION ILLUSTRATED WITH THREE DIFFERENT BUNCH CONCEPT ADJUSTMENTS

The crucial consideration in creating the Bunch concept for any offense is to get receiver #1, #2, and #3 in close proximity to each other at the snap of the ball in order to gain the advantages of this concept. The flexibility of the formation and motion systems we use can attain this goal when used together. There are a number of basic ways to create such bunched situations, regardless of whether your basic set is some kind of pro set, I, Wing-T, or whatever. Each of these different ways carries with it specific advantages and leverage that may not be found to the same degree in other methods of "bunching" a formation. Your basic system, personnel, weekly game plan ideas, specific Bunch routes you employ, and extent to which you employ them will all help you dictate which and how many of these Bunch variations you use.

Basic three receiver sets. Using three stationary receivers is the basic "bunch" set. Most pass routes are initially taught in such sets for simplicity of learning. Key teaching of techniques, skills, and reads are all begun in these sets.

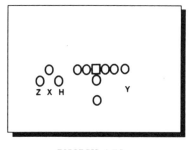

DIAGRAM 4-52

"SQUEEZE LARRY 7"

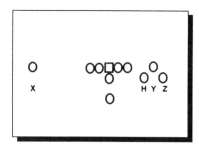

DIAGRAM 4-53

"SQUEEZE REX 6"

Once the key techniques and concepts are mastered, then the system's versatility allows the coach to create the "Bunch" any number of different ways, constantly changing who will be receiver #1, #2, or #3, and/or bringing receivers from a variety of places to participate in the Bunch.

Using a back as #3 from the backfield or through motion. By grouping (bunching) two receivers and bringing the third receiver from the backfield via motion or the set, can get three bunched receivers with different personnel in each position.

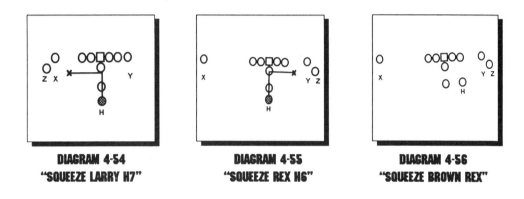

DIAGRAM 4-54	DIAGRAM 4-55	DIAGRAM 4-56
"SQUEEZE LARRY H7"	"SQUEEZE REX H6"	"SQUEEZE BROWN REX"

Using Wing sets. Wing sets and two tight end sets are currently popular at all levels. Such formations are good in the Red Zone and at the goalline because of their versatility in complementing your running game in those areas.

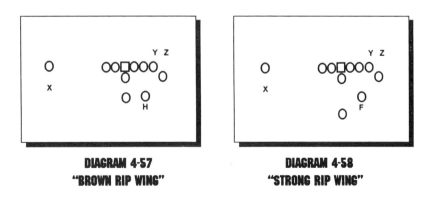

DIAGRAM 4-57	DIAGRAM 4-58
"BROWN RIP WING"	"STRONG RIP WING"

Using short, outside-in motion by a wide receiver. By bringing a wide receiver in motion toward an inside receiver, leverage for your crossing routes can be gained as you bunch your receivers.

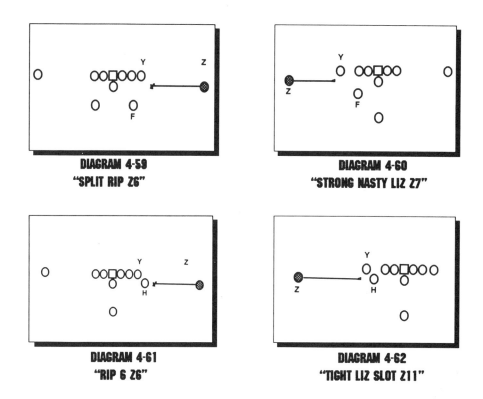

DIAGRAM 4-59
"SPLIT RIP Z6"

DIAGRAM 4-60
"STRONG NASTY LIZ Z7"

DIAGRAM 4-61
"RIP 6 Z6"

DIAGRAM 4-62
"TIGHT LIZ SLOT Z11"

Motion across the formation. By using receiver motion across the formation, the coach can disguise his intention to bunch his receivers until the last possible second, thus making special defensive adjustments that much harder to make.

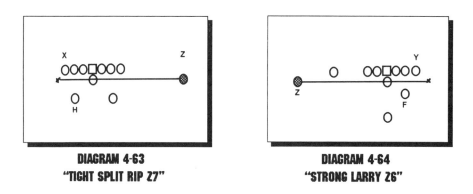

DIAGRAM 4-63
"TIGHT SPLIT RIP Z7"

DIAGRAM 4-64
"STRONG LARRY Z6"

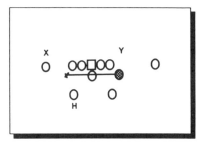

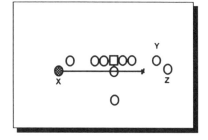

DIAGRAM 4-65
"SQUEEZE SPLIT RIP Y7"

DIAGRAM 4-66
"TWIN X6"

Using unusual motion. Using unusual motions with a fast change of direction built in can help create additional leverage for outside breaking routes. Two additional advantages are the confusion it causes a secondary as they try to make their checks, and the fact that a slow defender may get lost or momentarily freeze.

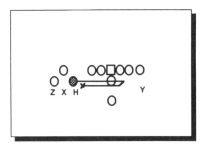

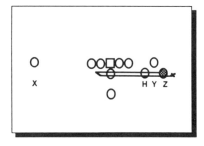

DIAGRAM 4-67
"SQUEEZE LARRY 7 H IDIOT"

DIAGRAM 4-68
"SQUEEZE REX 6 Z RETURN"

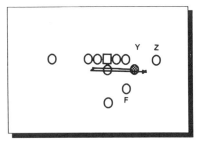

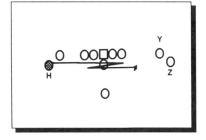

DIAGRAM 4-69
"SQUEEZE STRONG RIP Y IDIOT"

DIAGRAM 4-70
"SNUG REX 11 H CRAZY"

Motioning to nearly stacked alignments. Some formation and motion combinations can create a vertical stacking of your receivers near the same spot on the field. Certainly this could cause difficulty in bumping across for pass defenders and it will also be difficult for reading defenses to identify who is #1, #2, or #3 within the set. For sake of our own clarity, the number to which the motion man is given to motion tells him and everyone else exactly where he should end up, and which receiver he ends up being in the route definition (6 or 7, he's #3; 8 or 9 puts him at #2; 10 or 11 makes him #1). You will see this done numerous different ways throughout the illustrations in the text, two of which are illustrated below:

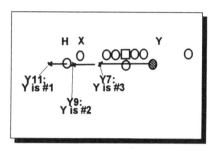

DIAGRAM 4-71
"SQUEEZE RIP 11 Y7, 9, OR 11"

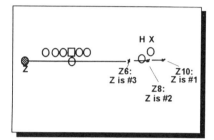

DIAGRAM 4-72
"CLUSTER LIZ 8 Z 6, 8, OR 10"

Assorted one back variations. The one back offense offers other creative ways to get three receivers bunched into a grouping. A double-wing concept, possibly using three tight ends, certainly provides a strong running edge in addition to the benefits this type of set brings the passing game.

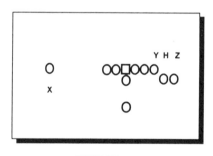

DIAGRAM 4-73
"RIP WING 6"

Offsetting a back as #3 provides some different kinds of advantages. One way to use an offset back is to use a tight end/wing combination away from the Bunch you have created to help minimize defensive adjustments to the three receiver side. The tight end/wing can also be used to double a dominant pass rusher in backside protection.

Another idea is to offset the back to the side you've bunched three receivers, then motion one of those receivers across, leaving the impression that you have motioned out of bunch, when in fact, a three receiver bunch is still in tact with the back serving as #3.

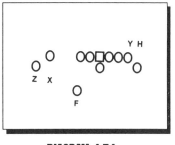

DIAGRAM 4-74
"SQUEEZE B LARRY 6"

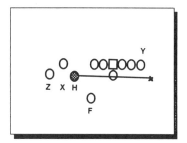

DIAGRAM 4-75
"SQUEEZE B LARRY 7 H6"

No back variations. If you choose to add a no back package to your approach then the opportunities for creating bunched receivers increases dramatically. One effective no back ploy is to create a pre-aligned Bunch, and then motion the fullback outside of it wide to create an extreme horizontal stretch.

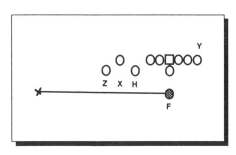

DIAGRAM 4-76
"SQUEEZE LARRY 7 F11"

You can also the motioning of a single back to create the third receiver in a bunch.

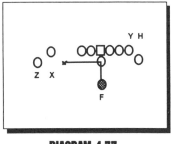

DIAGRAM 4-77
"SQUEEZE LARRY 6 F7"

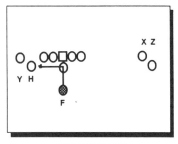

DIAGRAM 4-78
"CLUSTER RAY SLOT F7"

If you employ no back sets by alignment, then those sets could be realigned into bunched groupings. "Empty" and "Zilch" in our system are no back sets.

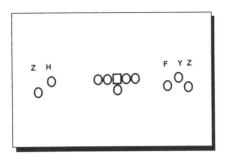

DIAGRAM 4-79
"SNUG EMPTY"

Summary

As you can see, any coach can adapt the Bunch principle to his offense. Within any offensive structure a bunching of receivers could be used to gain some offensive advantages. The "sky is the limit" as far as a coach's creativity in getting into bunched concepts. As a season progresses, your offense can evolve and take on new looks, yet continue to use the same plays and offensive structure. As opponents' strengths and weaknesses change week to week, offensive game plans of attack can specifically be tailored to meet your particular needs.

CHAPTER 5

First Things First: Pass Protection and Its Application to the Bunch Attack

Basic philosophy

Before discussing in detail the routes and techniques we employ in our "Bunch" package, it is imperative that some discussion of pass protection and its relationship to our offense take place. Pass protection is by far the single most important factor influencing the success you can achieve throwing the football. As a coach you must develop a sound philosophy in regard to your protection schemes and spend detailed time determining how to teach the techniques involved in protecting the quarterback. This chapter is in no way the complete statement on pass protection in our system, or in any system for that matter. What we will attempt to do is discuss several of the most basic protections that are used in the illustrations provided in this text. We do use other protection schemes in our package, but since the scope of this work is to introduce a basic bunch philosophy that can be incorporated into any offense (not to sell anyone on our offensive package), we will refrain from going into intimate detail on every protection we use and each technique we teach. Rather, we will speak to generalized protection schemes that are used to some extent in most styles of offense, so that no matter which offense you may run, hopefully some of this pass package might be incorporated into what you use.

There are several key philosophical considerations a coach will encounter when constructing a passing package and its protection schemes. The answers, in each case, will impact your choices of how you protect the quarterback. Our basic philosophy is dictated by the fact that our offensive package is a multiple package. Therefore we have a need for several types of pass actions, of which; quick, semi-roll, sprint, dropback, play action, and bootleg, are all illustrated in this work. We also employ two back, one back, and no back pass packages therefore we need several different schemes to protect the quarterback. Several aspects of the passing game follow which directly impact pass protection.

Uncovered principle

We believe in forcing the defense to "cover down" on our receivers. What we mean by that is that we will throw to any uncovered receiver that you give us, based on down and distance. Obviously if the situation is third and 12 yards to go, we will not throw to an "uncovered" receiver and then see that receiver tackled for a short gain that does not result in a first down. But, within a common sense approach to the game situation, we will throw to any receiver we feel you have not properly covered on any down, regardless of the run or pass called. The basic definition we use for "uncovered" defines a receiver to be uncovered if he can catch the ball and end up with a gain of 4 yards. In practice this amounts to the defender being off the receiver by 5 yards or more for inside receivers and 7 yards or more for outside receivers, depending on the arm strength of your quarterback.

By being willing to throw to uncovered receivers, you do several things for your offense. The most important gain is that every receiver you place in the formation requires a defender within a close proximity of him and therefore one or two deep safeties is a must, otherwise the receiver is likely to go right by any defender who is too closely aligned in relation to the talent and speed of the receiver he is covering. This means that four wide receivers will usually demand a minimum of at least five defenders in coverage, four closely aligned defenders and one deep safety. Using five defenders in coverage leaves only six potential rushers to protect against. The number of stunts, blitzes, and alignments available to the defense is more limited than if you allowed seven or eight defenders to align in the tackle box. Using this same logic, those teams wishing to make use of a two deep zone defense must now use six defenders verses four wide receivers, thus limiting the pass rush to five men. Another clear benefit of throwing uncovered is that it can keep you in favorable down and distance situations. Most coaches would gladly take an easy four or five yards on first down to set up their second and third down play calling sequence. Just as big a benefit is that defensive teams are less likely to blitz on second and five and third and two. Staying out of long down situations can be a tremendous help for your pass protection because the defense does not have leverage on your offense. Another benefit the offense realizes from throwing to uncovered receivers is that the defenders who now must align more closely, are more susceptible to option type routes, crossing routes, routes employing natural picks and rubs, and of course deep routes. Because of this, defensive teams have to work harder to create adequate coverage schemes which usually result in a more cautious pass rush schemes. The first principle we teach our quarterback and receivers is the uncovered principle because it has so many positive implications for our linemen in pass protection.

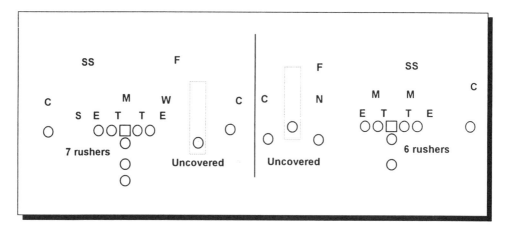

DIAGRAM 5-1
EXAMPLES OF DEFENSES LEAVING A RECEIVER UNCOVERED

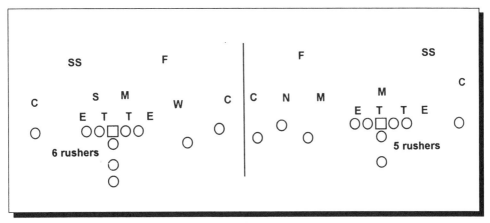

DIAGRAM 5-2
EXAMPLES OF THE REDUCED AMOUNT OF POTENTIAL RUSHERS WHEN ALL RECEIVERS ARE COVERED

Protection versus the blitz

The next consideration any coach wanting to pass the ball must deal with is to determine your basic philosophy versus the blitz. Will you chose to protect the quarterback to the best of your ability even if it means losing a receiver from the route, or are you going to depend on "hot" principles and the quarterback's ability to get rid of the ball to an available receiver before the pass rush gets to him? Our answer to this question is that we must be able to do both because of our desire to employ a multiple package, but we prefer to protect the quarterback first, if at all possible. We bring a receiver in to protect, and usually check to one of the blitz check plays we have game planned. Because our philosophy is to protect the quarterback first, our pass protection usually can remain quite firm and not experience extreme stress verses the blitz. From a coaching standpoint this does not mean that we do not attack blitz coverages, rather that we attempt to attack them with a fully protected quarterback (as best as we can) and a specifically designed and practiced response to any blitzes we can recognize. We do employ a "check and then release" philosophy for some of our receivers in order to better provide protection for our quarterback. *It must be noted though that the defense always has a way to bring "one more" than the offense can protect, therefore a clearly defined blitz package employing "hot" principles, planned, built in, or called sight adjustments, and max protected passes is essential for your offensive arsenal.* When we chose to bring a receiver in, or to keep a receiver in to check and then release, we attempt to do it away from the play if possible in order to not lose the play called. This is not always possible, nor preferable in all situations, therefore careful blitz game planning is essential. We rely on the quarterback to recognize potential blitz situations and to understand when the defense has more potential pass rushers than we have protectors. He simply calls a receiver in from the backside and runs the play or checks off. Because of this basic "protect first" philosophy we can help our pass protection in a large number of unfavorable pass blocking situations. We feel this is safer and more reliable than continually relying on "hot" schemes and more complicated pass protection schemes on every pass down.

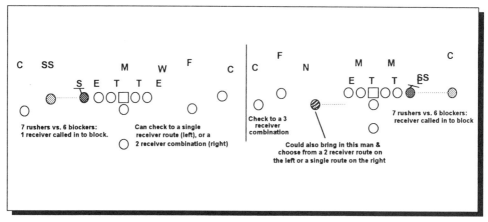

DIAGRAM 5-3
BRINGING IN AN EXTRA BLOCKER AGAINST BLITZ COVERAGE

Big on big

Most coaches who design pass protection schemes prefer to match up the offensive linemen in pass protection against the defensive linemen in order to avoid size and strength mismatches. Unless we decide by game plan that we need a lineman blocking a great linebacker, we strive to match "big on big" in most of our protection schemes. Besides the obvious size and strength factor, another benefit of this philosophy is that when linebackers do not blitz, the back who is assigned in protection can now either help with protection or release into the route. Either scenario has positive benefits for your passing game. We have a better chance of getting five receivers out when we match up protection this way. We also can provide for built in help verses the better pass rushers or one extra man looking to help wherever needed to strengthen our protection.

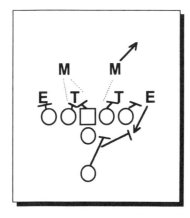

DIAGRAM 5-4
RUNNING BACK RELIEVED OF BLITZ
PICK-UP HELPS DOUBLE

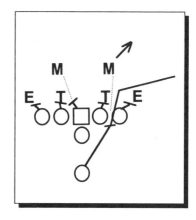

DIAGRAM 5-5
RUNNING BACK RELIEVED OF BLITZ
PICK-UP RELEASES INTO ROUTE

Use of zone and man pass blocking rules

When blocking protections are designed, another consideration for the coach is the decision as to how stacks, stunts, blitzes, and basic protection rules will be blocked. Will you rely on a "zone" blocking principle, blocking the man who shows up in your area, or a "man" blocking principle, blocking your assigned man regardless of where he rushes. Our preference is to zone block whenever feasible. We try to zone all stunts and twists involving two offensive linemen in assigned protection. We usually put our backs in man protection since they are in a better position to see the stunt develop and react to the changing angles of the pass rusher involved. There are times when we have our linemen stay in man protection, but for the purposes of this text we will consider protections that zone all stunts on the line of scrimmage.

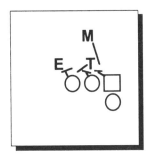

DIAGRAM 5-6
CENTER AND
GUARD ZONING A "FIRE" STUNT

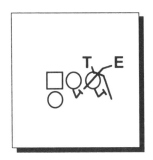

DIAGRAM 5-7
GUARD AND
TACKLE ZONING A "TWIST"

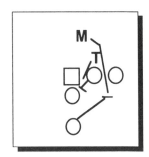

DIAGRAM 5-8
BACK ASSIGNED
TO LB MAN BLOCKS "LOOP"

Using simple protections

One principle we adhere to is to keep the protection schemes as simple as possible. The key to pass protection is matching up your blockers to the potential pass rushers. Recognition of potential pass rushers is key, and the simpler you can make your pass protection rules, the easier matching linemen to rushers will be. The simplest example of this would be a base scheme defined simply as "block man on". This is clearly an easy scheme to define and the rule provides an easy scheme for pass rush recognition. Another example of an easy scheme is the traditional sprint out scheme of "frontside REACH and backside HINGE". No matter how easily you define your protections there will be times that the defense can align in ways that make protection by the rules tough, therefore you will need a set of calls to adjust protection. A clear set of terms that allow the linemen to communicate is invaluable when it comes to dealing with the exceptions to the blocking rules. The complete set of terms we use to communicate will not be presented in this work, because we are only speaking of pass protections in a general sense to facilitate the incorporation of the Bunch principle into whatever offensive system you use.

Adjusting protections to different fronts

As discussed above, we believe in keeping our protection schemes as simple as possible. This necessitates a system of communication that allows for some flexibility for our linemen in choosing the best protection techniques to fit a particular front they are seeing or alignment problem they are encountering. We believe that such a system is a necessity for pass protection. It is very difficult to design a system that will stay absolutely unchanged versus all fronts and accounts for all possible problems defensive staffs can dream up for you pass offense. Our approach is to design a protection in such a way that it has the flexibility built into it, allowing adjustments to the front and allowing the linemen to use the best techniques available to them in any given situation. Toward this end, we have calls that turn the line back in the protection scheme to gain better angles, calls to fan the line out, calls that collapse linemen into gaps, and calls that would bring an uncovered lineman outside or backside to pick up potential rushers. What our specific calls are is not that important, rather the consideration of the premise that you will let your linemen on the field make the decisions that most directly relate to them doing their job better.

Protections for one and two back sets

Clearly, protection is directly impacted by two key formation considerations: how many receivers you use, and how many backs you decide to keep in the backfield. Since we use a multiple offensive package, making use of varied passing packages (of which "bunch" is only one concept), we use protections that are designed for both one and two back sets. What we strive to do is to design protection schemes that are defined similarly regardless of whether we are one back or two back. We try to keep the rules as standard, yet as simple as possible, with few exceptions to the rule. Usually the second backs can easily fit in to most protections without much adjusting of the overall scheme. The closer the rules for one and two back set protections are, the easier for all to understand how the protection will be applied to the defensive fronts you are seeing, regardless of the formation you are using.

Building simple pass protection schemes for Bunch

The illustrations we have chosen for this text illustrating the varied uses of bunched receiver alignments have been chosen for their applicability to most any offense. The basic routes and packages discussed can be used with six simple protections. As mentioned earlier, this is not our entire offensive pass protection package, but a selected set of illustrations that can be adapted to any package. Most offensive systems will already be using some, or all, of these protections, thus making adaption of this principle into your offense much easier. You can develop new calls, or use your existing protection calls and rules, and feel reasonably assured of success.

The protections illustrated in this text are as follows:

    90 PROTECTION—Quick, 3 step, firm on the line 6 or 7 man protection
    80 PROTECTION—5 step angled drop, Reach and Hinge 6 or 7 man protection
    70 PROTECTION—Sprint out, Reach and Hinge, 6 or 7 man protection

50 PROTECTION—5 step dropback, cup, turnback, 6 or 7 man protection
300 PROTECTION— Play Action dropback, Reach & Pivot, 6 or 7 man protection
200 PROTECTION— Bootleg Action, block down, backside guard pull, 6 or 7 man protection

The following diagrams illustrate the basic protection calls that we often have used in more than one of these protection schemes:

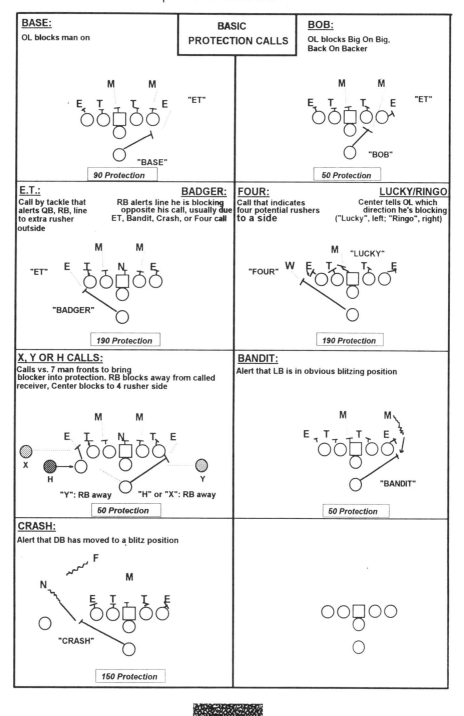

BASIC PROTECTION CALLS

BASE:
OL blocks man on

"BASE"

90 Protection

BOB:
OL blocks Big On Big, Back On Backer

"BOB"

50 Protection

E.T.:
Call by tackle that alerts QB, RB, line to extra rusher outside

BADGER:
RB alerts line he is blocking opposite his call, usually due ET, Bandit, Crash, or Four call

"BADGER"

190 Protection

FOUR:
Call that indicates four potential rushers to a side

LUCKY/RINGO
Center tells OL which direction he's blocking ("Lucky", left; "Ringo", right)

190 Protection

X, Y OR H CALLS:
Calls vs. 7 man fronts to bring blocker into protection. RB blocks away from called receiver, Center blocks to 4 rusher side

"Y": RB away   "H" or "X": RB away

50 Protection

BANDIT:
Alert that LB is in obvious blitzing position

"BANDIT"

50 Protection

CRASH:
Alert that DB has moved to a blitz position

"CRASH"

150 Protection

<table>
<tr><td colspan="3">

IF:
Tight End works with uncovered
tackle, check releasing off LB

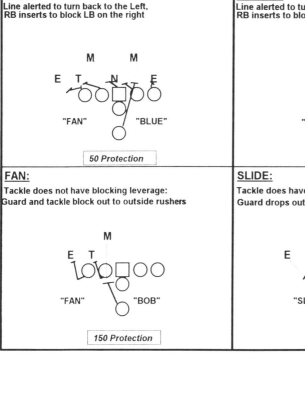

S drops, Y leaves
& tackle blocks E

"ET"

| 50 Protection |

</td></tr>
</table>

	BASIC PROTECTION CALLS	

IF:
Tight End works with uncovered
tackle, check releasing off LB

"ET"

S drops, Y leaves
& tackle blocks E

| 50 Protection |

TUFF:
TE blocks man on--
Should get help from RB
*Used to double a great rusher at End

"TUFF"

| 70 Protection |

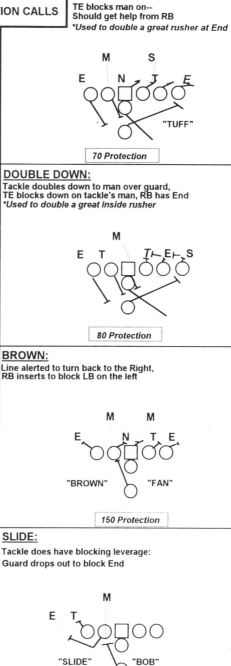

DOWN:
TE slams man on, and doubles down
to tackle's man.
*Used to double a great rusher at Tackle

"DOWN"

| 70 Protection |

DOUBLE DOWN:
Tackle doubles down to man over guard,
TE blocks down on tackle's man, RB has End
*Used to double a great inside rusher

| 80 Protection |

BLUE:
Line alerted to turn back to the Left,
RB inserts to block LB on the right

"FAN"   "BLUE"

| 50 Protection |

BROWN:
Line alerted to turn back to the Right,
RB inserts to block LB on the left

"BROWN"   "FAN"

| 150 Protection |

FAN:
Tackle does not have blocking leverage:
Guard and tackle block out to outside rushers

"FAN"   "BOB"

| 150 Protection |

SLIDE:
Tackle does have blocking leverage:
Guard drops out to block End

"SLIDE"   "BOB"

| 150 Protection |

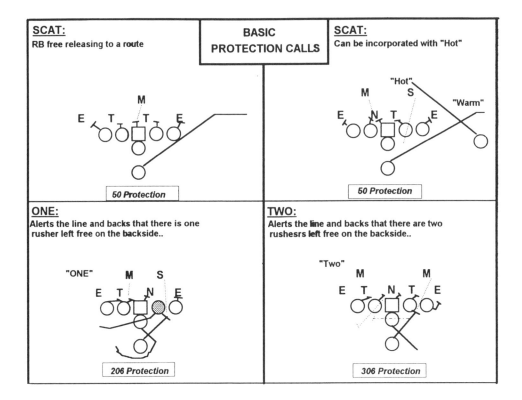

BASIC PROTECTION CALLS

SCAT: RB free releasing to a route

50 Protection

SCAT: Can be incorporated with "Hot"

50 Protection

ONE: Alerts the line and backs that there is one rusher left free on the backside..

206 Protection

TWO: Alerts the line and backs that there are two rushesrs left free on the backside..

306 Protection

90-190 protection

Our three step drop, quick passing game uses 90 PROTECTION rules. The basic definition of 90 PROTECTION is to block the man on using a quick pass set technique, firmly keeping the defender on the line of scrimmage and allowing no penetration to an inside gap. The backs are assigned to block the end man on the line of scrimmage unless given a call that changes their assignment. The center is assigned backside with the single back assigned call side. Since this is quick pass protection, the ball will be gone very quickly, therefore we are as aggressive as possible on the line of scrimmage to keep pass defenders' hands down. Some pertinent calls we use are:

BASE:	Line call indicating to block the man on
BOB:	Big on Big, Back on Backer, call to assign RB to LB, linemen to #1 and #2 DL on the L.O.S.
E.T.:	Tackle call indicating "extra" rusher to his outside, demands a decision as to how we are going to block him ("Eee"-"Tee")
BADGER:	Back call indicating he is blocking away from call, four weak rushers
X, Y, H:	Calls bringing X, Y, H into the protection scheme as a blocker
FOUR:	Call indicating four rushers to a side
RINGO:	Call putting center to right side, used to account for four rushers
LUCKY:	Call putting center to left side, used to account for four rushers
CRASH:	Receiver alert to potential DB blitz
BANDIT:	Receiver alert to potential OLB blitz off edge

The diagrams that follow illustrate 90-190 PROTECTION versus different fronts and indicate the basic use of each call.

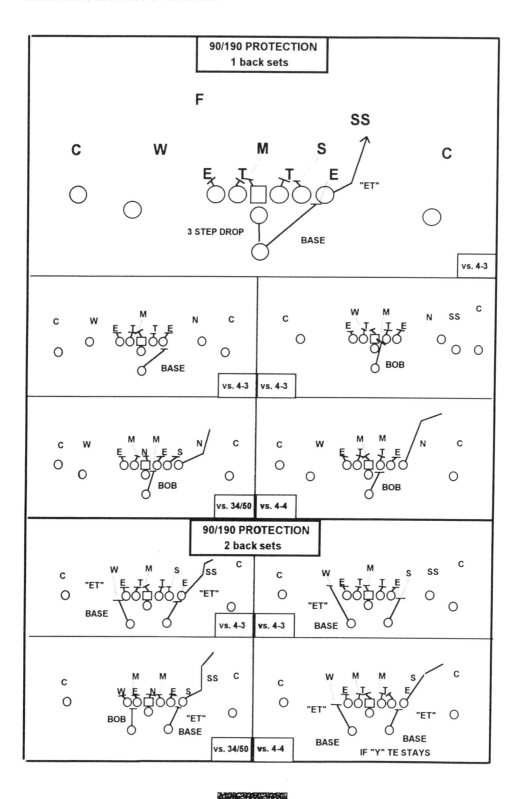

80-180 protection

Our half-roll passing game makes use of a 5 step, angled drop that keeps the quarterback in the guard-tackle gap. The pass protection we use is 80 PROTECTION. This protection is defined as onside REACH to the call side gap and backside HINGE and retreat. The back is initially assigned to block the end man on the line of scrimmage. A second back is assigned to block to the call side, checking playside LB's or helping on the end man with the first back, but may get called to the backside due to front calls that can be given. Any blocker frontside who does not encounter a pass rusher in his area is to pivot and work to the backside. The center is defined as part of the REACH unit if covered and part of the HINGE unit if uncovered. Most of the basic calls discussed still apply and can be used with this protection to adjust to fronts as needed. Other calls that apply include:

IF: inside receiver call, usually a TE, indicating he is working check release off the linebacker his side in tandem with an uncovered lineman

The following diagrams illustrate 80 protection and some common calls:

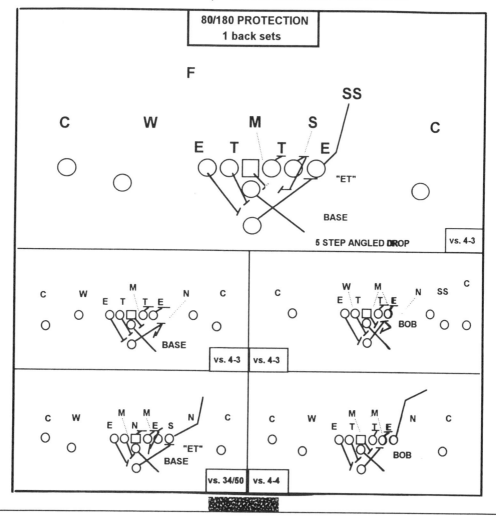

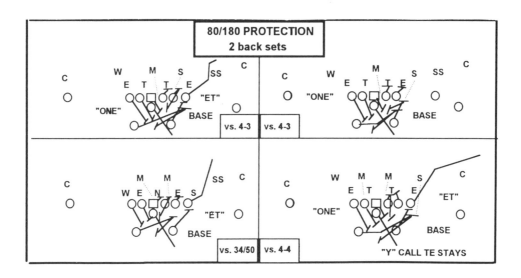

80/180 PROTECTION
2 back sets

vs. 4-3 | vs. 4-3 | vs. 34/50 | vs. 4-4

"Y" CALL TE STAYS

70-170 Protection

Full sprint out protection uses the same REACH and HINGE protection used for our 5 step angled drop. Therefore, to the line, **70-170** and **80-180** are the same basic protections, with a different quarterback launch point. The linemen need to understand how the difference in launch point effects the firmness of the protection and the rush angles. An awareness.of where they can let a rusher go is essential, yet by using the same basic rules we cut down learning, which allows for increased understanding of the finer points in each protection. We have calls that aid blocking on the edge toward the sprint , in order to account for a superior pass rusher to the sprint side.

TUFF: Playside inside receiver blocks man on, may get RB help (double team)
DOWN: Playside inside receiver double teams on next man inside using slam technique on man over him to set him up for RB
DBL DOWN: Playside guard-tackle double down on first DL inside tackle, inside receiver blocks down to next man inside, RB has the end man

Again, it is of special note that our other protection calls are still in use, therefore there is a high amount of carry-over from one protection to the next. The following diagrams illustrate 70-170 SPRINT PROTECTION.

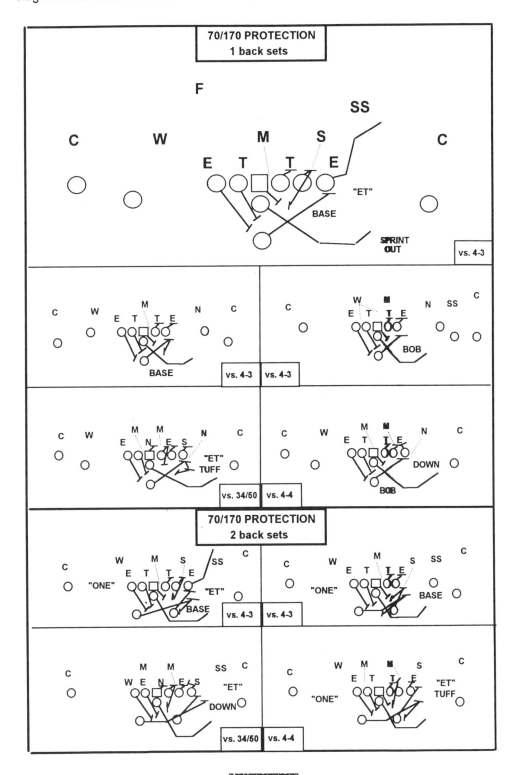

50-150 protection

Our 5 step dropback passing game operates using 50 PROTECTION. This protection is the simplest dropback protection scheme we use, and some years it is all we are able to use. It is standard cup protection by the line with the backs initially assigned to the end men on the line of scrimmage. It can be altered to turnback protection, with the insertion of the backs to the call side simply by using a call. Since turnback protection answers many protection problems you encounter with twists, stunts, and blitzes, this protection has great versatility and can be used safely verses most standard fronts. It does not answer every question that may arise in every pass package we use, but you can assure solid protection and simple rules by using careful formation game planning. This protection scheme is easy to adapt to four wide receiver, one back systems, to guarantee at least four receivers out. It also offers a two back maximum protection cup, capable of blocking a 7 or 8 man rush, using the tight end. Because dropback passing involves careful blitz planning, one must be careful what routes are used with this simplest of dropback protections. We create a set of calls that give this protection some versatility for our linemen and add some ways to strengthen the protection. As with the other protections, some of our calls have carry-over to this protection.

SCAT: call indicating the free release of a back, employed with a hot read by the quarterback (or warm dump, or Q-quick throw alert)

BROWN: call turning line back to right from first uncovered lineman, RB inserts himself into the protection

BLUE: line turns left

FAN: call for tackle-guard technique to block two outside rushers

SLIDE: call for guard to block outside most rusher

This is a standard protection (for any system) that is fairly simple, yet adaptable to many fronts. Again, special emphasis is needed in dealing with all the vast types of blitzes being employed by defenses these days. We tend to "protect first" and check to a given list of blitz checks rather than read "hot" and take our chances.

The following diagrams illustrate 50-150 PROTECTION and the uses of several calls:

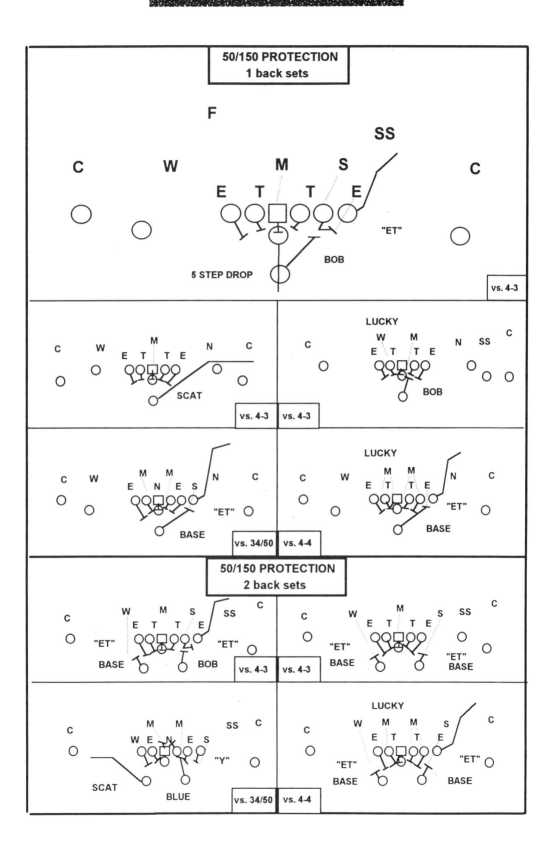

300 Protection

300, our basic play action dropback protection, can be used with several running plays in our system. If we want to play action pass off our basic outside zone "STRETCH" play which is 8-9 in our run system, then 308-309 indicates fake stretch right or left and set up. By changing the number, different play fakes can be accomplished. A play action fake off the inside ZONE would be numbered 306-307. A play action pass off a basic BLAST or LEAD play would become 336-337. 300 PROTECTION is defined as a call side zone step and pivot backside if no one shows in your area. Offensive linemen account for all defensive linemen in the front with the faking backs check releasing off the remaining linebackers call side. As with all protections, some special calls are needed to deal with special situations you may encounter.

ONE: call of backside lineman indicating how many defenders or potential rushers remain in the front, players pivoting, or backs can be responsible for them

TWO: two defenders left backside

One must also note that, as with most play action pass protections, stunts and blitzes put extreme pressure on these type of protections. Careful game planning as to down, distance, and situation on the field is important. The quarterback may read the blitz and everyone may be aware of where the problem rushers are, yet in the end it is always a "game of poker" when you match a play action pass against an all out blitz by the defense. Sometimes the rewards are great and sometimes the risks make you pay.

The following diagrams offer some standard 300 PROTECTION looks:

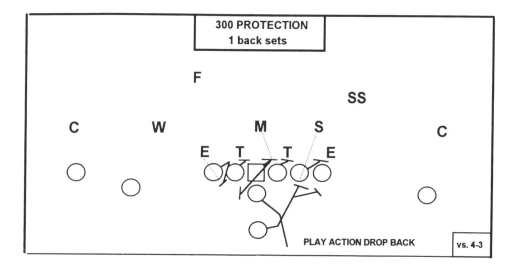

300 PROTECTION
1 back sets

PLAY ACTION DROP BACK

vs. 4-3

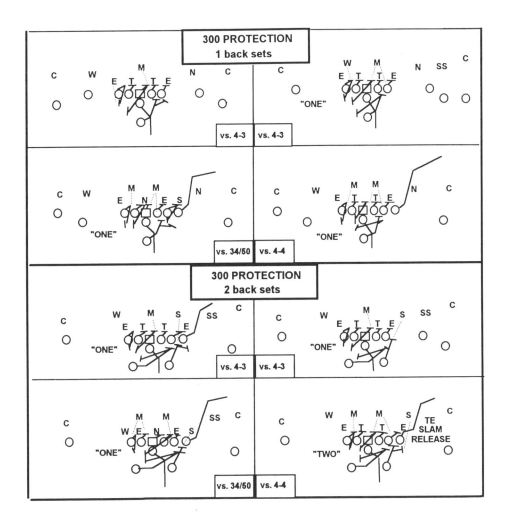

200 Protection

Bootleg action by the quarterback requires a bootleg 200 PROTECTION scheme. For us, bootleg action usually comes off an inside ZONE (206-207) fake or a COUNTER TREY (226-227) fake. Bootleg protection involves the line stepping to the gap toward the run fake, and the guard to the side of the run call using a sickle pulling technique, as the protector for the quarterback's bootleg action. If no one shows in an assigned area then the linemen keep working in the same direction (will be backside, away from where the QB ends up) by gaining depth and looking for extra rushers. The "one" and " two" calls are important, as is defining a rule for how to deal with a "two" call to the side of the boot. We assign the faking back (to the backside) the outside linebacker that would be a "one" call and rely on someone helping out to the "two" call backside. We also have simplified things by just checking out of bootleg actions when we get "two" calls, since usually that is indicative of the potential for blitz. As with other play action schemes there is large room for risk against defensive blitz schemes. There is also the potential for big gains with careful game planning and teaching of techniques and reads.

The following diagrams illustrate our standard bootleg 200 PROTECTION:

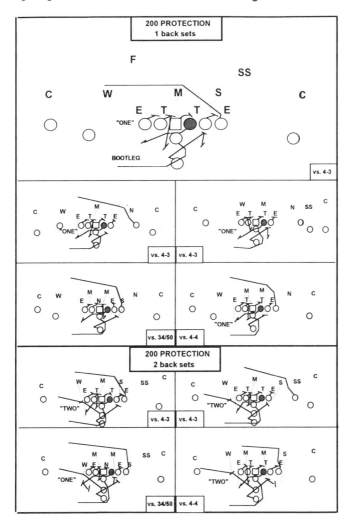

Summary

The purpose of this chapter has been to illustrate some standard pass protection schemes that can be used with a "Bunch" passing concept. Our intent has not been to sell you on our protection scheme. Nor have we attempted to cover every scheme or call we use. We have added this protection chapter to address the question we have been asked the most, which is, "How can we protect the quarterback in this pass package?" We have selected the illustrations in the succeeding chapters to better illustrate how the "Bunch" principle can be applicable to any offensive structure. The protections we selected are fairly common and are adaptable to any offensive system you may employ. The rest of the text illustrates the standard route packages and techniques used in the Bunch philosophy. The reader should be able to understand our system clearly enough to see what we are doing with our offensive structure, therefore realizing its potential for your offense.

CHAPTER 6

Building the "Mesh" Route Package

Introduction and basic attack concept

If there is one single package that could be considered a "base" route within the Bunch concept, it would be what we call the "Mesh" route. In its basic form, it provides a number of options that hold up well against most any coverage. Even better, its structure provides the flexibility to easily tag it a number of different ways to specifically break different coverages and techniques. Most of the Bunch attack concepts we have discussed up to this point can be realized in some part of the Mesh package. This adaptability will prove particularly helpful later in this section in discussing the employment of the Mesh in different situations and with different pass actions.

As with most any route that we use in a bunched environment, it is taught initially from normal, spread formations, then later refined as specific Bunch formations are applied. This provides a consistent, solid foundation for learning and building from a base of knowledge rather than just memorization of arbitrary routes and concepts. A full installation schedule is discussed and illustrated in Chapter 20, and you will see how all of this fits together for us and our players.

Technique and basic route mechanics

The following diagram illustrates our starting point in the teaching of this package:

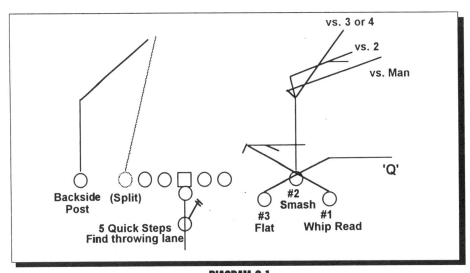

DIAGRAM 6-1
BASIC ROUTE DEFINITIONS FOR MESH ROUTE

Frontside:

#1: Whip Read. Mesh over the top of the flat runner at six yards, being certain to gain some push on the defender over you with your eyes and arm action. We do not want him squatting on you.

Your key is the defender over the #3 receiver; unless something happens to change your mind, you will push hard at him, threatening across the field to try to turn his hips inside. Near the original position of #3, drop your head and drive your arms to get a final burst, and spin out flat, accelerating away to the Whip. This should happen a depth of 6 to 7 yards and stay at that depth; keep it flat and do not gain depth upfield. If you see a zone defender outside you as you're accelerating out of the break, cut the throttle in the open hole and face the quarterback. Otherwise, assume it is man coverage, keep accelerating away, and look back at the quarterback once you're sure of coverage and know that you're open.

What would change your mind at the initial breaking point? If the defender over #3 works vertical and gets depth, then you will sit right inside him, face the quarterback, and look for the ball, after which you'll spin 180 degrees north and begin splitting defenders. Your rule is that if he is backing up and not reacting to your route, you can sit right there. Otherwise, assume that you are to spin out of it to the Whip.

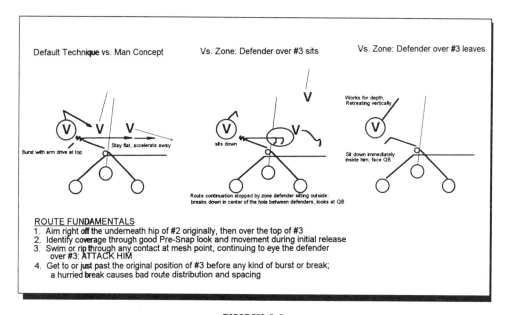

DIAGRAM 6-2
WHIP READ TECHNIQUES

Alerts to #1 receiver: Special tags. Certain tags added to the basic Mesh route will dictate that #1 should not use his normal Whip technique, but make different adjustments off the initial stem. The following tags address other receivers in the pattern but affect your technique as well. Note specifically that each of these dictate that you do not look to sit down versus a zone until you have passed a certain point.

Stem, Arrow, Spear, or Turn. After your initial release, continue inside of the defender over #3, sitting in the center of the hole between him and the next defender inside. If you have a man chasing you, continue across.

Hi. #1 will now rub over the top of you, and you will continue across, accelerating to get separation, looking at the QB when you're sure of coverage and the fact that you're open. If you see any zone defenders stopping your route past the mesh, sit in the center and look at the QB.

Under. Same initial dynamics as Hi, but now you will continue after the mesh in an attempt to rub over the top over a Shallow Cross route from the backside at a depth of six yards. Do not sit versus any type of zone until after you have passed this man.

Delay. Precisely the same as Under, except that you will sprint fully until you've cleared the backside TE area at a depth of 4 yards, because someone is delaying behind you. Do not throttle until 4 yards past the backside TE.

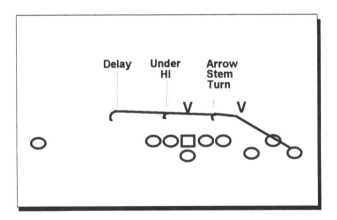

DIAGRAM 6-3
EARLIEST ZONE SIT-DOWN POINTS FOR #1 WITH VARIOUS TAGS

#2: Smash. Release cleanly, straight up the field, break at 10-12 yards based on coverage.

Versus Man coverage or Cover 1, eyeball your defender and push hard to the Post; get his hips turned. Plant your inside foot, arms driving, and snap your head back out, accelerating away to the corner.

Against Cover 2, angle your break as deeply as the hash safety's action will allow you without having him on your back; for normal safety technique, this will amount to splitting the locations of the cornerback and safety right down the middle. If he's a really wide, over-the-top safety, make sure you stay head-up to a bit outside him with your weave. Look the safety in the eye and push him deeper into his backpedal until you snap your head and plant your inside foot on your break; this will give you a bigger hole and keep him off your back. You may use a nod inside with your head as well.

Versus Cover 3 or any coverage where you see a deep corner outside of you (e.g., Cover 4), angle deep to the corner, trying to get over the top of deep ⅓ or ¼ coverage. Do not lose acceleration to make a distinct break.

#3: Flat. "Mesh" beneath the Whip Read; look him up and try to rub shoulders with him at about five yards (See special mesh technique adjustment from squeeze). Do not wander to this point; angle up to your depth, getting some deep push, and make a distinct, flat, break, snapping your head around, on your way to the mesh. Drive your arms and run through the mesh—you may get the ball as soon as you clear it (you are the 'Q' receiver). For this reason, you should have your hands in position to make the catch as your head snaps around, anticipating the quick throw. Make the catch, getting in the habit of seating the ball in your outside arm, and turn up the sideline, defeating one defender at a time. Be moving forward as you go down; because you know that this is a ball-control pass, you're extra aware of how vital the extra yard or two after the catch may be.

On 3d down and 4-5, push your route 1 yard beyond the marker before flattening; if we're less than five yards from the goal line, get 1 yard deep in the end zone. If you only get to the first down marker or the goal line, you risk get shoved back by the defender or brought back by the ball. You should locate this spot before the snap and get to it; don't guess.

Special Note: If the fullback has motioned wide to his sit down route, you must sit your Flat route down inside the last underneath defender you see and ensure that he cannot cover both you and the fullback.

Fullback:
Protection, call, or motion. By the definition of the route, you are most often the frontside #4 receiver who is to stay in and block with no check release; if you get no linebacker in your protection, sit and help. Certain, special situations change that.

You may, at times, be the #3 receiver frontside from an offset position; in this case you take on the same responsibilities and rules as any other #3 receiver. You could have the same tags applied to you as any #3 as well.

You may also have a called route from your #4 position; run the route as the last releaser into the pattern.

Other times, as our offense develops, we may employ a backside check with me in which we slide you to the weakside and check release you on a backside Flare. You'll know this by game plan.

The last possibility is to put you in motion wide. This will be done from the hashmarks, motioning you to the wide side of the field all the way to about six yards from the sideline to severely stretch the defense. Motion parallel to the line of scrimmage and, upon the snap of the ball, lose a bit of ground before turning up field on your flare route. In hot situations and/or uncovered instances, you'll get the ball right away. This type of motion always makes you a 'Q' receiver. If you have not received the ball at 4 yards, turn there and face the quarterback. This is the only motion that does not affect the numbering of receivers; you are still considered #4, even out wide.

Special technique adjustments for #1 & #3 from bunched alignments

Mesh mechanics. From compressed formations, attempting to rub shoulders at a determined distance no longer becomes functional; therefore, the rules change. The person running the high route (in other words, the one who would mesh over the top from a normal split; the Whip Read in a normal call, the Flat in a "Hi" call) must release related to the man over, or nearest to being over, the low man. He will release directly at that man's near hip (outside hip for a Whip Read, inside hip for a Flat), continuing to mirror that near hip until he brushes just by that hip going past. Do not initiate collision; stay on your landmark looking to run by. If he tries to run through you, keep your arms driving and eyes upfield. It is important that you mirror his movements, constantly adjusting your route to his hip in order to not allow him to slip directly or easily by you to his coverage. After this mesh, readjust and get back on your normal route course.

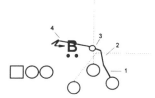

WHIP READ as high mesher

1- Initial release angle right at B's outside hip
2- Adjustment: B widens, realign on his hip, keep outside leverage
3- Possible mesh point; run through with eyes up
4- Continue on normal route, see coverage, adjust

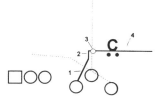

FLAT as high mesher

1- Initial release angle right at C's inside hip
2- Adjustment: C closes, realign on his hip, keep inside leverage
3- Possible mesh point; run through with eyes up
4- Continue on normal route, see coverage, adjust

DIAGRAM 6-4
BUNCH MESH MECHANICS

- **CARDINAL RULE:** *Do not allow the defender over the receiver for whom you're meshing to take the easiest route to him, unhindered. DO YOUR JOB.*

Timing and release. This type of route dictates a certain timing of receiver releases. #2 will always be allowed to release first, with the High man releasing under him as closely as possible while still staying clean from collision or hesitation. The Low man, then, wants to release behind and underneath both of these in getting into this pattern. He still must get good push, acceleration, and use good separation technique in his routes; he times things up correctly by deepening alignment just slightly and coming off the ball with a split second's hesitation, not by cutting down his speed during the route itself.

Backside:
Post or Split except for special calls. Post for wide receivers, "Split" route for backside tight ends or wide receivers with a Cover 2 look backside. Stay skinny inside a deep free safety, especially since you are a viable option against cover 4-type looks.

- *"Under" Tag.* The "UNDER" tag tells the backside receiver that he will be meshing underneath a frontside crosser at a depth of five to six yards. He runs a normal Shallow Cross route, trying to separate from man coverage, or find a hole to throttle in versus a zone. Important versus zone is that once he makes the catch in the hole, he must spin 180 degrees and look to split defenders going north and not dance around sideways.

- *"Delay" tag.* If the backside receiver is tagged to run a Delay route, he hesitates two to three counts, waiting for a receiver from the frontside to clear him. Having done that, he releases into the area behind that man, looking for a crease to get into so the quarterback can get him the ball. Again, he looks to split zone defenders going straight upfield after the catch.

- *Curl, Hinge, and other single route tags.* Other individual routes may be given to the backside man depending on what we are trying to do. In these cases, he employs the normal split and technique associated with these routes.

Quarterback reads for basic MESH route

- **CARDINAL RULE:** *When in doubt, be prepared to hit the Flat right off your fifth step; always force the defense to cover the flat. This is a ball control pass.*

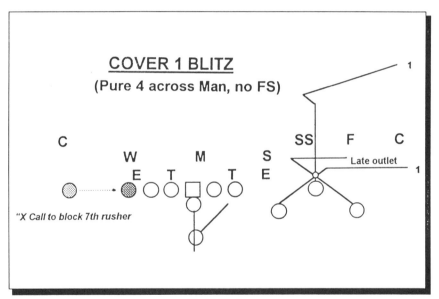

DIAGRAM 6-5
QB READS VS. COVER 1 BLITZ

1. If you have the right matchup and can get time, SMASH is the ideal choice because of its big play possibilities. Be aware, though, that you may not have a lot of time to throw against this coverage because they're bringing people.

2. Otherwise, hit the FLAT off the mesh off your fifth step, throwing it right through his hip and keeping him on the move. Make sure you don't blindly throw into a cornerback who has made the switch and is waiting in the Flat...you should know this by game plan.

3. The WHIP will always be working inside out against this coverage, getting open slightly later than the Flat. This is the outlet you always want to find if:
   - The Flat is your choice and doesn't get free; or
   - The Smash is your choice, but you can't wait it out because of pressure.

The Whip Read should not be a problem to find because he will be working right into your vision. Keep your feet alive if either of these two scenarios occur, bounce up and throw it to the side *away from* where he is covered, again allowing him to keep running away from coverage.

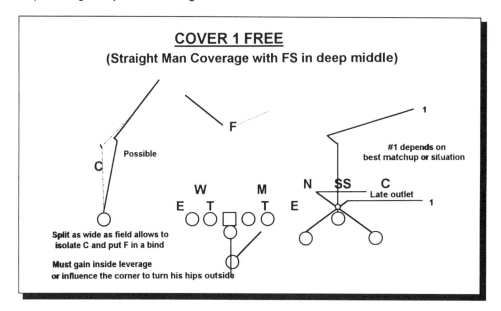

DIAGRAM 6-6
QB READS VS. COVER 1 FREE

1. Your first choice will vary by situation and matchups, but the SMASH should be able to defeat the FS. You should have time to wait him out if you think that you can get him free.

2. If we're playing a free safety who wants to overplay to Trips, we might take a shot at staring him off to the Smash and coming back to the Post...lead him and don't make him slow down for the football.

3. As with Cover 1 Blitz, the FLAT throw quickly off your fifth step is your guarantee and your money-maker. Understand the possibility of any type of Banjo or Switch that would defeat the route with outside leverage.

4. The WHIP outlet will still hold up well if any of your early options breaks down. The instant you see any sort of Switch or exchange taking place, you

know that the Whip will have leverage on his defender as he works back outside.

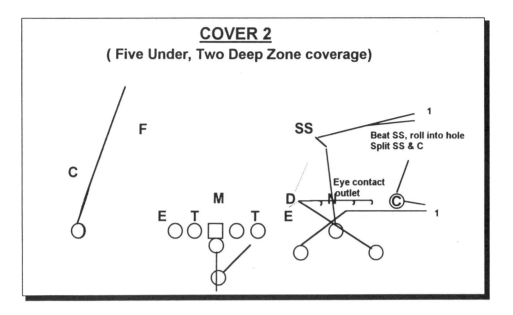

DIAGRAM 6-7
QB READS VS. COVER 2

1. The basic Cover 2 read is off the reaction of the cornerback; if he gives ground, hit the FLAT right off the Mesh, if he stays stationary or comes up on the Flat, throw to the SMASH in the hole, flattening the receiver slightly to the open area if need be. NEVER, under any circumstances, try to throw a Smash route over the top of a retreating cornerback.

2. The WHIP route is given the responsibility of getting open in some sort of zone void. If neither of the first two looks is available, you should be able to glance quickly to find whether the Whip is available or not. If he is making eye contact with you, throw to him as a stationary outlet in the hole; if you do not get eye contact, throw the ball away or shuffle your feet and wait for him to clear if you have time.

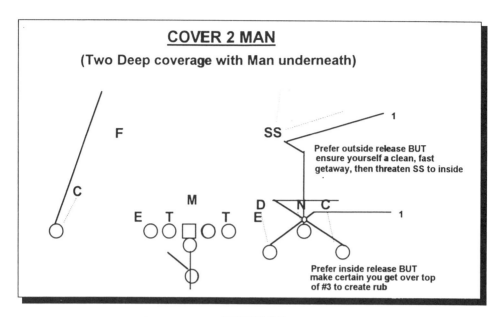

DIAGRAM 6-8
QB READS VS. COVER 2 MAN

1. Again, the first choice is a function of the down and distance situation. Certainly, however, we want to think in terms of SMASH if we can, if the matchup is favorable and the hash safety does not work too quickly over the top.

2. The FLAT should come off cleanly from the mesh, because his man will be playing inside leverage (beware of switches). A quick throw to him off your fifth step is a good guarantee play on third and medium.

3. Another good way to pop a man free quickly is through a HI tag, which will spring your #1 coming inside off the mesh. If the middle linebacker is not a factor working that way, this could be a big play.

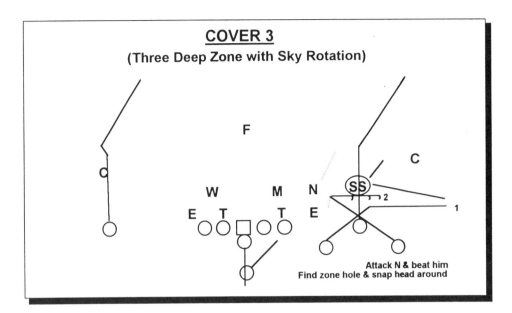

DIAGRAM 6-9
QB READS VS. COVER 3

1. You're basically working whoever is responsible for the Flat area, either the SS or corner if he's rolled up in "Cloud" rotation. Take five quick steps and hit the FLAT immediately, giving him the best chance to make good yardage up the sideline after the catch. If the flat coverage has jumped him, it will be obvious to you during your drop, and you'll pop up off your fifth step, shuffle, and hit the WHIP as he snaps his head around into the natural void that is created by the flat coverage widening to cover #3. Throw the ball right into the hole, stopping him with it, so that he can turn and begin splitting zone defenders vertically.

2. In very rare cases, versus either an especially slow corner who doesn't get depth on his backpedal, or an exceptionally active corner who wants to come up quickly to tackle the Flat, we can predetermine that we'll pump to the Flat and try to hit the Smash going over the top.

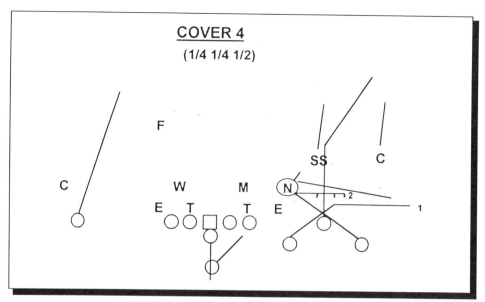

DIAGRAM 6-10
QB READS VS. COVER 4

1. Against this coverage, we have the first short defender outmanned. The faster you can read his movement and get the ball in the hands of the one he does not cover, the more we gain after the catch. This play will work much more effectively, however, if you can do that without advertising the fact that you are looking to throw the ball short. The deeper the deep ¼ defenders work as they run with the Smash, the better.

Thought Process Summary			
COVERAGE	**PRIME READ/MOVEMENT KEY**	**OUTLET**	**POSSIBLE CHECKS**
1 Blitz	Matchup: Smash or Flat	Whip	X Call - 7 man prot
1 Free	Matchup: Smash or Flat	Whip	Post if FS leaves
2	Cloud Corner: Flat or Smash	Whip	Shake vs. wide SS
2 Man	Matchup: Smash (hash Saf) or Flat	Whip	HI to get Shallow Crs
3	Cornerback: Flat to Smash	Whip	Stem Hide
4	Short defender: Flat to Whip read		Arrow Hide

Route tags and adjustments for frontside receivers

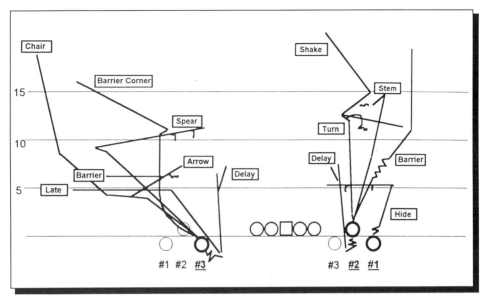

DIAGRAM 6-11
SUMMARY TREE OF MESH ROUTE TAGS

Adjustments for #1

- *HI.* You now have the low mesher part of the route and your assignment turns into a full-speed Shallow Cross. Use the mesh to gain separation vs. man, accelerating away, look for open holes to throttle in (after the mesh) vs. zone. In either case, notify the QB that you have identified the coverage and are ready for the ball by making eye contact with him.

- *HIDE.* Pause - push up 4 to 5 yards under control. Let #2 and #3 clear over the top of you, then plant and come underneath; try to brush underneath the Flat runner's shoulders. You want to get cleanly inside the first short defender, whoever he is, and find the next dropping linebacker inside. Go underneath him if he chases routes wide, sit if he sits. If you feel a man defender chasing you as you get your initial push, give a hard stick to the outside and accelerate in underneath. Catch the ball, tuck it, spin and split defenders going straight upfield.

Adjustments for #2

- *STEM.* Weave to a spot 3-4 yards outside your alignment for 4 yards, then push hard to 14-15. Use phony acceleration at the top to separate from any deep defender. Plant under control and come straight down the STEM, finding the next underneath coverage inside. Do not make a wide turn. Get depth to ensure that you're behind underneath coverage. The ball will be on its way as you come down the stem.

  Note: If you see two deep defenders playing deep ¼ over you, don't weave outside; use your split and your weave to get head up to inside the inside ¼ defender and BEAT HIM. Do not give him an inside course to the ball. This is the only way you can keep from being bracketed by deep ¼s. Catch, tuck, turn.

- *TURN.* Push straight upfield to 12, feeling the coverage as you go. If someone is chasing you, stick hard inside, plant inside foot and break outside, coming back downhill slightly. If you feel zone drops, turn outside at your 12 yard breaking point and get centered in the hole, making eye contact with the quarterback. This is a possession-down route, so be alert to adjust your cut 1-3 yards depending on where the marker is.

- *BARRIER.* Weave wide, approximately 45 degrees for four steps off the line. Straighten up; find the man covering the man inside you OR the Sky flat defender and move upfield at whatever speed necessary to impede/collision him. Once clear, accelerate straight up the seam, looking to outrun the Free Safety.

- *SHAKE.* Base Mesh route technique, but in the third step of your break back out to the Corner, drop your hips, plant your outside foot, and drive back to the Post, looking to get skinny over the top of the FS. Your head and shoulders must stay on a swivel throughout.

- *DELAY.* Basic delay technique; pause two to three counts to let people cross in front of you and defenders react. Then, seeing the coverage, come out into the open lane behind them, look for the ball and begin splitting defenders straight upfield.

Adjustments for #3

- *HI or HIDE.* These calls change you to the high mesher, rubbing over the top of #3 at about six yards. Once the mesh is cleared, snap your head around to the Flat and be prepared to get the ball.

- *LATE.* You run your normal Flat route, but hesitate a bit over a count before doing so, using the time to feel the initial movement of the defense, and work as the last receiver into the pattern.

- *ARROW.* Push outside hard to the flat for 5-6 yards on a normal Flat angle; convince the defender that you're going to the flat and turn his hips. Thrust head forward and numbers low on last, exaggerated step before break. Know Man or Zone quickly; vs. Zone, come out of break flat and under control, finding next inside zone dropper and looking to center yourself in the void. Vs. man, accelerate and angle upfield if you do not see stray linebackers dropping.

- *SPEAR.* This amounts simply to a deeper version of Arrow. Your initial angle will not be quite as flat, and your depth of break becomes 9-10 yards. You want to get behind the first layer of coverage. Your techniques out of the break are exactly the same as on Arrow, with the exception that vs. zones, you may have to run through the first open window and get the ball in the second one.

- *DELAY.* Basic delay technique; pause two to three counts to let people cross in front of you and defenders react. Then, seeing the coverage, come out into the open lane behind them, look for the ball and begin splitting defenders straight upfield

- *BARRIER.* Stretch your release to stay on the inside hip of #2; when he straightens, push up one step outside him and snap out to a flat break behind him.

- *BARRIER CORNER.* Get outside #2 when he straightens, straighten yourself slightly to push your defender back on his heels, nod inside and accelerate to the corner at 10 yards deep.

- *CHAIR.* Snap head around just like flat break for 3-4 steps, plant and accelerate upfield, getting width to a landmark 6 yards from the sideline. Use Fade landmark and technique.

CHAPTER 7

Attacking Coverages with the "Mesh" Package

Why Mesh is our first and most basic Bunch package

The Mesh, or "7" route package is the best and most useful package we employ within the Bunch concept, for these and other reasons:

1. Its basic structure and definitions allow it the most diversified kinds of variations to attack the widest variety of defensive adjustments and wrinkles.

2. The three core routes that make up the frontside of the route are three that we have seen have success against most any coverage, are routes we believe in and can complete with a high percentage, and have initial releases that are naturally complemented by a host of other breaks off of them that can take advantage of a defense's initial reaction.

3. The route can be built around a wide variety of pass actions, and can incorporate a full range of protections, from the least to the most restrictive.

4. By using different combinations of the "building blocks" associated with the package—formations, pass actions, protections, and tags—we can fashion good answers to most any game situation out of the Mesh. We can use it to emphasize quick throws against a heavy rush, or deeper throws when we have a mismatch.

For those same reasons, Mesh is perhaps the most popular "Bunch" route currently in use in the NFL. Offensive coordinators feel they can get a step or so extra separation for their athletes, which is vital at that level, and its basic route can be used to set up other things at key times.

The Mesh's flexibility has been specifically highlighted during two recent playoff games. In a 1996 divisional playoff between Indianapolis and Kansas City, the Colts used different forms of Mesh twice early in the game. In the first instance, they ran it out of a straight I formation, motioning Z in close, and using the fullback as the #3 Flat runner after a play fake. They used the same action later out of a bunched I Twins set, again off play action. Both times, the Fullback was clearly open in a lot of space, both times he dropped the ball. Because of the flexibility of their system and the route, though, they were able to come back to it in a crucial 3rd and goal situation, knowing it had been open before. This time they did it out of a four wide receiver Bunch with "Idiot" motion (the motion man running the Flat) and a straight drop back action, impeding defensive recognition while allowing them to stay with something that had already proven successful. Sure enough, the Flat came wide open again, and they scored a touchdown that proved to be the difference in a tight game.

An equally good example occurred in Super Bowl XXIX. San Francisco used Mesh—known in their terminology as "Spot"—three different times out of three different formations and two personnel packages. All three were complete, each to a different individual route, two of them for touchdowns.

Our first rule: Make them stop the basic combination first
These are two examples of why we always begin with the idea that a defense must do something specific to stop our basic Mesh combination before we will alter it. Hand in hand with this idea goes the thought that it then gets practiced, both its individual elements and the whole pattern together, over and over and over again. Your players then grow very confident and versed in its details.

A key benefit of having a basic route on which you can "hang your hat" in this manner is that it always gives you a *starting point* in attacking any opponent, and you can become very methodical in your adjustments. By starting from this core that you have practiced repeatedly, you come to know exactly what to look for in terms of what people will do to try to stop it. When you discover what in particular that is, your structure has given you a specific variation to go to as an answer, you and your players having understood that by defensing the initial combination in a certain way, vulnerability has been created to a specific adjustment you have already practiced.

This method of structuring, teaching, and organizing your offense around a core of well-rehearsed parts makes your adjustment process much more efficient and scientific, reduces guesswork dramatically, and eliminates numerous wasted play calls.

This chapter is devoted to exploring in depth some of the ways these adjustment processes off the basic Mesh start to occur against six basic coverage families:

Coverage	Basic Description
Cover 1 Blitz	Man coverage across with no free safety in the deep middle
Cover 1 Free	Man coverage across with a deep middle safety
Cover 2	Two deep halves safeties with zone coverage underneath
Cover 2 Man	Two deep halves safeties with man coverage underneath
Cover 3	Forms of three deep, zone coverage
Cover 4	Cover 2 technique weakside with two defenders playing deep ¼ or man coverage to the strongside

There is also a section which deals with some of the special coverage combinations which have evolved in defending Bunch, and how the Mesh package can be adapted to attack them.

Cover 1 Blitz

We work hard to instill in our players a certain *mentality* against the blitz: a mentality of opportunistic, confident *aggression*. Too many times coaches convey to players their own fear of the blitz, and the result is tentative, defensive play on the offense's part. The defense is then allowed to steal the initiative, and the offense is left playing not to lose instead of attacking.

We avoid this pitfall by taking the opposite track. From the first day we practice against the blitz, we preach that a blitz is our opportunity for a big play, a challenge to our athletes. This is done by talking over and over about the fact that we will "recognize, attack, and defeat" the blitz on any given play.

Fundamental to the recognition aspect is the quarterback understanding when the defense is playing the four across, blitz man coverage being dealt with in this section, and making certain that he gets seven people in to protect for it. We take this approach in our case rather that "hot" sight adjustments because we do not want defenses dictating our choice of throws to us. For example, oftentimes you see defenses blitzing on long distance downs while playing soft in their coverage. This is done to force the offense to make their quick or "hot" adjustment throw while they make the tackle well in front of the first down marker. By getting seven people in to protect, we can take our full drop and get full route development. (Refer to Chapter 5 for more specifics on protection.)

Another element of recognition comes from the receiver coverage calls and identification. The are trained to pre-read and call coverage each time out of the huddle (see "Principles and Disciplines of the Passing Game," Appendix C), a reinforcement to the quarterback as well as a focusing device for the specific techniques they will use.

The Mesh package, to us, is one of the best ways to attack Cover 1 Blitz, because there are so many types of routes and rub combinations that we can get to without sacrificing protection. Too often teams are limited to one or two kinds of routes that they check to against blitzes, which becomes easy for the defense to anticipate and defend. Often, the only blitz check a team will have is either a Hitch or a Slant, both of which can limit you. The Mesh in and of itself gives us a good arsenal of cuts and combination that we can use against blitz, all of which have been practiced extensively within the confines of the rest of our offense. A number of these concepts follow:

- *Basic combination.* We're not going to get too complicated against anybody and start using our variations until a defense does something to stop our basic Mesh combination (Kansas City couldn't against the Colts). We feel like the Smash is a very good one-on-one route in general and a great one-on-one route from Bunch, because it gives the receiver loads of room and natural leverage to the outside. Because blitz defenders are aware that they have no help in the middle, they often play with inside leverage so they do not give up the Post. That helps the Smash further. The timing is such that the Whip can function very well as an outlet running into a lot of space if some kind of switch or technique change-up is used to take away the Smash.

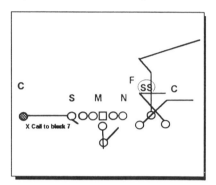

DIAGRAM 7-1
BASIC BLITZ COMBINATION #1
SQUEEZE REX 6 57

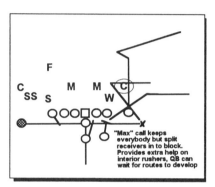

DIAGRAM 7-2
BASIC BLITZ COMBINATION #2
BROWN LIZ Z10 MAX 57

- *Under tag.* Two receivers crossing near each other full speed is very hard for man coverages to cope with; this is particularly so against Cover 1 Blitz, because often the middle of the field is void of linebackers who could otherwise help against the crossers. In all likelihood, they are blitzing if this coverage is called. With the "Under" tag added (it can be an audible at certain times), we look for the backside receiver who's rubbing full speed underneath #1 from the frontside. The quarterback takes five quick steps and looks to hit him in stride. If this happens, you're looking at big play because the receiver his running at full speed away from his pursuer with a lot of open area around him.

This is also a good call against the increasingly popular "zone" blitz where combinations of people rush while zone is being played behind, because the paths on which the Shallow Cross routes run give them the flexibility to stop in any holes that are left by that tactic.

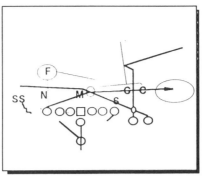

DIAGRAM 7-3
UNDER TAG TO DEFEAT BLITZ COVERAGE
SQUEEZE RAM X 57 UNDER

- *Emphasizing the Flat.* If the situation or our preference does not warrant holding the ball to throw the deep Smash, we can create good, high percentage, quick throws to the Flat that even the quickest of pass rushes will have trouble getting to. The Flat defender will have a lot of traffic to run around and through, and again the route is enhanced from Bunch because the athlete is given a wide open field to run in once the catch is made. Again, the Whip route as a misdirection route naturally complements the Flat's timing; if we get some type of defensive switch that blankets the Flat, the Whip runner should have a very good chance against the defender that has switched to him. The quarterback will see it and come back to him as he bounces up off his fifth step. Diagrams 7-4 and 7-5 show two ways we might emphasize the Flat, and its complement, the Chair, in accordance with other blitz-beating principles.

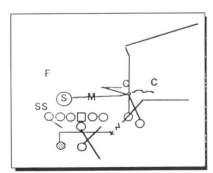

DIAGRAM 7-4
QUICK MOTION BY HB TO FLAT
SQUEEZE BLUE RAY H6 87

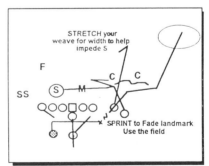

DIAGRAM 7-5
STEM CHAIR COMBINATION TO ATTACK
DEFENDERS JUMPING FLAT ROUTE
SQUEEZE BLUE RAY H6 57 STEM CHAIR

- *Key blitz-beater.* The Mesh package in a bunched environment also provides an opportunity to attack key blitzes by bringing our people late into the space created by the compression of receiver splits. The tagged receiver sets to pass block initially, then releases to his called route. This has to be choreographed and timed for the quarterback so he can get the ball out quickly, because you are potentially turning an outside rusher loose.

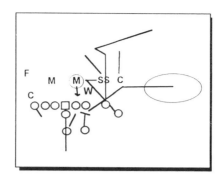

DIAGRAM 7-6
LATE TAG VS. KEY BLITZ
SQUEEZE BROWN RAY MAX 157 H LATE

Cover 1 Free

We always feel good about our chances with the Mesh route against man coverage because of the rhythm of our throws and the way we train our receivers to work their rubs. To attack it best, there are specific things we want to know about the type of man coverage we're getting. Those questions would include:

- Do they play *loose* or *tight* man coverage?
- Do they *switch* or *lock* coverage assignments?
- How do they account for the Fullback and backfield motion?
- Where are our best matchups?

The answers to these questions will dictate to us how we adjust out of the Mesh package.

- *Basic Flat/Whip combination.* This is an excellent combination to hit the fast Flat against *tight* man coverage, because of the proximity of the rubs. Using different kinds of motion helps us in this dynamic as well: motion by the Flat man helps us gain a step, as illustrated by "Idiot" and "Crazy" motion illustrations below; motion by the Whip runner helps him find the man he's trying to rub and get a good angle of release on him.

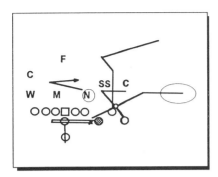

DIAGRAM 7-7
IDIOT MOTION TO HELP FLAT
SQUEEZE RAY 6 H IDIOT 57

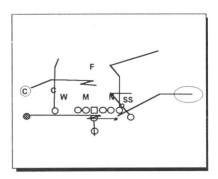

DIAGRAM 7-8
CRAZY MOTION TO HELP FLAT
LARRY 6 Z CRAZY 57

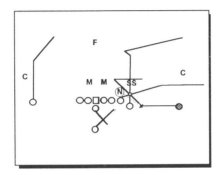

DIAGRAM 7-9
MOTION BY WHIP TO RUB FOR FLAT
RIP 6 Z6 87

- *Arrow vs. Banjo techniques.* As we've detailed already, one of our best concepts against switches is some kind of misdirection route (Chapter 3). Many times, if this man comes from the backfield, the outside banjo defender will not see the outside threat immediately, and will soften outside and drift. The Arrow route then has great leverage to get inside and underneath him.

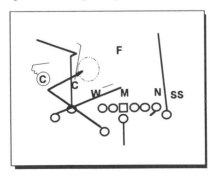

DIAGRAM 7-10
ARROW VS. BANJO
SQUEEZE B LARRY 6 157 ARROW

- *Loose man coverage: Hi tag, Under tag, and Hide.* If man coverage is playing loose, we want to release underneath him quickly and build some kind of wall that the defender has to run around, giving him a tough course to get a downward break on the ball. The timed nature of the throws makes this doubly tough for him. The Hi tag gets a Shallow Cross route from our frontside #1 underneath a wall built by the Flat and the Smash; the Under tag gets a rub for the backside crosser from the frontside; the Hide builds a wall out wide and gives the receiver a chance to push his man even deeper with a five yard release straight upfield.

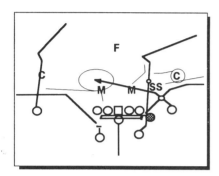

DIAGRAM 7-11
HI TAG VS. LOOSE MAN
SQUEEZE SPLIT RIP Y IDIOT 57 SWITCH HI

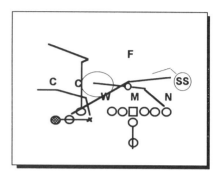

DIAGRAM 7-12
UNDER TAG VS. LOOSE MAN
SQUEEZE LARRY 11 H7 157 UNDER

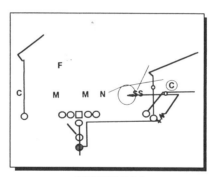

DIAGRAM 7-13
HIDE TAG FROM CLUSTER ALIGNMENT VS. LOOSE MAN
CLUSTER REX H10 57 HIDE

- *Turn tag.* This is a route that has a chance to beat most man techniques, using a good hard misdirection fake at the top of a 12 yard break. Often this route is being run against linebacker, strong safety, or nickelback coverage, so it is a better matchup than we would get on a comeback-type route outside, and it is a shorter throw, too. This becomes an excellent possession-down call if man coverage is the norm on 3rd and 7 to 10.

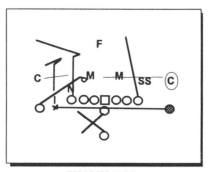

DIAGRAM 7-14
TURN TAG VS. MAN
SQUEEZE RAM Z9 187 TURN

- *Red Zone specials.* From the 25 in, where a lot of man coverage can occur, we have specific variations that we will go to, often built around play-action.

In the first example, we take advantage of the fact that the Fullback is often the least accounted for of the five possible receivers. A middle linebacker covering him will have to step up to deal with the play fake, find the Fullback somehow, and run around the Whip Read to get to his man.

The second also uses the Fullback in more of a +5 play, where it is even harder for the defense to account for the Fullback. We keep regular personnel in the game and line up in a two back set initially to avoid nickel adjustments and substitution by the defense. The halfback then shifts to a strong wing, helping to insure that a safety in the middle cannot jump the fullback, who motions quickly to the weakside, running a fast Flat as #3. With the Whip as a pick, we should get at least a step on coverage.

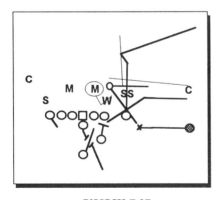

DIAGRAM 7-15
PLAY-ACTION MESH IN RED ZONE
SQUEEZE STRONG RAY Z10 336 MESH

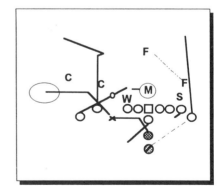

DIAGRAM 7-16
FB MOTION SPECIAL
(SHIFT) SQUEEZE RAY 6 F7 187

The third and fourth red zone examples are both bootlegs that the San Diego Chargers had great success with, and can be used in sequence out of the same formation.

In the third example, we use Idiot motion and hesitation—a "Late" call—with a Counter fake away to try and momentarily paralyze the defender covering #3. This defender has so much to look at that it is easy for him to get lost. If he goes flat-footed at all, he's dead, because it is timed up so that the quarterback snaps his head around on the boot action just as the Late breaks free.

In the last illustration, we motion a man to the inside of the leg of the tackle either from the outside in, the opposite side, Idiot motion, or, as in this case, the backfield, and try to get him lost opposite a play fake to the motion side on a "Sneak" call. If a free safety is trying to cover this man in a motion adjustment, he will never get close. Even if the man defender finds the Sneak, he will have to run through a cross coming from the backside. The quarterback boots to his side, snapping his head around to find the Sneak. If the Sneak gets jumped, he looks for the hi Cross coming into his vision. This play is similar to the one that beat Miami in 1995.

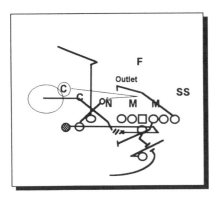

DIAGRAM 7-17
LATE TAG OFF BOOT ACTION
SQUEEZE LARRY 11 H IDIOT 226
MESH UNDER LATE

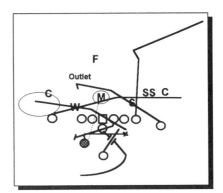

DIAGRAM 7-18
SNEAK TAG OFF BOOT
SQUEEZE WEAK RIP F4 206
MESH UNDER SNEAK

Cover 2
In working against Cover 2, the frontside safety and cornerback become the focal points of what we do. We start with the basic premise that the Smash must be trained to beat the safety, which enables us to isolate the corner on two receivers. Variations, then, are built in response to different techniques by those two people that do not allow us to work that two receiver combination efficiently. Throughout this process, we have in mind the thought that the Whip will often serve as our guaranteed outlet who should be able to get open regardless and keep us out of bad plays.

1. Basic Mesh. The basic Mesh concept against Cover 2 is to throw the fast Flat unless the cornerback really jumps on him. If the Flat get jumped, a huge hole is opened behind for the Smash. Our steadfast rule is that the Smash *never* gets thrown over the head of a cornerback who is retreating at all. If you don't make the read this clearly defined, two bad things happen:

- The Flat becomes less effective because it is not getting thrown off the natural, quick rhythm that allows it to gain yards after the catch. The result is catches that are made and tackled immediately for three yard gains, or broken up by defenders who had dropped, settled, and had time to break up on the ball.

- The passer will misjudge how much ground the cornerback can cover, and the throw for him becomes a very fine, sort of touchy throw that he'll often underthrow because he's trying to drop it in a bucket instead of throwing in his natural rhythm to a receiver in a large void. This type of fine throw results in a lower percentage of completions and more interceptions.

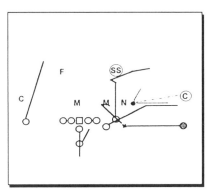

DIAGRAM 7.19
BASIC MESH VS. COVER 2
RIP SLOT 210 57

2. Motion concept vs. jam. One of the best things that we've done with the Bunch concept has been to use quick motion against jam techniques. If the cornerback puts his hands on #1 to engage a jam, the quick motioning #3 is in position to freely release to the Flat outside the entire defense into *a lot* of open space. The ball has to be thrown *in a hurry,* sometimes off the third step.

This concept can be used with any route package containing an inside Flat (e.g., the Slant in Chapter 8, or the Flood in Chapter 17), and is applicable to any coverage where the outside most defender jams hard (e.g., Cover 3 Cloud).

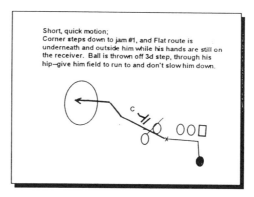

DIAGRAM 7-20
BASIC DYNAMIC OF QUICK MOTION VS. JAM

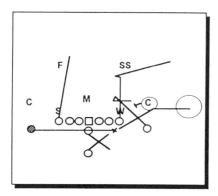

DIAGRAM 7-21
MOTION CONCEPT VS. JAM W/WR
SQUEEZE RAM X6 87

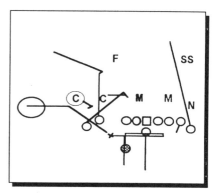

DIAGRAM 7-22
MOTION CONCEPT VS. JAM W/ FB
SQUEEZE B LARRY 6 F RETURN Y157

3. *Playside hash safety working fast for width.* The best way for a defense to take away the Smash is to predetermine that safety work hard for width over the top of him. This creates three specific opportunities that we want to exploit with tagged routes.

First, the widened safety has lessened his ability to "sit on" and break toward the #2 receiver should he break short and to the inside; he's playing with deep outside leverage only. The "Stem" variation takes advantage of this because it looks just like the Smash for 10-12 yards and pushes that safety deep into the outside hole. He then has no play on the hooking type break. In the illustration below, the Stem will be our choice unless the second short defender widens and deepens into his hole, in which case, the Under route from the backside will naturally be free, and in the quarterback's vision.

Secondly, we can also give the appearance of a normal Smash by #2 and break his route off a different way, using the "Shake" tag. Here, he's eyeballing the safety all the way, even driving three steps toward the Smash corner, then planting and driving back inside to the deep hole in the middle. The backside receiver should have taken the other hash player with him, leaving the middle open for a deep shot. The quarterback's mechanics change to seven steps to allow the route to develop.

The last variation involves #3, but gets to this same hole. Using a "Slip" tag for #3, preferably out of the backfield, we get to the same place a bit later down the middle. Play action is often helpful here to keep linebackers underneath from being able to run with the Slip route vertically, thus closing down the hole.

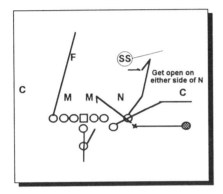

DIAGRAM 7-23
STEM TAG VS. WIDE HASH SAFETY
TIGHT RIP SLOT Z10 57 STEM

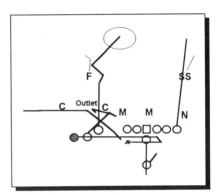

DIAGRAM 7-24
SHAKE TAG VS. WIDE HASH SAFETY
SQUEEZE LARRY 11 H IDIOT 157 X SHAKE

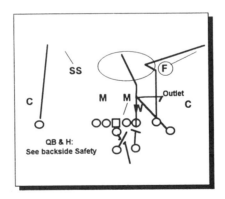

DIAGRAM 7-25
SLIP TAG FOR #3 VS. WIDE HASH SAFETY
SQUEEZE BROWN REX 336 MESH H SLIP

4. Corner plays "Match" technique or tries to play in between. Hard, or "pressed" cornerbacks are naturally coached very hard against this combination of routes, and one ability they try to develop is to play deep enough to get under the Smash, but just close enough to break quickly on the shorter route, either to tackle it for a short gain or break it up altogether. Within this idea, they can also play "Match" technique, in which they pattern read for a flat threat, and, seeing none initially, work hard for depth to close down the deep outside hole. We will attack this by changing the timing of the route and inviting that cornerback to turn and run to the Smash. This happens through the use of a "Late" call, slowing down the Flat receiver just over a count. With the corner turned and deepening, we time this up so that the quarterback hits the Flat just as he's coming out of the hesitation and hitting his stride, and can therefore make yards after the catch, beating a corner who is not squatted and breaking up on him, but trying to recover from his retreat and running in open space.

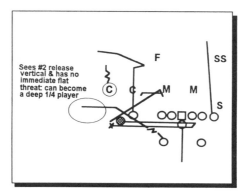

DIAGRAM 7-26
"LATE" TAG VS. IN-BETWEEN OR MATCH TECHNIQUE CORNER
SQUEEZE SPLIT LARRY Z RETURN 157 LATE

Cover 2 Man

As with any form of man coverage, we concern ourselves with matchups and getting separation within those matchups against Cover 2 Man. Very often, our best matchups occur on the inside, because teams get locked into linebacker or nickel coverage on #2 and #3 when playing this. A lot of our attack, then, will be directed at these people, often underneath with the idea that we will make yardage after the catch.

Rubs are excellent against this scheme, because many times the man coverage technique is tight with inside leverage. If teams try to neutralize our rubs with switching techniques, the Whip will serve as a solid outlet, because he is spinning back out away from a man who has switched with inside leverage.

1. Basic combination: Rubs for the Flat. We can use a few specific enhancements to help us gain an advantage for the Flat route. One of these is to motion the Flat full speed from the other side of the formation into a Bunch. Another is to use "Return" motion by the Whip route, to twice redefine assignments for bumping defenders, create some confusion, and help this Whip runner get better leverage to impede the man covering the Flat. If this return man is a tight end, you have given the defense a bigger body through which to run. Lastly, keeping the Flat-runner in the backfield in a conventional two-back set helps us, because our standard personnel grouping is more likely to keep defenses out of Nickel packages, forcing a linebacker (rather than a nickelback) to chase #3 at a downhill angle. The first of these ideas is illustrated in the first diagram below, the others in the second:

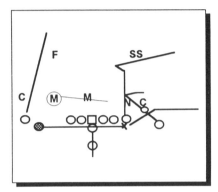

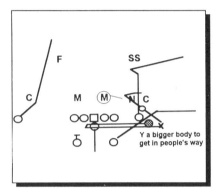

DIAGRAM 7-27
FAST MOTION FLAT
SQUEEZE RIP 9 H6 57

DIAGRAM 7-28
RETURN MOTION WITH BACKFIELD FLAT
SQUEEZE SPLIT RON Y RETURN 57

2. Misdirection routes. This is a solid concept against active man defenders who really run hard to defend the outside routes, especially when they recognize that we are using motion to do this. In this way, we will sequence the basic combination with an Arrow tag out of the exact same look, to try and prey on their recognition. "Spear" accomplishes the same purpose, only at a deeper depth with a deeper quarterback drop. An important coaching point on these routes is to have the receiver prepared to use some kind of violent escape move as he spins back underneath on his final break; defenders will be schooled to grab or gain contact with their back arm as they try and play the ball with their front arm in breaking on an outside route. We have to be equally physical in knocking their arms down to beat him cleanly back inside.

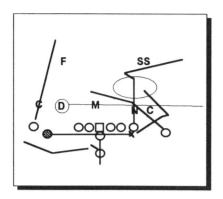

DIAGRAM 7-29
SEQUENCED ARROW OFF MOTION
SQUEEZE RIP 9 H6 57 ARROW
(SEQUENCES WITH 7-27)

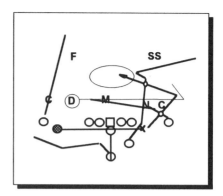

DIAGRAM 7-30
SPEAR VS. 2 MAN
WEAK LOU Z6 57 SWITCH Z SPEAR

3. Fullback motion to open the middle for Arrow. Against a 4-man rush, we can break the middle wide open against this coverage by removing the middle linebacker with Fullback motion. We then use a singled up, misdirection break to beat another man defender inside into that big hole, where the potential exists for monumental R.A.C.

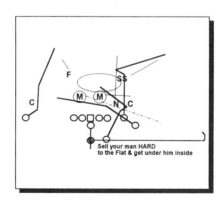

Sell your man HARD
to the Flat & get under him inside

DIAGRAM 7-31
ARROW INTO OPEN MIDDLE WITH FB MOTION
SQUEEZE BROWN REX F10 57 H ARROW

4. Hi tag to create a rub for #1 crossing. If we feel like our outside receiver can release underneath the trail technique initially, we feel like this has a chance to be a great R.A.C. play also, again with the middle linebacker being controlled by the Fullback, who now check releases weak. He handles him by picking him up if he blitzes, or taking him wide out of the area to which we're throwing if he Flares, seeing no blitz.

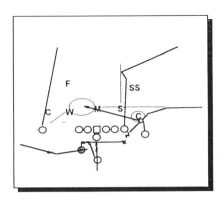

DIAGRAM 7-32 HI RUB FOR SHALLOW CROSS
SQUEEZE WEAK RIP F6 57 HI

5. Flare by #4. Again, we look to take advantage of a Fullback not well accounted for by defenses. A Fullback against a middle linebacker may be the greatest mismatch in athleticism on the field for you. Here, the Arrow by #3 and adjusted Cross by #1 build a wall for that linebacker to have to chase. The quarterback is taking five quick steps and dropping the ball a foot in front of the Fullback's numbers so that it can be caught while the back is moving upfield, not slowed down.

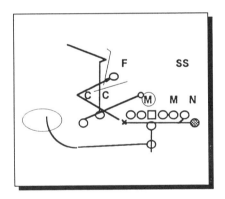

DIAGRAM 7-33
#4 FLARE CONCEPT VS. 2 MAN
SQUEEZE LARRY 6 H7 157 ARROW FLARE

6. Barrier Corner (see Diagram 3-9). This is an opportunity for us to try to get a lengthy completion, especially against a tight hash player. The Barrier technique is a good all-purpose concept against man coverage, either switching or locked, and the Barrier man goes on to occupy the hash safety, leaving the Corner route open in space.

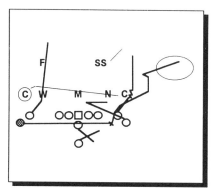

DIAGRAM 7-34
BARRIER CORNER VS. 2 MAN
TWIN X6 87 BARRIER CORNER

Cover 3

Cover 3 is another case in which we will force a defense to do something to stop our basic combination initially. To do this, they have to find a way to stop the rhythm Flat route first, and in doing so, a good hole normally ensues for the Whip Read. Generally, adaptations within Cover 3 to stop the basic route fall into one of three categories: wide flat player concepts, collision or walling techniques against the Whip Read, and overloaded frontside structures. It is against these three that we will tailor our Cover 3 Mesh adjustments.

1. Basic Flat/Whip Read. The following diagrams are illustrative of different ways we package our basic combination vs. Cover 3: the first is a basic version, the second, a use of quick motion to change the three receiver side in a hurry in hopes of outnumbering their coverage and gaining further advantage from a half-roll action, and the third, a bootleg version using "Idiot" motion. In this case, the motion and the action are both done in hopes of getting the flat coverage to hesitate and/or lose track of where #3 is. The Idiot motion makes it look as if the motion man is being used the seal the backside for a Counter play away.

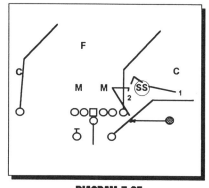

DIAGRAM 7-35
BASIC FLAT/WHIP READ VS. COVER 3
SPLIT RIP Z6 57

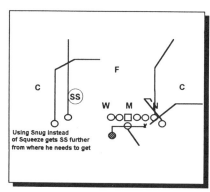

DIAGRAM 7-36
MOTION TO CHANGE FORMATION STRENGTH
SNUG STRONG LARRY F6 87

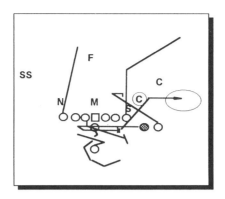

DIAGRAM 7-37
BOOT ACTION WITH IDIOT MOTION
SQUEEZE RAM X Z IDIOT 227 MESH

2. Wide flat player/Cloud corner concepts. The first of three things a three deep secondary can do to defense the original Mesh combination is to play a wider flat player, taking away our rhythm throw. This width can come from a Sky safety who runs to the flat quickly, or from a Cloud adjustment in which the cornerback is given flat responsibility and plays with outside leverage. Three basic tags are used in this event: the Hide, the Turn, and the Arrow.

With the Hide, we allow the Flat route to run his normal outside course to take coverage with him, then bring #1 into that hole late over the defender's original position, making sure he beats the next defender inside. Other devices can enhance this basic mode of attack:

- Motioning the Hide man may help the development time up better, and help get him lost.
- A "Switch" call makes this happen faster, because the Flat gets out quicker.
- Wide motion by the Fullback can also create more horizontal stretch and bigger openings.
- "Snug" adjustment could open our holes a bit wider inside for the R.A.C.

These ideas are incorporated into the following diagrams:

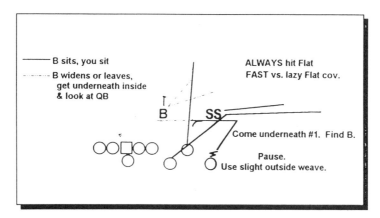

DIAGRAM 7-38
BASIC TECHNIQUE OF HIDE TAG

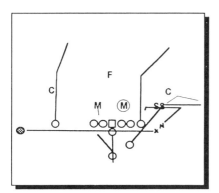

DIAGRAM 7-39
HIDE TAG OFF MOTION
WEAK LARRY Z6 57 HIDE

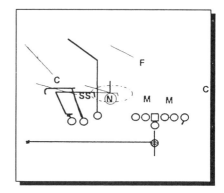

DIAGRAM 7-40
HIDE WITH SWITCH & WIDE MOTION
SNUG LARRY 11 F11 157 SWITCH HIDE

3. Attacking coverages that collision, wall off, or squat on the Whip Read. The second area of defensive focus against the basic Mesh is to look for and physically impede the Whip Read. Usually this will be done by the second short defender, who will try to "look him up" through pattern read principles, or will just plain try to knock him down. Sometimes this second short defender will line up with outside leverage, and the middle linebacker will work hard to the strong side to try and bracket the Whip inside-out. In any of these cases, they've left themselves vulnerable in either the second level hook area, or right over the ball, both of which we can exploit.

- *Getting behind the short defenders in open creases: Stem and Spear.* These cuts are problematic for pattern-read teams to defend, because the original *pattern* that they *read* looks just like the basic route, not differing until the final break. The Stem is designed to get into a window behind and between the first and second short defenders. Because it is a stationary throw and a hook-ing-type pattern that allows the receiver to adjust toward where the hole exists, Stem becomes a high-percentage throw.

The attack area for Spear begins in the window behind and on the other side of the second short defender, and can also be completed one window further over, giving you a certain flexibility against middle linebackers that drop toward your frontside.

Play action is a key element that can be used to enhance these schemes, pulling the linebackers up further and opening zone holes wider.

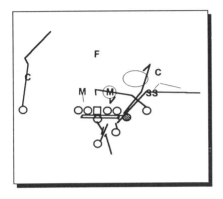

DIAGRAM 7-41
STEM OFF PLAY ACTION
SQUEEZE STRONG RIP Y IDIOT 336 MESH STEM

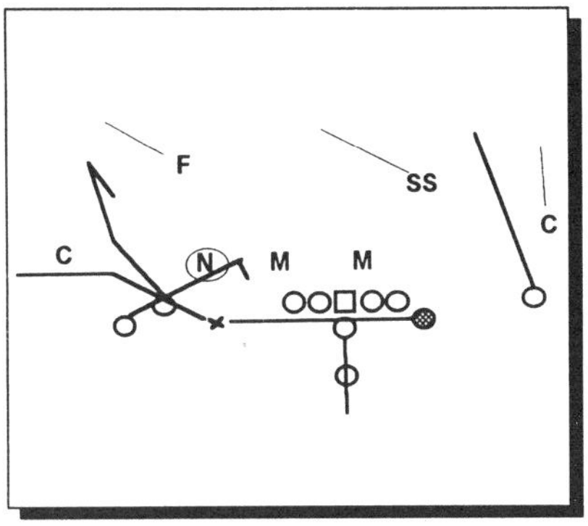

DIAGRAM 7-42
STEM FROM SNUG
SNUG RIP 11 Y7 157 STEM

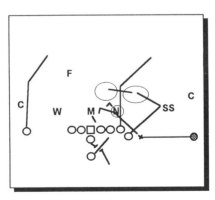

DIAGRAM 7-43
SPEAR TAG OFF PLAY ACTION
RIP 6 Z6 306 MESH SWITCH SPEAR

- *Frontside Delays.* The hole created by a squatting, second short defender is also naturally exploited by a delay route, late, into the area between the Whip and Flat releases. Often, we will put the Delay man in motion to hide him and help time up the release.

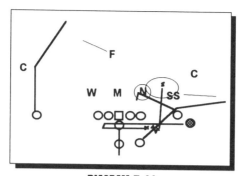

DIAGRAM 7-44
DELAY TAG FOR #2 FRONTSIDE
SNUG BROWN REX Z IDIOT 57 Z DELAY

4. Dealing with overloads. The last general category of zone adjustment to the basic Mesh is to overload the underneath coverage structure to the three receiver side. Generally, this is done by bringing a weak linebacker or nickel player over from the backside.

Two primary built-in ways exist within the Mesh package that exploit the voids left backside, both of which involve putting *two* receivers on the *one* remaining backside linebacker.

With a "Curl" tag for a wide split, backside receiver, we create a horizontal stretch on a single backside linebacker. The Shallow Cross coming from the frontside ("Hi" tag) is our guarantee player if the backside linebacker works underneath the Curl.

The "Delay" tag for a tightened *backside* receiver attacks a slightly different area of the defense, but operates on the same idea, working particularly well against linebackers who react to shallow, crossing receivers.

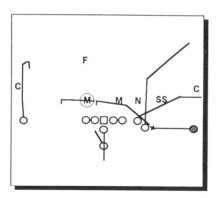

DIAGRAM 7-45
"CURL" TAG WITH BACKSIDE
NASTY RIP 6 210 157 HI X CURL

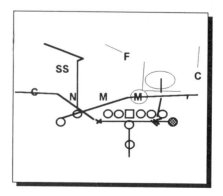

DIAGRAM 7-46
BACKSIDE DELAY TAG
SQUEEZE LARRY 6 H7 157 HI, Y DELAY

Cover 4

When a defense plays Cover 4 against Bunch, they have given themselves leverage against deep routes and effectively doubled anyone on the backside that we might ordinarily try and isolate away from Bunch overloads. At the same time they have made themselves a bit more vulnerable underneath to the strong side, giving linebackers more ground to cover. It is a logical adjustment by a defense which has been hurt by Smash cuts. This scheme turns into a brackets coverage on a deep receiver if he's the only one releasing deep.

Therefore, our principle ideas of attack out of the Mesh package versus Cover 4 will revolve around putting underneath defenders in a bind, though in certain situations we can get a deep shot as well. Our basic Mesh concepts against Cover 4:

1. Basic Flat/Whip combination. Because the underneath people are so structurally strained, the fundamental Flat/Whip combination is probably better against this coverage than any other; it amounts to a two-on-one advantage for the offense. As always, we force the fast Flat first in our thinking, coming back to the Whip if the Flat coverage really runs. If we prefer the Whip for some reason, a "Switch" call gets the Flat route, and thus the flat coverage, outside more quickly and visibly, widening the hole for the Whip.

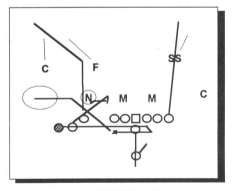

DIAGRAM 7-47
BASIC FLAT-WHIP COMBINATION VS. COVER 4
SQUEEZE LARRY 11 H IDIOT 157

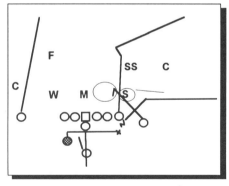

DIAGRAM 7-48
SWITCH CALL TO FREE WHIP
SQUEEZE WEAK RIP F8 57 SWITCH

2. Getting to the hole left by fast flat coverage. One benefit that comes from having a passing game that always looks for fast Flat routes is that defenses get very conscious of running to that area, creating a stretched out defense in general, and big holes for easier throws just inside the vacating defender specifically. Especially against this coverage, we want to have built-in ways to exploit that. One way is with the "Hide" tag, out of a wider, "Snug" formation designation that stretches zone holes further:

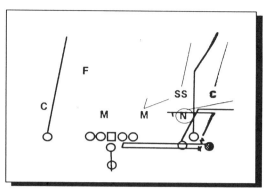

3. Four receivers frontside. The lack of underneath help in this coverage makes it impossible for it to handle four receivers to one side, especially with three of them running underneath cuts. We can do this within the Mesh structure by tagging the Fullback as #4 to the Flat. This dictates that #3 run an Arrow, and it along with the adjusted, crossing #1 are eye contact outlets in the unlikely case that the flat coverage is able to run through people to get to the Fullback. As is illustrated in the following diagram, we like to half-roll to this to shorten the throw, and get the ball off very quickly so the Fullback can get the sideline after the catch and make more yardage.

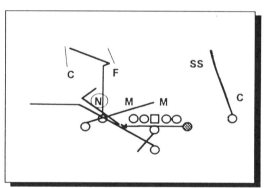

4. Motion to stretch the defense and change deep lanes. By motioning the Fullback outside of the Bunch, we can force the deep ¼ players to redefine their coverage lanes, and change up what would have been a bracket coverage. #2 can now release vertically and not get easily doubled inside and out. Out of the Mesh, we will employ two different tags for him to take advantage of this: the "Stem", which is a really excellent possession pass because the underneath coverage has been stretched as well, and the "Shake", which fakes a Smash (which is what they may very well have been told specifically to *stop* if they are playing this coverage) and turns the inside $^1/_4$ player outside before breaking underneath him into the deep middle hole.

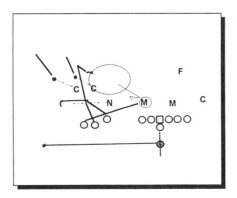

DIAGRAM 7-51
STEM VS. STRETCHED COVER 4
SNUG LARRY 11 F 11 157 STEM

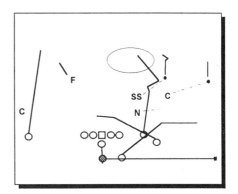

DIAGRAM 7-52
SHAKE VS. STRETCHED COVER 4
SQUEEZE BROWN REX F10 57 SHAKE

Special coverages

1. "Triangle" concept. This defensive idea is basically similar to a basic 3-way banjo, with the exception that an assumption is made that all three players cannot release short and have good distribution, therefore, the middle defender is assigned to the first deep, or vertical, release. The inside and outside defenders are responsible for first inside and first outside releases, respectively. If the middle defender knows he has free safety help inside, he can play outside leverage and really shut off routes like Smashes and Fades.

We feel like "Stem" and "Turn" are both very solid, basic tags against this, because the middle defender has been softened in alignment to stay out of traffic and gain deep leverage for his assignment. Both of these routes are designed to drive such a defender deep and break in front of him, and open lanes will exist once this break is made, because the area has been vacated by defenders chasing the other releases. If a very active linebacker came from inside-out to try and bracket our vertical releaser short and inside, we would favor the Turn over the Stem. That illustration follows:

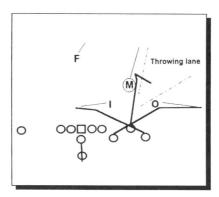

DIAGRAM 7-53
TURN TAG VS. TRIANGLE
SQUEEZE R 10 57 TURN

2. Banjo #1 and #3: Lock onto and jam #2. In practicality, this does not work out to be especially different for us in terms of our reads, though it does make a good, clean release by #2 more vital. In most cases, our basic misdirection route concepts hold up well against this kind of technique.

There is one special combination of tags we can use, however, to get #3 wide open. By calling "Barrier," we tell #2 to release outside, through the inside hip of the outside defender. Because of the lock technique, the middle defender goes with him as well. #1 releases inside as he normally would, taking the inside defender with him. Because the outside releaser for the outside defender is also the middle defender's man, we have temporarily, at least, left the defense with no one on #3, who is free for an inside break. Even if the outside defender can recognize this and not get totally lost, he will have a tough time running through two people and making any sort of inside break on #3, running the Middle Read from two positions removed. A great jam by the middle defender actually causes more problems than it solves for the defense, because a big mass of bodies is created for the outside man to have to run around.

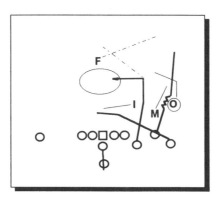

DIAGRAM 7-54
SPECIAL COMBINATION VS. BANJO LOCK #2
SQUEEZE REX 6 57 BARRIER H MIDDLE

3. Cover 3 Cloud, Lock #2. This is a concept used to try to gain the best of two worlds: multiple frontside zone drops with a Cloud corner playing outside leverage for the Flat, and a hard jam on #2 to try to disrupt our entire release dynamic. Fortunately, a basic tag exists that can defeat this, and can even be used as a check should the quarterback sense it in his pre-snap read (it looks just like 3 Cloud, with the tip-off being that the defender over #2 is likely to be tighter, with inside leverage, engaged in eye contact on #2 instead of scanning around). That tag is "Arrow." As with normal Cover 3 Cloud, we're using the cornerback's outside leverage against him and coming back inside. The inside into which the Arrow is breaking is even more open, because the second short defender left to run with our #2 receiver. If the corner tries to collapse in with him, he's liable to run right into #2 and the defender chasing him on the way. Other basic concepts for attacking Banjo and Triangle coverages hold up well against this as well.

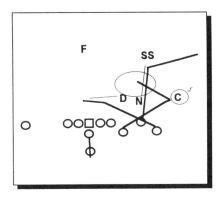

DIAGRAM 7-55
ARROW VS. 3 CLOUD LOCK #2
SQUEEZE R 10 57 ARROW

4. Cover 2 Robber. In Cover 2 Robber, defenses will generally show some kind of Cover 3 look, and then try to roll late to a Cover 2, with the free safety stepping up to rob the intermediate to short middle area. For this reason, Arrow and Stem tags need to be avoided if we can anticipate this coverage, because they have the potential of getting thrown right into a Robber player.

The weakness of the defense relates to the movement of the players and the ways you can use their momentum and reaction against them. The strong safety, for example, is really hustling to get back to the hash from the outside-in, so he has a difficult time breaking back out over the top of a Smash route if he gets pushed hard by the receiver to that middle hole (See also Diagram 17-9). For that reason, the basic 7 route, the Mesh, is very good. The strongside corner, rolling up to the flat, is more likely to jump any kind of flat route *hard* and fast. So, any kind of cut designed to beat the next short defender inside and turn out into that hole the cornerback left quickly is good; the basic Whip fits here, as does a "Turn" tag.

5. Cover 3 Key Robber. In this coverage, the free safety is schooled to rob the middle immediately if he sees all Post threats disappear. It is a good built-in adjustment to shut down crossing routes at different levels. We will attack this by luring him into the Robber position with an "Under" tag, bringing both outside receivers underneath, and bringing #2 into that vacated hole late on a "Shake" route.

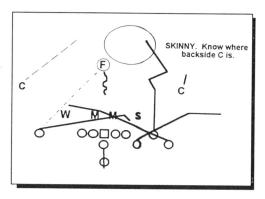

DIAGRAM 7-56
SHAKE TAG VS. KEY ROBBER
SQUEEZE REX 6 57 UNDER Y SHAKE

6. ¼ ¼ Man. Certain eight-man front defensive structures will bring the free safety to the strong side to play deep ¼s with the cornerback, while leaving the backside corner locked up in man coverage. This defense does not, then, have a true deep middle safety, which has to be the primary thing we want to exploit. What we have to keep in mind, though, is that the benefit of this coverage to the defense is that it allows them to maintain the integrity of their eight man front, meaning they can rush four people weak. Protection is vital.

Route-wise, our emphasis will be the backside, built-in Post, after a good look off to the Bunch side.

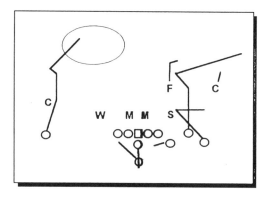

DIAGRAM 7-57
BACKSIDE POST VS. ¹/₄ ¹/₄ MAN
SQUEEZE R 10 Y57

7. Cover 3 "Safety Slot Zone" adjustment. Some Cover 3 looks will use as a change-up a switch of assignments between the strong safety (normally in flat coverage) and the second short defender, running the latter to the flat while the safety lurks and tries to rob the area that a careless quarterback would think had been vacated. Two elements of the basic Mesh structure should hold up against this adjustment, if your players have been properly disciplined: first, the "hi" release of the Whip Read should impede the second short defender attempting to run to the Flat, making the first option still a good one. Secondly, the quarterback should have never lost vision of the safety, since he, in Cover 3, is his primary key. Lastly, the Whip Read, has been taught to read the defender *over #3,* which in this case would be the second short defender who has run to the flat. This man having run out, his basic read tells him to just sit right inside instead of spinning out. There will be a hole there, because the safety is in no position to sink down inside. Where you would get into trouble against this technique is if he carelessly whipped back out by force of habit, thinking he was free, and the quarterback, equally careless, threw it there, right into the slot zone safety's trap.

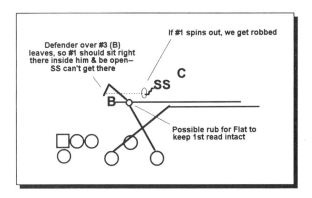

DIAGRAM 7-58
BASIC MESH RULES AGAINST SAFETY SLOT ZONE ADJUSTMENT

CHAPTER 8

The Slant Route

Introduction and basic attack concept

The Slant represents another way to hit a timed break out route using a quick drop, in this case three steps (sometimes two). If cornerbacks want to jam hard, it is an even quicker way to spring someone outside (see "Motion Concept vs. Jam" in Chapter 7). It is also an excellent blitz beater. At lower levels where protecting and throwing five step patterns can be impossible, this could be the simplest and most effective way to employ the Bunch principle. This is also an excellent percentage pass to use on first down if you are looking to balance your run/pass ratio in that situation to keep defenses from packing in on you. It is easily applicable for anyone who has within their offense a basic quick passing game.

Technique and basic route mechanics

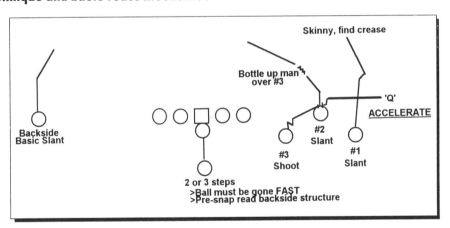

DIAGRAM 8-1
BASIC SLANT ROUTE ASSIGNMENTS AND DISTRIBUTION

Frontside:

#1: From Bunch, #1 wants to get a bit of an outside weave, if possible, to give himself more room to the inside. For this reason, he'll take his route up to six yards before nodding and planting his outside foot to the break. The nod (a change of direction without losing speed) is important in getting separation from a man defender. This particular receiver has to keep his angle very "skinny," and not get inside very much at all. Against man, he's looking to beat the cornerback and stay out of the free safety's reach. Against zones, he wants to get the corner (whether soft or rolled up) off his back and find an open vertical seam in which to run.

#2: This is a "purpose" receiver in that his objective is to create opportunities for the other two receivers to get open.

He zeroes in on the man over the inside, or #3, receiver, and attempts to bottle him up, impeding his progress to the outside. He gets one step of push straight upfield, then releases to the outside hip of the man over #3, adjusting his course while maintaining leverage to his outside hip. Again, he has to drive his arms through any collision, and then drive through on an angle that will place him over the ball 20 yards deep. After he clears the underneath coverage, he wants to flatten so that he doesn't congest the area in which #1 and #3 are operating. Because he is a clear-out type of receiver, he is the one who must get off the ball the quickest.

#3: He has a "Shoot" route, getting into the pattern last and releasing behind the other two receivers, just a half count late. His whole key is acceleration and separation once he gets into his route. He'll be flat initially to clear the traffic, but once he gets beyond the #1 and #2, he'll get two steps of push upfield before planting his inside foot and accelerating flat. He has to snap his head around while at the same time continuing to accelerate away because we want him to get the ball as quickly as possible and let him run.

Backside:
#1: He has a normal Slant technique on the backside, with a wide 12 yard Slant split, and may very well get the ball against defenses that have overloaded the frontside. If you can put a breakaway person in this position, this is where the opportunity to make huge plays occurs when defenses sell out to cover the trips side.

Quarterback:
We want him to throw the ball right through the Shoot runner's hip as fast as he can get it out there and give ourselves the best opportunity for yardage after the catch unless the defense has somehow been able to really jump the route. Often on Flat and Shoot-type routes, a one-tenth of a second delay in the ball's delivery costs the man 5, 7, or more yards of run after the catch. That's why, with so many of our routes, we build in the look to the flat right now and emphasize hitting it as quickly as possible; we want the ball in our receiver's hands while defensive people are still dropping, before they have a good break on the ball. So often when you look for a deeper route first and then try and come back to the flat, defenders have settled and are ready to break on the ball, and the pass is either broken up or the receiver is tackled almost immediately.

We also know that because of the angle of this particular type of throw, our quarterback can't try to lead him, because the receiver will never catch up to it; but if the thrower's feet step right through the man's hip and the throw is on a line, we're likely to get a catchable ball that will not break his stride.

Slant variations for attacking coverages

Motion by #3 and quick play action right at the man covering #3 are two of the ways we enhance this basic combination vs. man coverage teams. Motion can create confusion for man coverage schemes that "bump" assignments (switching assignments as motion men pass rather than locking on and chasing), or can simply gain a step of leverage for the Shoot route by going in motion quickly. Play action can drastically hinder a linebacker playing run first (especially on first down), and he will have taken a step up, then have to try and work laterally and around bodies to chase a fully accelerating receiver. These two ideas are illustrated in diagrams 8-2 and 8-3:

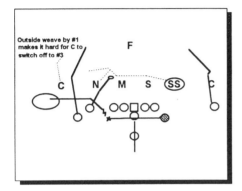

DIAGRAM 8-2
MOTION BY #3 VS. MAN
SQUEEZE RIP 11 Y7 190 SLANT

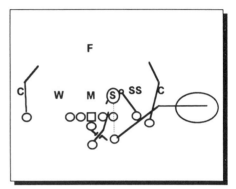

DIAGRAM 8-3
PLAY ACTION VS. MAN
SQUEEZE BROWN REX 90 VEER SLANT

As teams become proficient at anticipating and running to the Flat receiver, either in Cover 3 or man, a "Chair" tag for #3 off of the normal Slant development becomes an effective deep shot. The space created by Bunch really enhances the Chair's possibilities.

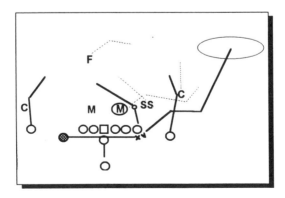

DIAGRAM 8-4
CHAIR TAG VS. MAN COVERAGE
SQUEEZE RIP 9 H6 90 SLANT H CHAIR

Against two deep coverages that like to jam the outside receiver, we'll employ the same motion concept vs. the jam that we did with the Mesh, putting #3 in motion either across the formation or from the backfield. If their coverage or technique allows them to jump the flat, the #2 receiver should occupy the next underneath coverage man inside, and with #1 staying skinny up the seam, having created a bit of space with a good outside weave, we should have a lane through which to get him the ball. Our hope against two deep with a softer corner, is to: a) occupy the hash safety with our #2 receiver as he bends inside him after clearing the mesh, and b) widen the Cornerback with the Shoot, giving the #1 a big lane to run in. In all honesty, there are many times when this isn't a great route against a softer Cover 2. Nonetheless, it is extra important in this case that the depth of #1's route is correct so that we are able to come back to him after the shoot is taken away. If he hurries his route and only gets 4 or 5 yards depth, he's gone by the time the QB can get back to him.

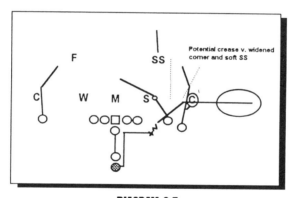

DIAGRAM 8-5
SLANT VS. COVER 2
SQUEEZE REX H6 90 SLANT

A final idea we will use related to the Slant in this environment is to use Bunch and motion as a decoy to create overreaction that opens up the backside Slant. By motioning the Fullback wide of the Bunch side, the defense is forced to either slide underneath players or the free safety that way to compensate. This opens up lanes for the backside Slant to both get a catch and big opportunities to run after. Again, the possibility of the free safety vacating the middle makes this a touchdown play inside the 25. By game plan, we may shorten the Slant a bit to get it off more quickly against the blitz.

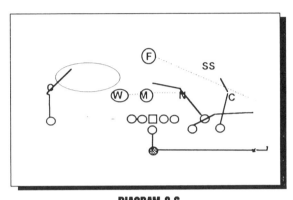

DIAGRAM 8-6
OPENING UP THE BACKSIDE SLANT WITH MOTION TOWARD THE BUNCH
SQUEEZE REX 6 F10 190 SLANT

CHAPTER 9

The "Fade" Route

Introduction and basic attack concept

The Bunch Fade was designed specifically to give two deep coverages real problems when we're aligned on the hash. This was the concept that originally began our evolution into a full Bunch package. By compressing both of our receivers inside the wide side hash, we've given our Fade a full 1/3 of the field to run to, and have put the cornerback in a real bind. If the corner sits in his flat area and waits for the Out break from the inside, there's a huge hole for us to hit the Fade. The hash safety will have likely compressed his alignment with the receivers. Having begun his backpedal, he will find that he can't make up ground fast enough to get to the Fade; we've thrown it to a spot, and our man is running away from this hash defender.

If the corner gives ground and starts to sink with the Fade to reduce the hole, our quarterback is trained to get the ball outside to the Break Out quickly. That receiver will be outside the cornerback with the ball in a hurry because of the Bunched alignment, and he'll have a lot of field to run to, giving us a great chance for good yards after the catch. This dynamic is illustrated in 9-1.

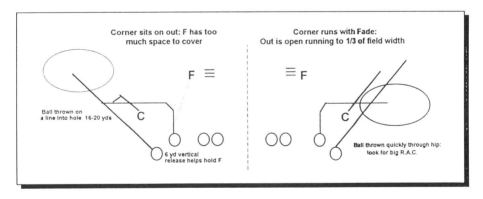

Corner sits on out: F has too much space to cover

Corner runs with **Fade**: Out is open running to **1/3 of field width**

F ≡

≡ F

Ball thrown on a line into hole 16-20 yds

C

C

6 yd vertical release helps hold F

Ball thrown quickly through hip: look for big R.A.C.

DIAGRAM 9-1
WIDE FIELD BUNCH FADE CONCEPT

We still may employ this version of the Fade against a man or deep ⅓ corner if we think we can create specific kinds of matchups. Often, because we're throwing to a spot, our man can make better adjustments or just plain beat the defender to that spot in a foot race; the bunched set makes the corner's job a little less comfortable because he may not be as sure of his operating area. If you find a man who stays in his backpedal too long, or can't accelerate well as he turns and runs, your chances are good. At other times, deep ⅓ or deep ¼ coverage is often a good scheme to emphasize the Out part of the route against, because he can outrun the flat defender into space.

Technique and basic route mechanics

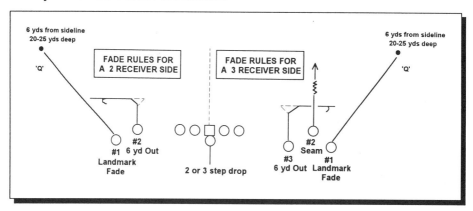

DIAGRAM 9-2
BASIC FADE ASSIGNMENTS AND ROUTE DISTRIBUTION

Route rules (they work the same both front and backside):

#1: SPRINT to the Fade right now; do not mess around with an inside jab or any conventional Fade technique—release cleanly and beat your man to a spot within six yards of the sideline. Find the ball and beat your man to it, use leverage and box out techniques, catching the ball at its highest point. Be careful that as you turn to look for the ball, you do not slow yourself down. Near the goalline, we may predetermine that we'll throw the ball over your outside shoulder to increase your leverage there.

#2: (3 receiver set) As with #2 in the Bunch Slant, this is a clear out receiver. Align on the ball if you have a choice, get off the ball fast and clean, and run a Seam straight up the field. Make it very difficult for the man covering #3 to jump outside you; widen for a time, if need be, to bottle him up, and then get back on your straight course. Be alert versus 2 deep coverage if the safety anticipates the Fade and flies off the hash; bend inside and you'll have the ball drilled to you as you clear underneath coverage.

#3, or #2 in 2 receiver set: Align off the ball whenever possible, and make certain that you get off about a step behind #2; you want to maintain this relationship so that you can run right underneath him. Lean on the inside of the man covering you, push to get him turned before making a flat, accelerated break out, right off the hip of #2. Against Zone, roll out to your break, still underneath the Seam; sit inside any underneath coverage which has settled outside of you (e.g., a Cloud corner). Snap your head around and look for the ball as you clear underneath traffic.

Quarterback:

If we've determined that we're zeroing in on the Fade, get the ball up in the air and outside RIGHT NOW. Give your receiver the chance to be an athlete and make a play. Allow your receiver to use the leverage we've given him; DO NOT miss inside. Make sure you don't loft the ball to the extent that you allow the free safety to come out of the middle and make a play.

If we're working a 2 man side vs. 2 deep coverage and the cornerback jumps the Out quickly, then you may have to throw the ball on a line through the big opening that will occur so that the receiver can get it caught and tucked before the hash safety gets to him.

If we're looking for the Out (which will likely be predetermined by game plan), hit him on time as he breaks underneath the Seam; the throw will be much like the Shoot.

Fade variations and attack concepts:

1. Prioritizing the Fade vs. prioritizing the Out. Diagrams 9-3 and 9-4 show how we generally prioritize the route based on coverage. Generally, against hard corners, the Fade is the priority into the hole behind because of the bind the cornerback is in; we can always come back to the Out if he runs with the Fade and squeezes the open hole.

If the corner is soft, we feel like the Out can outrun short defenders into wide space, so it becomes the first thought. The Fade only becomes good in this case if the cornerback's technique is suspect in certain ways.

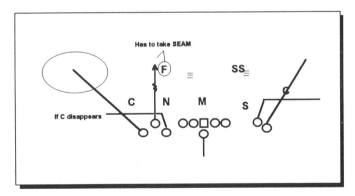

DIAGRAM 9-3
BUNCH FADE VS. BASIC COVER 2: FADE AS THE PRIORITY
SQUEEZE EMPTY 190 FADE

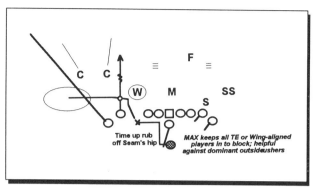

DIAGRAM 9-4
BUNCH FADE V. COVER 4: OUT AS THE PRIORITY
SQUEEZE LARRY 6 F7 MAX 190 FADE F OUT

2. Balanced 2 X 2 Fade. By using a Bunch set with two receivers on either side, we can pick a matchup or work off of the free safety. This is an excellent way to attack in the middle of the field, in which case the field width is your ally either way, or against combination coverages, where you can get leverage by picking the favorable side and not have to guess.

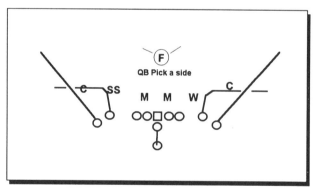

DIAGRAM 9-5
BALANCED 2 X 2 FADE
TWIN 90 FADE

3. Short motion to leverage a trail technique defender. Versus a trail technique defender, short motion from the outside in can be used to build a sequence with Shallow Crosses off the same motion; a very inside-conscious corner who has been beaten across underneath and has become obsessed with taking away your inside will give you great leverage back outside off of this motion.

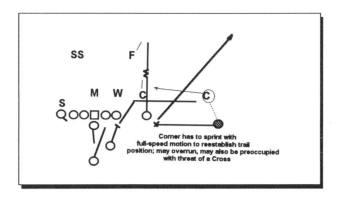

4. Motion specials. One particularly effective tool throughout Bunch is to motion outside and/or deep routes across, full speed, to gain an advantage if his man loses a step while adjusting across with motion or if the opponent bumps man assignments and we can snap the ball with him halfway stacked behind another receiver and either confuse their bumps or create a natural pick. When this motion is done from the backfield, is helps even more because you're matching a linebacker, who may be surprised by or late reacting to the motion, chasing a superior athlete.

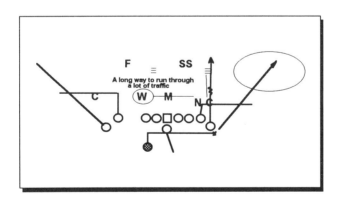

DIAGRAM 9-7
MOTION SPECIAL VS. PURE MAN COVERAGE
SQUEEZE LARRY 6 F10 90 FADE

CHAPTER 10

The "Triangle" Package

Introduction, basic attack concept, and teaching progression

As with the previous three routes, Triangle was a standard route in our offense that we merely realigned to create an excellent Bunch package. The hallmark of Triangle is its flexibility, and it gives us, with the way we teach it, the ability to create a lot of different types of problems and looks within the same basic rules. It was originally developed as a goalline package as a way to package three common individual Red Zone cuts together and attack from the five yard line in. Triangle has generally been used with a half roll protection, throwing from behind the frontside tackle, to create a really shortened throws since we're only using half of the field anyway.

We found, though, that Triangle provides us with some good weapons up and down the entire field; a Fade that can be employed in the same manner as the three step drop Fade or done from an inside position to create natural picks for it, a Whip route that is a consistent man-beater and a good possession route, and an Option route that gives us an excellent chance to get behind and between zone drops.

When we first teach the route in our pre-season practice, we set the ball at about the four yard line and line three groups of assorted receivers in a standard trips set. We'll have three cones set up in the end zone: an "Option Cone" two yards from the end line (translated to the field, about 10-12 yards deep), a "Whip Cone" two yards into the end zone (5-6 yards from the L.O.S. in the field), and a "Fade Cone" in the corner. We emphasize that each of these three routes, as represented by cones, has to be occupied, or run. We tell them that as a base definition, #3 will have the Option, #2 the Whip, and #1 the Fade. That's if we just call "Triangle." If we call Triangle and tag a receiver with some other route, then the man next to him has to take his route. For example, in what we call a "Rip 8" formation, Z is the #1 receiver, H is #2, and Y is #3, inside. So, if we call regular 80 Triangle from this look, Y has the Option, H the Whip, and Z the Fade. But if we call "80 Triangle, H Option," now Y knows that he has to take H's Whip route. "80 Triangle, Z Whip" tells H that he has to take Z's Fade.

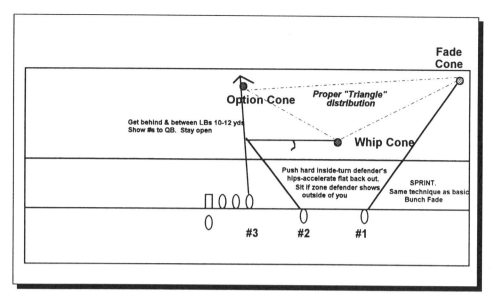

DIAGRAM 10-1
TEACHING BASIC TRIANGLE

When teaching technique, the bunched Triangle Fade is done just like the 3 step drop version; the only difference is if it's being done by an inside receiver, in which case he should start with a lateral step to let the interference get into action before racing to his spot. Often his defender will freeze and go flat footed as he hesitates. In throwing it, we tell the quarterback to imagine a barrel positioned in the very corner of the end zone, and to try to drop his pass right into that barrel.

The Whip runner really wants to turn the hips of the defender inside of him, pushing as though he was crossing. He must feel coverage early so that he can accelerate all the way out vs. man or look to throttle quickly in the first hole vs. zone. He must flatten and not drift upfield. Generally he wants to release underneath the Option route, and thus be off the ball if possible.

The Option route can be developed or taught in a variety of ways; most basic to it, however, is the man releasing straight upfield (or getting back over his original alignment if he gets bumped off his course) and pushing to his depth. We want him to work behind and between zone drops, breaking inside or outside away from coverage.

The priority for the Quarterback will generally be determined on a weekly game plan basis, depending on where we want to use it and what type of coverages and matchups we're dealing with. Most often, the Fade or the Whip will be what we're looking for first with the idea built in that the Option is responsible for getting himself open and being available upon eye contact for the quarterback as an outlet if our first look breaks down.

Triangle variations to attack coverages

Diagrams 10-2 and 10-3 show basic frontside Triangle distributions. 10-2 shows the route dynamics against a basic Banjo: if the linebacker and strong safety are playing this technique against #2 and #3, the linebacker will get in a lot of trouble. The switch will occur when the Whip pushes inside the Option route initially, and the linebacker will then almost immediately find himself having to chase the Whip back outside while at the same time having to run around a safety running upfield with the Option.

Diagram 10-3 illustrates how a backside "Under" tag can be used versus zone defenses that run hard to the frontside with the half roll. It also shows a technique we commonly use in Bunch offense to create difficulty for the defense: motioning someone behind and just outside the last receiver just before the snap and running him on a deep and/or outside route. It can confuse bumped man coverage assignments, or create a natural impediment to a defender who is trying to chase the motioning receiver.

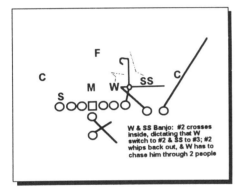

DIAGRAM 10-2
BASIC TRIANGLE DISTRIBUTION
SQUEEZE RAM X 80 TRIANGLE

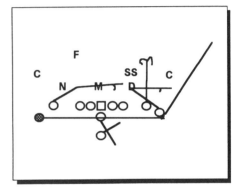

DIAGRAM 10-3
TRIANGLE WITH AN UNDER OUTLET
TWIN X10 80 TRIANGLE

One of the first of these variations that we employed when we ran Triangle from Bunch was "H Fade" with H as the #3 receiver; this enhanced our Bunch Fade concept by giving him the same room to run to with two receivers outside him running interference. This is better against tight man looks than loose ones, because loose man defenders can run around the traffic better. We also found that this gets open very early and that the ball has to be thrown on a line, not lofted. A lofted pass provides the rubbed defender too much time to recover over the top.

Within this variation, we can make life more difficult for inside defenders by putting #3 in the backfield and using play action to gain a step as he releases wide. Both of these ideas with #3 running the Fade are illustrated below:

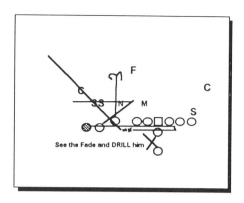

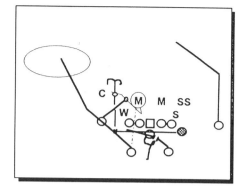

DIAGRAM 10-4
TRIANGLE WITH #3 RUNNING FADE
SQUEEZE LARRY 11 H IDIOT 180 TRIANGLE H FADE

DIAGRAM 10-5
TRIANGLE W/ BACKFIELD FADE AND PLAY ACTION
SQUEEZE SPLIT RIP Y7 341 TRIANGLE H FADE

One individual goalline route that has been extremely effective for us from normal sets through the years is a variation we call "Marker". When a receiver sprints toward the corner of the end zone, the defender had better sprint with him because he knows they're basically trying to get to the same spot to get the ball. A well-coached defender will also key the receiver's eyes; he knows that when the receiver looks for the ball, it's coming, and he'd better turn back to find it and defend it.

The "Marker" cut takes advantage of this. In running the Marker, the receiver runs hard initially straight for the deep corner of the end zone as though he's running a Fade. Two yards deep in the end zone, he looks back to the quarterback briefly, as though he's trying to find the ball. As noted, the defender almost has to look back, and when he does, he's lost. Our receiver has planted off his inside foot at five yards deep in the end zone, and is hustling back to the front pylon of the end zone (hence the name, "Marker"), where the quarterback is throwing the ball low and to the spot. We've even experienced success on this route to the point where it worked on back-to-back touchdown and two-point conversion plays against well-coached secondaries (not that we would normally recommend that particular play sequencing).

Because of what the defense has to do and does to stop the #3 Fade variation of Triangle, incorporating this Marker variation off that same look made complete sense. In stopping a #3 Fade off a rub, the defender has to sprint recklessly to the Fade spot once he has righted himself; he's in no position to break on a downhill break away from him. This is a terrific variation inside the eight yard line.

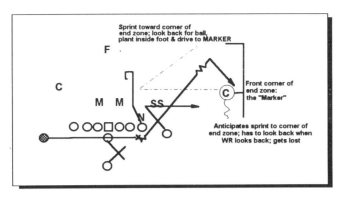

DIAGRAM 10-6
"MARKER" VARIATION OFF #3 FADE RELEASE
SQUEEZE RAM X6 80 TRIANGLE X MARKER

One good way to make the Triangle package very functional on longer distance downs is to feature the Option route working outside-in from the #1 position. He has clear-out receivers underneath and outside of him and the freedom to find holes between and behind people. He also may prove harder to find for dropping zone defenders coming from there. If this is the call, the quarterback and Option receiver are told to work the first short defender inside the cornerback. Of course, if he really works underneath the Option, we'll know to go right to the Whip, also trained to find a hole within the natural Triangle distribution. In the particular case of the diagram below, Y has been used as #2 running the Fade, because as a big body he can function really well as a "picker" should we get man. The Option rubs right underneath him.

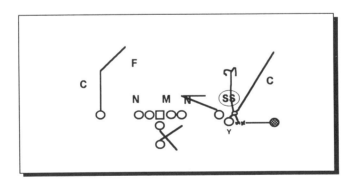

DIAGRAM 10-7
OPTION ROUTE WORKING OUTSIDE-IN AS #1
SQUEEZE RON 10 H10 80 TRIANGLE H OPTION

Another variation that has real merit against specific defenses is using #1 as the Whip runner. When you run short motion to gain leverage for crossing routes enough, defenders get used to anticipating them and squatting on them. Here, we bring #1 from wide in short motion, anticipating over-reaction to the cross, and bring him back out on a Whip running underneath a clearing pick by the Fade, now run in the route exchange by #2. The Option route then naturally fills any inside void as an outlet.

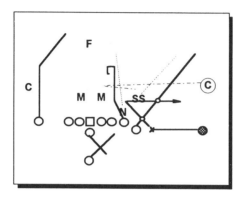

DIAGRAM 10-8
WHIP MOTIONING IN AS #1
RIP 6 Z6 80 TRIANGLE Z WHIP

CHAPTER 11

The "Vertical Switch/Choice" Route Package

Introduction and basic attack concepts

From spread four receiver sets, this is probably the one route that has been most identified with our offense for the past several years. It is an adaptation of the Run and Shoot Switch route that traditionally is run on the backside. We made it a frontside route to help our quarterback see the reads develop a little better, and it proved very successful. Outside receivers running crossed releases to landmarks on the field and giving them the ability to read on the move has consistently posed problems for most every kind of coverage we have faced. The deep structure of the coverage is put under tremendous pressure from every direction. For that reason, this is the kind of play that can quickly become the big play that breaks a game for you no matter what is being done defensively.

This Vertical Switch concept also has great potential as a weapon from Bunch, and we gave the package another dimension by evolving to a "Choice" route for #3. Now, instead of purely being a deep shot, the Vertical Switch can be employed in one of two distinct ways: 1) to create leverage for a deep route vs. man coverage with a pick for one of the two vertical routes, or 2) to develop a ball-control route vs. zones with the #3 receiver with an option-type route, and using the vertical players to pry open a hole for him to get into once they have cleared. The Choice route, because of the timing of the route's development, has a good chance to get lost behind the vertical releasers and either pop open outside or in a hole inside. It is very difficult for a defense to supply their deep defenders with the help they need and still cover the Choice man. If, for example, a Cover 2 cornerback sinks and gets depth quickly to try and shut down the Outside Vertical, the Choice breaks wide open into a lot of space. A version of this package used to create holes to throw the Choice route, was one of the key ways the Washington Redskins during the Joe Gibbs era hurt zone adjustments to Bunch throughout the late 1980s and early 90s. Again, we feel especially solid about it, because the Bunch version is only a minor variation on a route our players already have great confidence in.

Technique and basic route mechanics

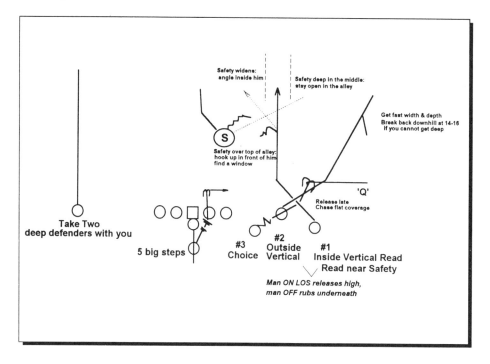

DIAGRAM 11-1
BASIC TECHNIQUES FOR SWITCH ROUTE

Frontside:
#1 and #2: Vertical switch technique. The #2 receiver releases at the outside defender's feet for a point six yards from the sideline; the #1 receiver works to two yards inside the hash mark. Reads are still in effect for the hash receiver: feel what the nearest safety is doing and get wherever he *isn't.* If he stays deep in the middle, then you will naturally have an *alley* in which to stay open; feel the hole between the layers of defense and expect the ball between 18 and 22 yards deep. Should he widen and cross your face, or if there is no safety present to read, break inside sharply into the hole in the middle. If the safety drops the middle, hook up in the front of him at about 14 yards, working to a lane between and behind linebackers.

#2 treats his route just like a Bunch Fade. The person ON the line of scrimmage releases high and runs his route through the near shoulder of the man covering his partner to create a pick. The man OFF the line of scrimmage releases behind and accelerates to his landmark. He should look to find the ball quickly, after trying to rub his man off on the other receiver. In this instance we will predetermine who we want on and off the line of scrimmage; vs. defenses with no free safety, we will certainly favor the rub to the outside man coming in to that vacated middle; he may flatten a bit once he clears the mesh to keep his separation. If he feels for some

reason that the coverage over him has deepened to the point where he cannot get past it, he breaks back to the sideline at a depth of 14 to 16 yards.

#3: Choice Route. If ever in doubt, use the following basic rules of thumb: first, just GET OPEN, get where defenders are not, and face the quarterback. Secondly, proceed out of your break into the space outside, chasing the flat defender until you see him settle and stop you.

Your initial release steps should get you centered between and behind the positions of #1 and #2; during these steps you need to quickly determine man or zone in front of you (we can also use motion to help define this before the snap). If you see zone, push upfield, angling slightly toward the underneath flat coverage to push him wider, and then snap around to an open settle point between him and the next underneath defender inside. If the flat coverage disappears (running with someone), your basic rule of thumb would tell you to keep going to the sideline. You should create a lot of motion with your arm drive, but not much acceleration upfield; be patient and get in the hole, seeing what's in front of you. The hole will happen naturally.

Against man, continue a step wider on your release, then push upfield 4-5 yards after you've established outside leverage on your man. Lean in, then accelerate flat and away. Make sure that you do not shorten your route, and that you get some push inside to create separation; there's no hurry because you're often the second read against man coverage. Do what you need to do to beat him and get some depth. All your releases should take you underneath #1 and #2.

Fullback:
Check-thru read. Check and double check your protection responsibility. If you get nothing, leak through the line over the center and sit in a hole, facing the quarterback. If you get a man chasing you, run away from him into the quarterback's vision.

Backside:
Take two. Sprint up your landmark 9-10 yards from the sideline, and do not look back. Your goal is to take two deep defenders with you.

Quarterback:
Five big steps if your initial priority is a deep route. Five quick steps if you're thinking *Choice* first; this will be designated by tagging the route with the word "Choice".

Against man, we generally want our first priority to be taking a shot at the deep route we've predetermined, either the deep Split or the Fade off the rub. You should come up out of your drop ready to give the ball to this man as soon as he clears the rub, seeing the open space into which you'll throw. In the case of the inside route, you'll recognize whether there's a Free Safety to take your throw away early on—this is a throw that you do not want excessive air under, lest the defender be able to close on your receiver.

If your deep man does not get out cleanly, or gets clamped as he does, shuffle your feet, turn your hips, and hit #3 breaking away from his man.

Against zone, look off downfield during your initial steps, then come back down and throw the ball into which area you see #3 breaking. Hit this on time, while the underneath people are still dropping, before they can react and close. If he gets jumped from the inside out, which you should see in your scan, turn and look up your hash receiver, whose read should have him hooking in the next open window inside. The fullback is a last resort outlet who should be working into your vision.

If we're seeing much of a 2-deep zone with the safeties playing wide, we can certainly look for the Inside Vertical in the hole as a first priority; this can even be a good 2-deep *audible* at certain times.

Vertical switch variations for attacking coverages

Deep shots. Versus blitz coverage of any kind where there is no free safety in the middle, we want to work a rub off this route for the outside receiver working into the deep middle. If he cannot get clear or gets stopped by some kind of secondary switch, the Choice route should still be a solid possibility.

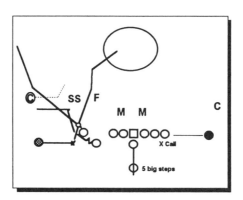

DIAGRAM 11-2
VERTICAL SWITCH VS. COVER 1 BLITZ
LIZ SLOT Z11 158

Against those forms of man coverage that have deep inside help (e.g., Cover 1 Free, Cover 2 Man), we favor the creation of a rub for the Outside Vertical instead. The Inside Vertical Read should occupy any safety inside, leaving us a chance to isolate the Outside Vertical with the rub as a bonus. Even if the defense is somehow able to successfully switch assignments in a very crowded environment, our receiver will still have an advantage in acceleration, running to open space. A half-roll action, as is illustrated here, can help make the throw an easier one, either for the Outside Vertical deep or the Choice route short.

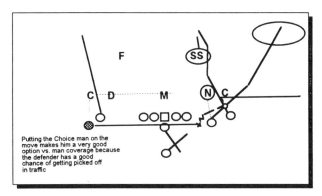

Putting the Choice man on the move makes him a very good option vs. man coverage because the defender has a good chance of getting picked off in traffic

DIAGRAM 11-3
RUB FOR OUTSIDE VERTICAL VS. COVER 2 MAN
TWIN X6 88

Versus Cover 2, we will go back to favoring the Inside Vertical if we want a deep shot. When the Inside Vertical happens from outside-in motion, the hash safety that we want to influence tends to see the Outside Vertical—who is lined up closer to him and gets off the ball quicker—first, and thus reacts with width to his outside route. This opens the hole in the middle. What can help open this hole also is play action, which should pull linebackers forward and make this less of a fine touch throw for the passer.

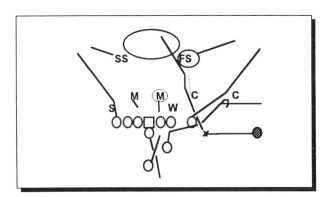

DIAGRAM 11-4
INFLUENCING A COVER 2 HASH SAFETY AND LINEBACKERS
SQUEEZE STRONG RAY Z10 336 SWITCH

Another way to get a deep throw is to try and get all safeties out of the middle altogether with motion, again to create a hole for the Inside Vertical. If a man coverage team, especially deep in their own territory, makes adjustments to motion with their free safety, this is the way to attack.

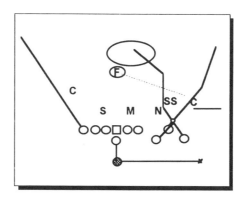

DIAGRAM 11-6
BACKFIELD MOTION TO OPEN MIDDLE FOR INSIDE VERTICAL
SQUEEZE RAY 6 F10 58

One tag that we've had great success with in running the Vertical Switch from regular sets is giving the #3 a "Split" route. He is simply told to run deep and get open anywhere on the other side of the free safety or other side of the ball. Primarily, this pries defenses open for the Inside Vertical—wide open. We can get the benefits of Bunch principle football added to this concept by aligning the three receivers in a "Snug" set:

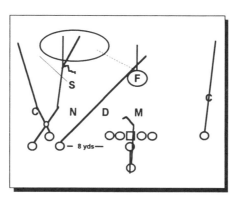

DIAGRAM 11-7
VERTICAL SWITCH WITH A SPLIT TAG
SNUG LEX 7 158 SPLIT

Ball Control Varieties. One of the best things that you can do for the runner of an Option-style route to gain medium third down yardage is to put him in motion. It provides him a chance to see coverage happening, naturally times his release into the pattern better, and gives the defense a chance to lose him. Calling "H Choice" after the number changes no assignments, but tells the QB that the Choice is now the priority. An example of how we might do this in a third and three or third and four to six situation might look like this:

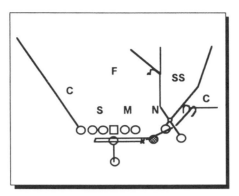

DIAGRAM 11.8 MOTIONED CHOICE ROUTE ON 3D AND 3
SQUEEZE RAY 6H IDIOT 58 H CHOICE

If we play a team that has active linebackers that try to close down our intermediate and deep passing games by running with vertical releases, a great ball control tag to use is Arrow for #3, and bring him back slightly late underneath the areas they vacated. The run after possibilities are great, which makes this a good call on third and 7 to 10 when you do not have time to hold the ball for longer throws.

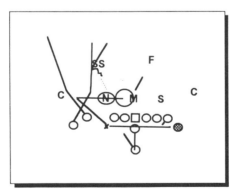

DIAGRAM 11.9 ARROW TAG FOR #3 VS. ACTIVE LINEBACKERS
SQUEEZE LARRY 6H7 158 H ARROW

CHAPTER 12

The "Smash" Route

Introduction and Basic Attack Concept

The Smash route, the package name we have given to the combination of a "Fin" by #1, a "Smash" cut by #2, and a "Middle Read" by #3, is a popular way to attack two deep coverages that puts tremendous pressure on the structure of those defenses, creating problems for both the playside safety and cornerback. The basic route combination puts two deep threats on the safety, or two threats in the corner's area. It holds a fundamental place in our basic passing game as the "6" route.

By employing this package from bunched sets, two added dimensions can be given the route. First, the featured Smash cut by the #2 receiver has more room to run, and secondly, the outside Fin route can become an option-style route with the built in ability to take advantage of any softness in the defense's interior. This second feature allows this package to be very effective against all coverages, not just Cover 2.

It also makes Smash a multi-dimensional package that has different parts you can emphasize for different situations: for example, you might use the Smash cut for long yardage shots or as a featured Cover 2-beater, the Middle Read on possession downs against zones, and the Fin route for medium distance situations and ball control. Other structural tags that will also be illustrated can also be easily used. Having passes that function in this way, along with formation flexibility, allows you to be comprehensively prepared for games without having to put in huge numbers of different pass plays.

Because of the man-beater features built into all three of the frontside cuts and the manner in which the route's design uses the field, the Smash package can become a staple-type play in the Red Zone as far in as the 15 yard line or so. Using maximum protection, which you sometimes have to do in this area, will give the quarterback time to wait for the Smash cut to come free.

Technique and basic route mechanics

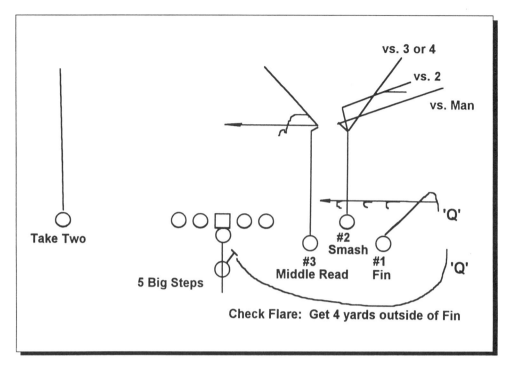

DIAGRAM 12-1
BASIC ROUTE DEFINITIONS FOR SMASH ROUTE

Frontside:
#1: Fin. Release slightly outside and run a lazy six-yard out, feeling the coverage and where the openings will be. In simplest terms, you want to get open from this point and look to the quarterback when you're sure, being DISTINCT in everything you do to communicate your intentions clearly. In general, work back to the inside if you can, and keep in mind that you must run away from man coverage and settle versus zones.

If you have a soft corner, stay where you are unless a short defender widens quickly, in which case you just slide inside him to the next hole. Versus a hard out-side corner, you'll spin back in immediately, trying to get a feel for whether he's chasing you or is or dropping into a zone.

#2: Smash. Release cleanly, straight up the field, break at 10-12 yards based on coverage.

Versus Man coverage or Cover 1, eyeball your defender and push hard to the post; get his hips turned. Plant your inside foot, arms driving, and snap your head back out, accelerating away to the corner.

Against Cover 2, angle your break as deeply as the hash safety's action will allow you without having him on your back; for normal safety technique, this will amount to splitting the locations of the cornerback and safety right down the middle. If he's a really wide, over-the-top safety, make sure you stay head-up to a bit outside him with your weave. Look the safety in the eye and push him deeper into his backpedal until you snap your head and plant your inside foot on your break; this will give you a bigger hole and keep him off your back. You may use a nod inside with your head as well.

Versus Cover 3 or any coverage where you see a deep corner outside of you (e.g., Cover 4), angle deep to the corner, trying to get over the top of deep 1/3 or 1/4 coverage. Do not lose acceleration to make a distinct break.

#3: Middle Read. Release upfield for 12 yards, favoring an inside release, seeing coverage develop in front of you. If there is no safety deep in the middle, you will break deep down the hole, splitting the defense. Otherwise, you will plant off your outside foot and break to the inside, accelerating across the field if you have man coverage, looking for a hole to sit in versus zones. Some key points to keep in mind:

- Against any kind of man coverage, safety or no safety, you must give a hard misdirection move to the outside to get separation.

- Make certain that you make engaged eye contact against any Cover 2 safety.

- Versus any kind of zone, get to a hole and be distinct. Do not wander laterally. Once you have found a hole, make eye contact with the QB and come straight back down through the hole.

Fullback:
Check Flare, making sure on your Flare that you get at least four yards wider than the Fin, wherever he is, to get the proper route distribution and maximum stretch of the defense.

Backside:
Take two. Sprint to the Fade hole, aiming at a landmark six yards from the sideline. Do not look back; you want to take two deep defenders with you.

Quarterback:
5 big steps. You have the same basic high-low read off any hard cornerback that you do in the Mesh and other routes. Hit the Fin if the corner deepens in any way, throw to the Smash in the hole if the corner squats. The contingency here is that if the cornerback takes away the Fin and the safety works over the top of the Smash, you know instantly to shuffle your feet, turn your shoulders, and come back to the Middle Read inside.

Against a soft cornerback, your priority becomes the Fin using good eye contact, again with the idea built in that the Middle Read becomes your outlet. If you ever feel like you don't have time to get all the way back to the Middle Read, don't hesitate to hit the Flare in stride, dropping the ball a foot in front of his numbers.

We can make the Fin first priority regardless of coverage by adding the word "Fin" at the end of the call; we can do the same thing for the Middle Read in certain cases, which makes the Fin the outlet.

Smash variations to attack coverage

Against straight man-type coverages, the routes of #1 and #3 will turn into full-speed crossing routes breaking off of misdirection moves, and #2's Smash is an excellent cut against man as well. Therefore, we can really emphasize any of these parts to the quarterback depending on weekly game plan and situation. In the case illustrated below, we're looking for the Fin route, and again using the principle of putting an option-style route in motion to help coverage get picked off and lost. The "Z Fin" at the end of the route tells the QB what his first priority is.

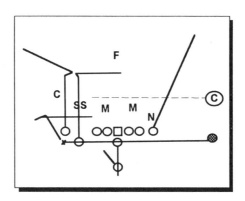

DIAGRAM 12-2
MAN VERSION WITH MOTION TO HELP THE FIN ROUTE
SQUEEZE RIP 9 Z11 156 Z FIN

As noted at the top, we feel like we can have consistent success against straight Cover 2 with this route, because the safety and cornerback are really in a 3-on-2 bind. The safety especially has to really make a quick commitment against a bunched set, because if he wants to play the Smash route, he has to really sprint wide in a hurry to cover all that space. If the safety from the backside gets too nosy in trying to help on the frontside Middle Read, we can tell the QB to look him off, or pump frontside and throw back to the backside Fade.

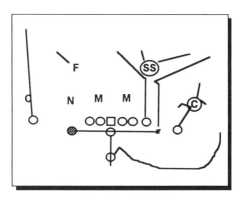

DIAGRAM 12-3
SMASH ROUTE AGAINST COVER 2
SQUEEZE RIP 9 H8 56

We can make a good route better against Cover 2 Man simply be using a "Switch" call which gives #2 the Middle Read and #3 the Smash. This creates a rub for the Smash by running the Middle Read "high" over the top of him.

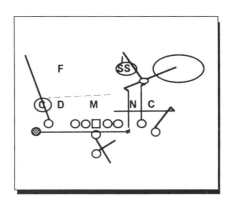

DIAGRAM 12-4
"SWITCH" CALL AGAINST COVER 2 MAN: RUB FOR SMASH
TWIN X6 86 SWITCH

This rub is doubled by a "Twist" adjustment, which tells #2 and #3 to run their regular routes, but only after crossing releases initially. As illustrated in Chapter 3, this causes a real problem for defenders who want to Banjo.

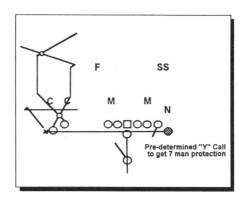

DIAGRAM 12-5
"TWIST" CALL TO CREATE A DOUBLE RUB FOR SMASH
SNUG LARRY 6 H11 Y156 TWIST

Another structural tag that comes into play out of Bunch is the "Change" call, which tells #1 and #3 to trade assignments off of switched releases. This generally is used to help either the Fin or a zone-beating Middle Read get lost in the wash, to make coverages that "pattern read" extensively a little uncertain about what they're reading. In the case below, we have made the Middle Read the first look by tagging "Z Middle" onto the end of the call.

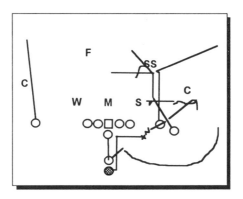

DIAGRAM 12-6
BASIC "CHANGE" CALL
SQUEEZE REX H6 56 CHANGE Z MIDDLE

The last variation is the use of a "Wrap" tag, which tells #1 and #2 to trade assignments off of crossed releases. Against normal Cover 2, this may help hold the cornerback in the short area for longer and enhance the possibility of the Smash route getting open behind it.

In the following example, we have also used max protection to illustrate a way the Smash package might be used in the Red Zone or as a blitz audible.

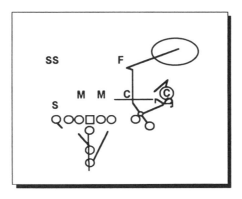

DIAGRAM 12-7
"WRAP" CALL WITH MAXIMUM PROTECTION
SQUEEZE RAY MAX 56 WRAP

CHAPTER 13

The "Dig" Route

Introduction and Basic Attack Concept

If you were to survey a large sample of cornerbacks and ask them what they felt was the single most difficult route to defend man to man, a very high number of them would likely respond "Dig," or an equivalent term. The combination of being turned and driven to the Post and then accelerated directly away from make this pattern a very difficult one for an individual defender to cope with. For that and many other reasons, one pass that is common to most all playbooks in one form or another is the Dig combination; a Dig route with a Post to clear the free safety and some form of underneath crossing routes to control line backers.

Within our particular system, the basic Dig package is called the "1" route, which, in its basic form, looks like this:

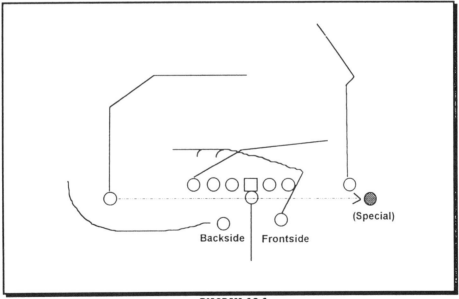

DIAGRAM 13-1
BASIC "1" ROUTE DISTRIBUTION

For us to adapt this combination to Bunch and get what we wanted from it, only a minor structural adjustment was required. The Dig cut moved from the backside to the frontside #1, working a wrap principle release with the Post, now the frontside

#2. Everything else stayed the same. We call this structural adjustment by saying "Special" after the call (e.g., 151 "Special"), and the basic distribution ends up looking this way:

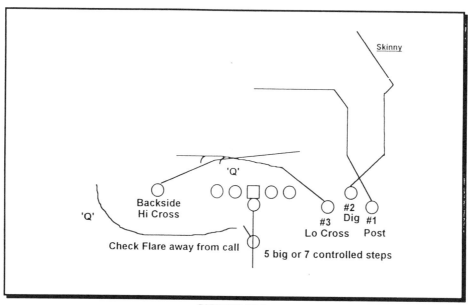

DIAGRAM 13-2
BASIC DISTRIBUTION OF "1 " ROUTE WITH "SPECIAL" ADJUSTMENT

This does not change the reads or the mechanics for the quarterback whatsoever, and the new learning for the receivers is really minimal, since they are only reapplying in a different place parts of a whole that they have already learned elsewhere (e.g., the wrap release technique).

The added dimension we get from using this variation in Bunch is twofold. First of all, we take a cut that by itself is already very tough on both man and zone, and make it even harder to cover by adding a rub (making it harder to chase) and bringing a deep crossing receiver from one man further outside than normal (making it harder to find or pattern read to).

Secondly, it creates a different kind of environment for any deep middle safety that can work to our advantage. In a normal Dig distribution (Diagram 13-1), a safety in the deep middle will only rarely sit on the Dig and leave the Post open behind him; he's seeing them both in his peripheral vision and backpedaling to stay deeper than the deepest. He does not have to react to either quickly because this is developing on either side of him, and because of the spacing involved.

In the case of the "Special" adjustment, though, he encounters a different problem. He sees crossed releases initially; if he is well coached, he will communicate to the cornerback to switch to the outside releaser, and he will pick up the inside releaser. The in side release drives at him to the Post and engages him; it is the route he is trained to defend from his position. If he locks in on this man and hesitates at all when the Dig route breaks flat in front of him, and if he forgets about the outside release that he has passed to the cornerback, the deep Post route will be behind him before he can recover. So, against indecisive safeties who do not want to work hard for depth, this can be a way to better open up the Post cut. Diagram 13-5 is an illustration of this dynamic.

The crossing routes rubbing underneath can also work very well for us in many situations, either as a primary look or an outlet entering the quarterback's vision.

Basic Route Rules and Technique (refer also to diagram 13-2)

Frontside
#1: *Dig.* Take your initial crossed release to a depth of about five yards. After that, make sure you get *distinct push straight upfield* to a depth of 10 or 11 yards. Plant and drive hard to the Post, engaging the free safety with eye contact, being a salesman. At 15 to 16 yards, give one final lunge and, with your lower body under control, plant off your outside foot and *flatten* across the field. If you feel man coverage, accelerate across to get separation. If you see zone drops in front of you, cross at 60% so that you stay open in the zone lanes longer. Look for the ball through one of these "windows" between linebackers as you cross.

#2: *Post.* Take your initial crossed release, getting some width. Straighten up to a depth of 12 to 13 yards and give a hard outside drive to the corner for three steps or so. You want the free safety to think that you've disappeared to the outside. You also want to be making strong eye contact with the cornerback, trying to turn his hips outside.

Plant off your outside foot with a final nod outside, and accelerate on a skinny course into the deep crease. Keep accelerating and looking for the ball.

#3: *Shallow Cross.* Shallow Cross at 5 to 6 yards, looking to rub underneath the backside cross. Work to get into the quarterback's vision. You are also a "Q" receiver.

A "Lo" call will make you the high crosser instead, rubbing over the top of the backside receiver.

Fullback
Check Flare away from call. You are the Q receiver. Work to get a wide stretch of the defense backside.

Backside Cross. Your basic split is 6 to 8 yards. Look to cross over the top of the frontside Shallow Cross, then settle into a hole versus zone or accelerate away versus man. Try to get into the QB's vision.

A "Lo" call tells you to be the underneath crosser at 5-6 yards, and a "Q" receiver.

Quarterback
Take five big steps and see the windows developing. If you see that linebackers are not getting depth initially, then wait to throw the Dig through a window bouncing off your fifth step. Make sure you do not telegraph where you're going with the ball, thereby giving a linebacker a chance to make a break to the ball. If you see the two interior linebackers really working fast for depth, don't hesitate—go right to one of the crossers underneath as they make eye contact with you.

In certain cases that we have determined during the game, we can make the Post the first choice by adding the word "Post" to the call, in which case you key the free safety. If he does not bite, come back down immediately to a crossing outlet or a wide Flare.

A "Lo" or "Cross" call at the end of the play makes the Shallow Cross the first look, which shortens your drop to five quick steps.

Dig Variations to Attack Coverages
Versus zones, one thing important to our teaching is the idea of "windows," or creases between linebackers through which we can throw. It is for this reason that the Dig only crosses at 60% speed vs. zone. By not running through these windows full speed, he stays open longer, can adjust to throws behind him better, and makes the QB's job easier. The quarterback must know where these "windows" can occur according to receiver alignment. The windows as they would occur in "Squeeze" calls as opposed to "Snug" calls are illustrated here:

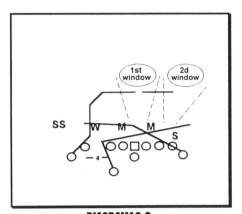

DIAGRAM 13-3
AVAILABLE ZONE WINDOWS
FROM "SQUEEZE" SETS

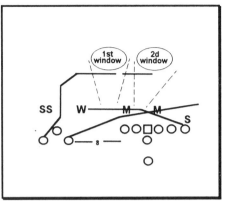

DIAGRAM 13-4
AVAILABLE ZONE WINDOWS
FROM "SNUG" SETS

Against Banjos that try to diminish the effect of our rubs, we find that the misdirection concept of having the Post break back inside after being switched to a defender with out side leverage is a good one (Chapter 3 discusses this idea in more detail). This idea is illustrated along with how we work a free safety in this package below:

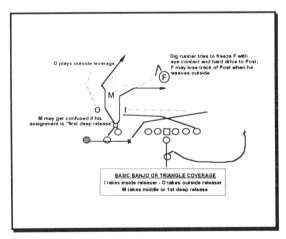

DIAGRAM 13-5
DLG COMBINATION VS. BANJO
SQUEEZE LARRY 11 H7 151 SPECIAL POST

These two receivers together also work very well against blitz coverage with no free safety; this can even be a blitz check. We can max protect once this coverage has been identified, giving the quarterback ample time to pick either route, depending on the technique of man defenders. Diagram 13-6 shows how to teach this idea to give us a great chance against a Banjo switch or straight man technique:

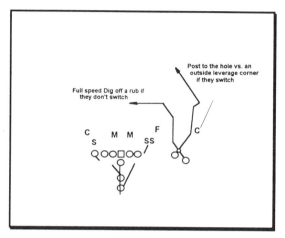

DIAGRAM 13-6
DIG COMBINATION VS. COVER 1 BLITZ
SNUG RAY MAX 51 SPECIAL

Another way to exert deep pressure out of this package is to tag an "Up" route for #3, which tells him to release behind the other two, creating a wall for his man to run around, and accelerate wide and deep to the Fade landmark. The free safety is put in a bind here.

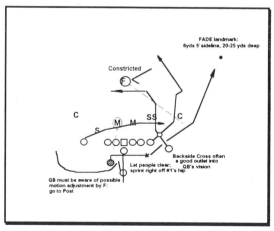

DIAGRAM 13-7
"UP" TAG TO PROVIDE DEEP THREATS VS. COVER 1
SQUEEZE WEAK RIP FG 51 SPECIAL F UP

If we want to emphasize the shorter routes, we can create problems for man or zone defenders. In the following example, we tag the backside receiver "Lo" and effectively create a wall of two rubs for him as he crosses against man coverage. It can also have use against zones when frontside linebackers, seeing no immediate frontside threat in their area, work hard to get underneath the Dig; this creates a big void for the backside crosser, who is hard for frontside coverage to find at times.

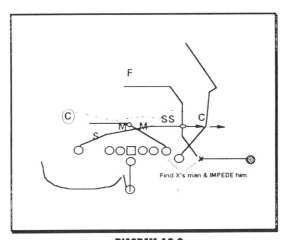

DIAGRAM 13-8
"LO" TAG TO CREATE RUBS FOR BACKSIDE CROSS
RIP 6 Z6 51 SPECIAL X LO

The other widely used element with the Dig route that we will also do from Bunch is play action. It becomes very difficult for linebackers to play run at all and still be able to get back to defend the Dig. This is one application we would use from a bunched set:

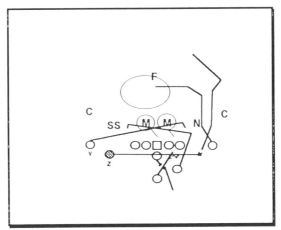

DIAGRAM 13-9
PLAY ACTION DIG COMBINATION FROM BUNCH
WEAK LOU Z6 336 DIG SPECIAL

CHAPTER 14

The "Cross" Package Off Four Verticals

Introduction and basic attack concept

Because the Shallow Cross is a fundamental part of our Bunch concept, we thought it vital to have a single structure that could package that route a number of different ways, while not creating any new reads or learning problems. Once more, a route that has long been part of the basic fabric of our offense fit this description, as it can painlessly be converted to something with great possibilities out of Bunch. In this case, it is our "9" route, which starts as a traditional "four vertical" route with outside receivers running to landmarks along the numbers, and inside receivers running to landmarks near the hashes.

From there, receivers can be tagged to run combinations of crossing routes within the package. Because of the way in which it is constructed, this route probably gives us more different types of ways to attack with less new learning than any of the other eight routes in our base dropback package.

Within this package, you create a number of positive situations that hold up regardless of how you distribute the crossers:

- *A good opportunity to throw against two deep zones.* A route, specifically the "Middle Read" is built-in to split the safeties if that look is shown, most often with another deep outside route on his side.

- *Multiple man-beating crossing-style routes at various levels.* Often this is happening off one or more rubs. One particular advantage of this type of route is that it is much harder for defenders to switch, or banjo, two receivers crossing from opposite sides because they have already built up momentum in chasing their initial receiver. It is also harder for them to communicate such a switch from opposite sides of the ball once the play begins.

Against man, the crossers will always release underneath people to get where they're going, and so natural rubs are occurring all over the place, sometimes as many as three for a receiver on one play. With all this going on and all that he must run through, a loose man defender has virtually no chance to make a play on a receiver who is underneath him and accelerating across the field immediately. If you have one playmaker on your team, you can create some situations where you do not have to throw the ball 15 yards downfield off a lengthy drop to convert long yardage situations. If you hit this man on the move on what is a short, timed throw right in front of the quarterback, you have a great chance of making the first down, or even breaking a big play. You've at least put the defense in a position in which they're forced to execute, sometimes with athletes that aren't as good as yours. A strong argument can be made that many times the chances of your best player breaking a five yard catch for fifteen or more are greater than your chances of being able to protect long enough to throw downfield, and throw accurately against defenses which are rushing hard.

The chaos that can be created by the rubs gives you something viable to use even with very limited speed. You're still going to get separation for consistent gains. This route is etremely valuable in high schools because there are substantial numbers of defenses that rely exclusively, or almost exclusively, on covering man to man.

- *A high-low combination on a zone defender.* The combination of a Shallow Cross with a Middle Read distributed somewhere behind it isolates a particular underneath defender. If he gets depth, a hole exists to throw the Shallow Cross. More likely at the high school level is for him to sit at a shallow depth and sort of muddle up the underneath player by default, which creates a big crease to throw the twelve yard cut behind him.

- *A place to get rid of the ball quickly in case of heat.* Shallow crosses coming off rubs into the quarterback's vision make a very convenient and effective throw if he gets heat. His "Q" receiver is right in front of him.

Basic teaching progression
Diagram 14-1 shows how the "9" route is initially installed in practice. This route uses an alternative numbering system, numbering *all* receivers consecutively, from the frontside (in these illustrations, the *right* side) to the backside, 1 through 4 (see diagrams 3-2 and 3-3, which illustrate different methods of numbering receivers). It is a *landmark route,* which means that all receivers have a definite spot on the field to which they're working. For #1 and #4, those *spots* are along the numbers on the field, or eight yards from the sideline. They run "Go" routes or Fade against a hard corner. #2 and #3 work the frontside and backside hashes, respectively, running to a spot one to two yards inside their hash. The fullback's rule, as it will be throughout the 9 route, is to Check Flare to the numbers away from the call. The quarterback takes five big steps, throwing to #2 or #3 off the free safety if there is one deep safety in the middle. If there are two deep safeties, he picks a side, often the wide side, and works outside-in off the hash player on that side. He forces him to cover either the numbers receiver or the hash receiver, and throws opposite.

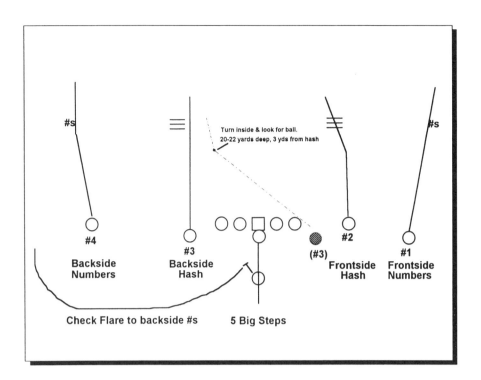

DIAGRAM 14-1
INITIAL TEACHING AND ROUTE DISTRIBUTION FOR THE "9" PACKAGE

Once this foundation is established, we begin to add tags that tell receivers to cross. One receiver tagged (e.g., "59 Y Cross", which we'll eventually shorten to just "59 Y") tells him to cross at 6, and the man next inside of him to run a "Middle Read". Everybody else keeps their normal landmark as dictated by basic 9 route rules. Getting them to these landmarks helps to maintain a horizontal and vertical stretch of the entire field, even though we're initially lined up in a bunched-up type of set. Diagram 14-2 illustrates a one receiver cross by an outside receiver, while 14-3 shows an inside receiver being tagged as the single crosser.

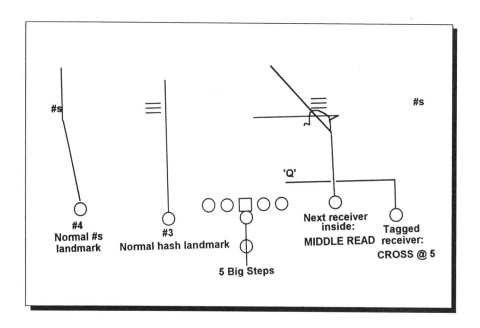

DIAGRAM 14-2
SINGLE RECEIVER CROSS: OUTSIDE RECEIVER TAGGED

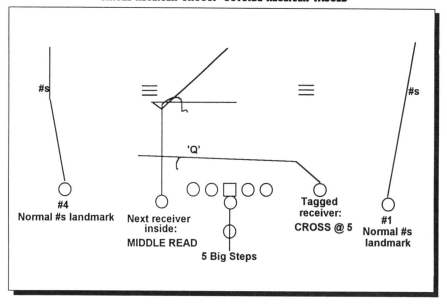

DIAGRAM 14-3
SINGLE RECEIVER CROSS: INSIDE RECEIVER TAGGED

Two receivers tagged (e.g., "59 ZH Cross," or just "59 ZH") tells the two receivers to cross, rubbing shoulders at 6 yards. The receiver first in the tag (in this case, Z) is the "hi" receiver, brushing over the top of the second tagged crosser. Whoever is just inside the first tagged receiver is assigned the Middle Read. Diagrams 14-4 and

14-5 A, and 14-5 B illustrate this type of tag, and show how a different looking route distribution can be gained—causing a different kind of problem for defenses—by using the exact same tag with a different formation.

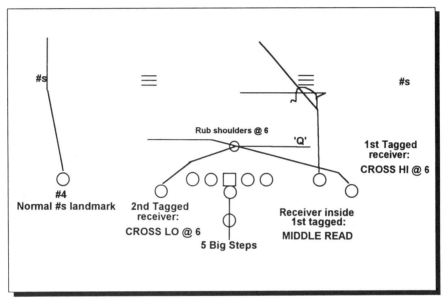

DIAGRAM 14-4
TWO RECEIVER CROSS OUT OF A BALANCED FORMATION

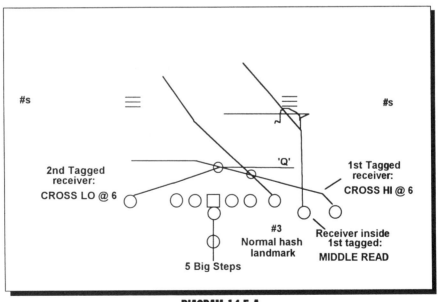

DIAGRAM 14-5 A
TWO RECEIVER CROSS OUT OF A TRIPS FORMATION

Technique coaching points

1. Definition and technique for "Middle Read". Release upfield for 12 yards, favoring an inside release, seeing coverage develop in front of you. If there is no safety deep in the middle, you will break deep down the hole, splitting the defense. Otherwise, you will plant off your outside foot and break to the inside, accelerating across the field if you have man coverage, looking for a hole to sit in versus zones. Some key points to keep in mind:

- Against any kind of man coverage, safety or no safety, you must give a hard misdirection move to the outside to get separation.

- Make certain that you make engaged eye contact against any Cover 2 safety. You freezing him and beating him to the inside is crucial to the success of this play against Cover 2. Give him a hard *nod* if necessary to keep him off your back.

- Versus any kind of zone, get to a hole and be distinct. Do not wander laterally. Once you have found a hole, make eye contact with the QB and come *straight back down through the hole.*

2. #3 aligned opposite final hash landmark. Of primary, vital concern for you is to get off the ball first and fast, and to get through traffic before crossers coming beneath you do. Focus, then, on finding a clear path of release (preferably inside) and on escaping jams both at the line of scrimmage and on the move. If possible, align on the line of scrimmage.

Once clear, keep sprinting at an angle across the field until you get within 3 yards of the opposite hash, at which point you turn inside and straighten up, looking for the ball in case you've been neglected by the defense. This turn should happen at a depth of about 20 yards.

3. Read and technique dynamics for a one receiver cross. The key to the quarterback and the two receivers involved will be to identify the first and second short defenders *inside the cornerback.* Our basic plan for this route is to get both the Cross and the Middle Read inside the first of these, and to beat the second.

The Middle Read will beat the first defender inside, whether by hooking inside him versus a zone, or beating him with separation if he's a man defender. If this first defender is stubborn about squeezing inside, we can move the Flare frontside to widen him. The Cross has come underneath all this, and looks to challenge the second defender to his inside hip with his crossing action, forcing that defender to react one way or the other. If he reacts to the Cross laterally at all, a wide lane opens for the Middle Read behind and outside him. If he has worked wide or deep in his drop and does not react to the Cross, then the Cross naturally comes open just inside his drop, and can make the catch and turn upfield.

The quarterback is keying all of this in his drop, having looked off backside coverage initially for a very brief time. By the time he hits his fifth step, his read will have played itself out, and he delivers the ball immediately.

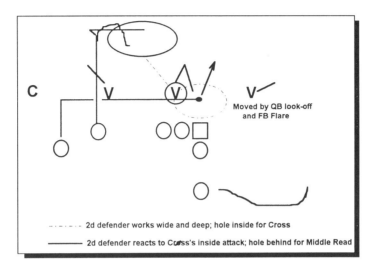

2d defender works wide and deep; hole inside for Cross

2d defender reacts to Cross's inside attack; hole behind for Middle Read

DIAGRAM 14-5 B
ONE RECEIVER CROSS READ DYNAMICS

4. Read and technique dynamics for a two receiver cross. Both crossers should release underneath any other receivers before getting into the pattern. The lo crosser, in particular, wants to be in no hurry, even pausing if he's lined up close to the interior of the formation so that he can see things developing and size up the best course. For as long as possible, the two crossers want to run as though they're going *straight at each other.* About three yards before they would otherwise collide, the hi crosser adjusts his course just over the top of his own man, looking to brush by his upfield shoulder. Both receivers are keeping their eyes up and arms driving , not staring at defenders or each other. Once past the mesh, either of them may settle in any zone hole they see.

The quarterback goes into the play with the idea that he will hit the lo crosser as soon as he looks back after the mesh. If short defenders are squeezing this man, he will bounce up and look for the Middle Read behind this in the lane that will naturally be created.

Nine route variations for attacking coverage
Zones. Regardless of how we do it, our basic one receiver crossing read should hold up very well against any type of zone. By using a "Snug" call, we can widen the two

receivers out a bit, attacking a little different part of the defense, and possibly opening up better lanes for the run after catch (Diagram 14-6). We like to use trips variations of the one receiver cross when we play a zone team that runs linebackers upfield against vertical releases; we can get the whole underneath cleared out with our two inside releasers, and really open things up for the Cross (Diagram 14-7).

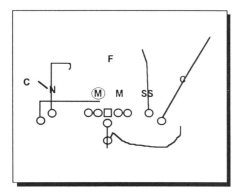

DIAGRAM 14-6
ONE RECEIVER CROSS FROM SNUG
SNUG TWIN 159 X

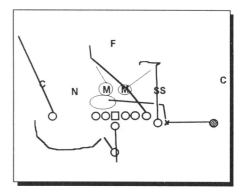

DIAGRAM 14-7
CROSS UNDERNEATH DEEP LINEBACKERS
RIP 6 Z6 59 Z

Another solid ploy against zones is to fake a run to the side you're bringing your crossers, pull up behind the tackle and hit one of them in the hole. Against man coverage where you feel confident that the side away from the fake will get cleared out, you can also throw the lo cross back across the field; certain teams will leave that wide open. Diagram 14-8 is an illustration of that:

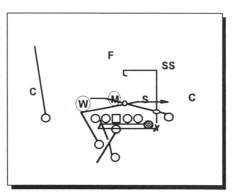

DIAGRAM 14-8
TWO RECEIVER CROSS WITH PLAY ACTION
SQUEEZE WEAK RIP Y IDIOT 337 ZF CROSS

Man. Against man coverage, of course, we are trying to create as many opportunities for the defense to get picked off covering our featured receiver as possible. Our quarterback is thinking in terms of leading receivers with his throw, not making them slow up to catch it. In Diagram 14-9, we take advantage of the fact that cornerbacks often play soft against a tight end/wing combination, because they probably have outside-in force responsibility on runs. Against man coverage, therefore, we can get the wing underneath a rub to the inside, leaving that cornerback a long way away from the man he's trying to cover. If they were to play zone against this particular combination, we still feel like we have a pretty good chance of having someone open because of the horizontal stretch created by the fullback Flaring wide to that side.

Diagram 14-10 shows a distribution that creates three potential rubs for a Shallow Cross: one underneath the Middle Read, one underneath #3 running to the hash, and one underneath the hi crosser coming from the other side. No matter what technique or tightness of man coverage a defender plays, we feel like he has a chance of encountering difficulty from one or more of these rubs. The outside in motion which changes the receivers' relative positions can also, many times, leave the outside-most defender in a softened, outside leverage position, which also works to our advantage.

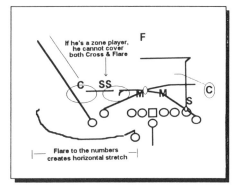

DIAGRAM 14-9
WING CROSS AGAINST MAN COVERAGE
SQUEEZE B LARRY 6 59 XH

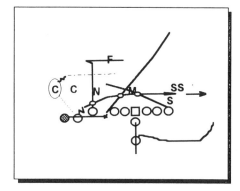

DIAGRAM 14-10
CREATING THREE RUBS FOR A CROSS
SQUEEZE LARRY 11 H7 159 YZ

Arrow Tag for #3. Changing the #3 receiver's responsibility to an Arrow route is very useful against both zone and man. Against the former, it serves as a trail-type route into a hole vacated when the other two routes were jumped. If, for example, a defense is trying to cause problems for your basic one receiver combination by walling the Middle Read with the first short defender and jumping the Shallow Cross with the inside linebacker, a big alley opens up for the Arrow. The timing is such that the quarterback can start on his normal reads, and then know that he'll go to the Arrow as soon as he sees the first short defender close down on the Middle Read. This is illustrated in Diagram 14-11.

Versus the latter, it isolates an athlete running a misdirection route on one defender in a space that has been cleared out by the Cross and the Middle Read. When quick motion into a bunch hides the Arrow behind stacked releases, it has an even greater chance of success. This application is demonstrated in Diagram 14-12.

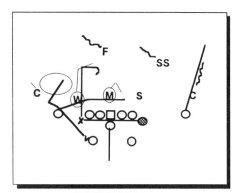

DIAGRAM 14-11
TRAIL-TYPE ROUTE BY #3 VS. A ZONE
SQUEEZE SPLIT RIP Y7 59 X, H ARROW

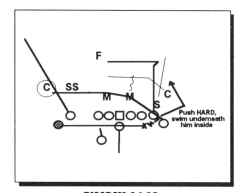

DIAGRAM 14-12
TRAIL-TYPE ROUTE BY #3 VS. MAN
SQUEEZE B LARRY 6 Z6 59 H, Z ARROW
GOOD COMPLEMENT TO ROUTE IN 14-9

CHAPTER 15

The "Hinge" Route

Introduction and basic attack concept

To have a consistently successful passing game at the high school level, it is important to exploit the fact that a great percentage of zone coverages at that level do not cover the flat very well. Often 50 defenses will rush the weakside end while playing 3 deep behind it. Many times weakside linebackers in even fronts will take 2 steps up each play and never work laterally for width. Even Sky Safeties on the strong side can tend to be run players first or be slow-footed at this level.

It is for that reason that we have been able to make a living throwing simple Hitches time after time through the years; it is also for that reason that the Mesh package was structured as it was, to attack the flat quickly. Easy throws occur with chances to make yardage after the catch.

If you want to pass and do not force people to cover you on the edges, you'll allow even bad coverage teams to compress you horizontally. Thus you will find people in close proximity of your route development, and the defense's job is 30% easier. Establishing a wide, horizontal stretch by pounding the flats produces benefits related to both pass and run.

While it, unlike many of the other routes here, requires a quarterback who can throw the ball with some zip through space, the "Hinge" route is another way to attack this area while taking advantage of the wide field created by Bunch. Because the angles of release are identical, it is an excellent complement to the Bunch Fade. Hinge takes advantage of cornerbacks who have been forced to turn and run out of their backpedal quickly because of the Fade threat.

Upon the snap, the horizontal and vertical stretch starts happening so quickly that it becomes difficult for a flat defender to look up the receiver and drop at the right angle to take away the route. It provides a totally different mode of release for the underneath defenders to look at and cope with. With much exposure to Bunch at all, they start to gear themselves for quick crosses and rubs inside. Two players (the flat coverage, whoever that may be, and the next underneath defender inside) not used to getting width must recognize the release, get width in a hurry, and then find where people are in order to successfully defend this route. Certain forms of play action complicate this process further.

For us, the Hinge is our "2" route package (once more, little new learning because the same base route structures are merely reapplied), which gives the Frontside #1 receiver some kind of outside route (a Speed Out at 10-12 is the base definition), and the #2 has a Choice route. Giving the #3 receiver (in cases where it's run from Trips looks) a "Flag" automatically with the Hinge call gives us a weapon with which to attack a Cornerback who squats on the Hinge. It cannot be run with as flat an angle as a normal Smash or Corner route; he has to literally angle toward the front corner of the end zone (out of his break) to try to get well over the top of the cornerback so that the Hinge and Flag cannot be played by a single defender. If we see the cornerback jumping the Hinge and a Free Safety coming out of the middle to get over the top of the Flag (which could well happen against moveout actions), we'll come off to the backside Post. The base trips route really stretches a defense both horizontally and vertically at the same time, as well as providing a unique package of releases that they may not be as accustomed to defending out of Bunch sets.

Technique and basic route mechanics

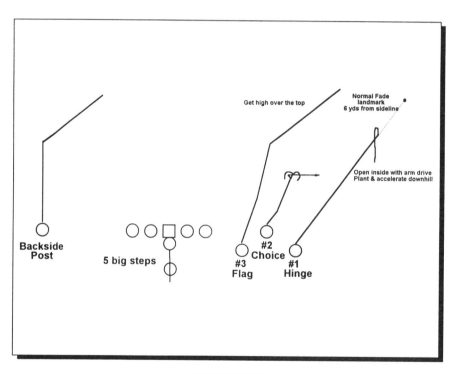

DIAGRAM 15-1
BASIC HINGE ROUTE DISTRIBUTION AND ASSIGNMENTS

Frontside:
All three receivers need an outside weave as they come off the ball to get where they're going.

#1 releases toward the same landmark six yards from the sideline that he would on a Fade. For this reason, you have to be careful about running this route into the wide side of the field. The angle and the length of the throw could become unreasonable, unless the landmark is adjusted. Getting full push, he breaks his hips down beginning at 13 yards, and plants his outside foot at 15. During this time, he's making a last, bursting *lunge* forward at the defender and doubling the speed of his arm drive briefly. This is the non-verbal detail of the route that gets us an extra step of separation. He opens and spins in to face the quarterback (tightly), and pushes almost straight back downhill, separating himself from the DB. The ball should already be ⅓ of the way to him. We find that the advantage of running this "Hinge" technique of opening inside and spinning outside gets us a more consistent angle of break back to the ball from receiver to receiver than if we used a traditional "comeback" technique where the receiver tried to plant on his inside foot and redirect his momentum all the way around to the outside.

If the "Choice" is tagged as the primary receiver, #1 will convert his Hinge to a Fade against a rolled up cornerback. Otherwise, run the Hinge with an outside release regardless of coverage.

#2, who is running the Choice, "chases" the flat defender during the first few steps. If he gets outside of him, great—the Hinge will now have no one underneath it. If not, he pushes at the inside leg of the flat defender for 4 yards to create some space between himself and the second underneath defender, whom he'll have to beat on his Choice route. Built into the teaching of the Choice route is the idea that the depth of his route works in concert with the route just outside of him, and whether or not he is primary or the secondary option in the route, so that the route's timing develops properly. As a general rule, he will be his deepest when he is the secondary read as he is in this case. Any secondary Choice route looks to break at a depth five yards less than the route outside of him. In the case of a 14 yard Hinge where he is a secondary receiver, he straightens and pushes to a depth of 9-10 yards before turning inside or out, because the QB has to come off the Hinge before throwing to him. If he had a shorter "Speed Out" of 10-12 yards tagged outside of him as a secondary receiver, the depth of his break would shorten to 5 or 6. Any time he is the primary receiver, which is designated by saying "Choice" after the route call (e.g., 152 H Choice), the route occurs at a depth of 5 to 6.

#3 wants to make certain that he releases OUTSIDE of the second underneath defender to keep that man from finding the Choice route quickly. After this, he wants to work his Flag route for depth and speed, trying to get over the top of the deepest outside defender, running on a course that would take him 35-40 yards deep at the sideline.

Backside:
Run a basic Post, looking to get into the hole in the middle where the free safety might leave if he works hard toward the trips side.

Quarterback:
Take five big steps, having located the first short defender inside the cornerback before the snap. Key his movement as you drop; if he works for width extremely fast to the point where you feel that he is in the Hinge's throwing lane, find the Choice runner, keep your feet alive, and throw to him in the hole when you get eye contact. Otherwise, whether it is man, zone, or whatever, you will be throwing the Hinge to a spot 12 yards downfield as you bounce up from your hitch step.

If the Choice route is tagged, then it becomes your primary read, and your drop changes to 5 *quick* steps. Find him in the hole off of eye contact. If he gets squeezed from the outside in, bounce up and hit the Hinge in the open lane.

"Hinge" coverage attack principles and variations
In general, we prefer this route to be run against some kind of soft corner (Cover 1 with loose man, Cover 3, and *especially* Cover 4 because its underneath coverage is limited) so that we can push the deep cornerback to his deep responsibility and break open in front of him. In all these cases, the keying of the first short defender inside the cornerback holds up, because he is the only one that can take away the Hinge throwing lane no matter what coverage they are playing.

Hinge can also be very effective against Cover 2, if our receiver can get an outside release and the corner turns to run with him in an attempt to close the deep outside hole. In this way, Hinge becomes an excellent route to use in sequence against Cover 2 teams that you have established the Fade against, because the cornerback will really work to run with the Fade and give you an easy completion in front of him.

Because these same reads and principles hold up so well for the Hinge versus all kinds of coverages, creating different variations to create specific additional problems for teams from week to week becomes especially easy, and there is absolutely nothing of consequence new for your players. Among the different variation concepts that can be used to enhance the route are the following:

1. *Double Hinge.* The "Double" call creates a two mirrored Hinge/Choice combinations on either side of a 2 X 2 Bunch formation, allowing the quarterback to choose the side he likes. This choice can be based on field width, matchups, or defensive structure. *(Diagram 15-2)*

2. *Motioning the Hinge receiver from the opposite side.* By motioning the Hinge receiver from the opposite side of the formation, a tight bunch of people is created

just before the snap that is hard for the defense to define, especially in terms of who's #1, #2, and so forth. What can happen is that a "wall" of sorts is built, either for a man defender chasing him or bumping to him, or a flat defender trying to adjust for width with the motion. *(Diagram 15-3)*

3. *Under tag for the backside receiver.* If underneath coverage really tries to over-compensate to the frontside when they see the quick stretch that's being created by the releases, they naturally open up a huge hole that an Under route can get into. This is very easy to add because we have trained our quarterback to find stationary outlets from the first week of practice. This can also serve as a 'Q' receiver if you're worried about quick pressure. *(Diagram 15-3)*

4. *Half roll action.* This route is easily incorporated into any kind of half roll package, because its throws are all naturally suited for that kind of action. This may be the preferable way of running Hinge if your quarterback's arm strength is limited, because it shortens the distance of the out-breaking pass. Half roll variations may also give you a better chance to run this play to the wide field and take advantage of space. *(Diagram 15-3)*

5. *Two back formations.* Staying in a more standard set may provide some benefits for this route in that it keeps teams out of overloaded underneath adjustments in the area you're trying to throw. To do this, though, #3 must be lined up in the backfield initially, which makes it impossible for him to get where he needs to be on the Flag route. So, we will use a "Switch" call (see Appendix B) to give #2 the Flag and #3 the Choice. *(Diagram 15-4)*

6. *Play action to the frontside.* A run fake directly at the side you are attacking with the Hinge is very beneficial because you can freeze the very man you're reading (the first short defender inside the cornerback). Hinge off your best run action can then become a good first down call. *(Diagram 15-4)*

7. *"Flag" tag for #2.* High-low on the cornerback. If you're not worried about flat coverage, you can turn this route into more of a deep threat by tagging a Flag route to #2 and telling your quarterback to take seven steps, throwing the Flag over the top if he sees the cornerback levelled or closing on the Hinge. Otherwise, he can throw his normal Hinge. Again, the rule must be emphasized that the QB never try to throw over the top of a retreating cornerback. *(Diagram 15-5)*

8. *Sprint-out run-pass option.* Sprinting out to the combination described above is a great way to take advantage of the space and leverage created by Bunch. The quarterback's option to run becomes more potent because he's likely to find more room outside if he wants to take off, and defenders will be pursuing him at unfamiliar angles. *(Diagram 15-5)*

9. *Speed Out tag for #1.* Changing #1's technique to a Speed Out at 10 yards rolling to 12 with a drop of 5 quick steps by the quarterback allows you to attack this wide space a little quicker with a little more of a rhythm throw. It may not use the space outside horizontally quite as well as the Hinge, however. *(Diagram 15-6)*

10. *Wrap tag to free up the Choice route.* In this case, we are again using motion to try to get one of our players lost in the defensive shuffle as we did in diagram 15-3. This time, however, it is the Choice route we're trying to get lost. By bringing him late out of the bunch, he can see what's going on in front of him and let the defense get where they're going to get, then easily slipping into the hole. He is the quarterback's first look because we have tagged it that way. Sometimes this adjustment, though, will serve to paralyze and impede the flat defender, which creates that much more of an opening to throw the Hinge. *(Diagram 15-7)*

11. *Special Wrap with #2 Flag to beat Man coverage.* This is a concept we originally adopted from Homer Smith of Alabama, though it may be older than that. The initial release looks like our "8", or Vertical Switch route, after which the receiver who has released inside breaks back out to his Hinge, rubbing underneath the outside Flag runner into space. Man coverage with no Switch will probably collide or impede each other, while a Switching tandem is left with no one covering the outside because the outside switcher left with the Flag route. *(Diagram 15-8)*

12. *Maximum protection.* This is an excellent route to use on blitz downs with maximum protection, because many times the extra underneath receivers are not crucial to the play's design. So maximum protection, either by call or a quarterback audible, gives you a chance to hold the ball longer and wait for a route that is very tough on man coverage. *(Diagram 15-8)*

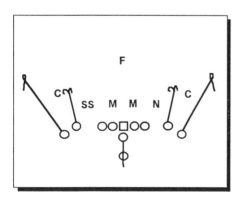

DIAGRAM 15-2
DOUBLE HINGE VARIATION
TWIN 52 DOUBLE HINGE

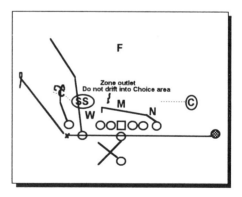

DIAGRAM 15-3
MOTION HINGE WITH UNDER TAG OFF
HALF ROLL ACTION
SQUEEZE RIP 9 Z11 182

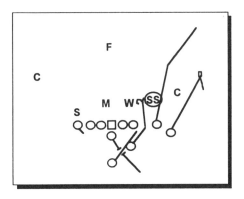

DIAGRAM 15-4
TWO BACK, PLAY ACTION
HINGE WITH SWITCH CALL
SQUEEZE RAY 308 HINGE SWITCH

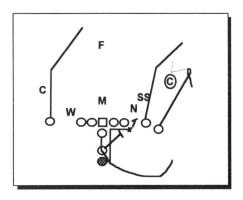

DIAGRAM 15-5
SPRINT OUT HINGE WITH
WITH #2 FLAG
SQUEEZE REX H6 72 Y FLAG

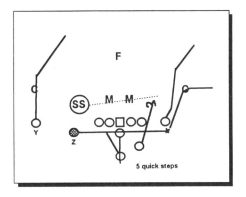

DIAGRAM 15-6
SPEED OUT TAG FOR #1
WEAK LOU Z8 52 SWITCH Z OUT

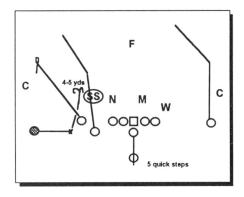

DIAGRAM 15-7
WRAP TAG WITH CHOICE AS 1ST LOOK
LIZ SLOT Z11 152 WRAP Z CHOICE

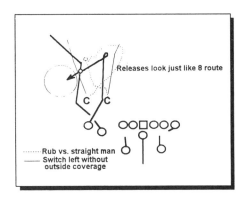

DIAGRAM 15-8
SPECIAL HINGE MAN-BEATER WITH MAX PROTECTION
SQUEEZE SPLIT LARRY 152 WRAP Z FLAG

CHAPTER 16

The "Over" Route

Introduction and basic attack concept

The OVER route is another basic package within our system that we merely adapted to Bunch. It provides a great backside attack against those who make large-scale adjustments to Trips, including Cover 3 Cloud-type looks. From a bunched alignment, these routes get to the backside areas very quickly; it is a package that has a chance of gaining large chunks of yardage at a time. OVER is an excellent Red Zone and/or 3d and long call, and can incorporate many different actions and tag adjustments to give it further advantage. It is also very hard on switching man coverage because the outside defender gets no outside releaser coming to him.

Technique and basic route mechanics

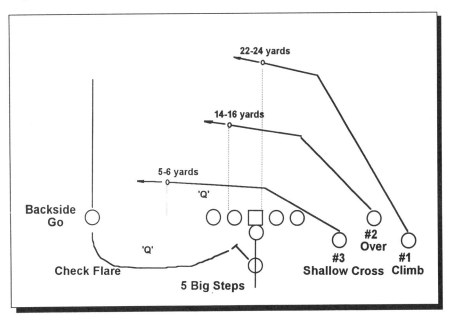

DIAGRAM 16-1
BASIC OVER ROUTE ASSIGNMENTS AND DISTRIBUTION

Frontside:

#1: CLIMB: work toward a landmark 22-24 yards deep over the ball. From Bunch, this will function much like a Split route, except that you want to flatten after you reach your final depth...you can be a great scramble outlet .

#2: OVER: climb to a point 14 yards over the opposite guard and flatten. Cross at 60% vs. zone, looking for the ball in open windows, accelerate away and separate vs. man.

#3: SHALLOW CROSS: 5 to 6 yards, underneath linebackers. Do not throttle down in a zone void until you are well past the backside tackle area.

Backside:
#1: GO route, sprint straight upfield, do not get forced inside. Do not even turn to look for the ball unless you completely run by your man. By split or by weave, run this up a line six yards from the sideline.

Fullback:
FLARE. Lose depth and shoot up through the original position of the backside receiver.

Quarterback:
Take 5 big steps and a hitch step...look off to the Climb for the first step or two. Turn and find the "window" through which you'll throw the Over, anticipating hitting it off your pop-up step. If you see drops that are working underneath the Over, turn quickly to the Shallow Cross and get it to him immediately so that he can make yards after the catch while defenders are still dropping . If you see the free safety really jump the Over, you can throw the Climb over the top IF YOU'RE ABSOLUTELY CERTAIN. On all of these throws, you must hit receivers in stride vs. man coverage and not make them slow down for the ball. This is the key to making big plays with this route.

Over variations for attacking coverages
Against zones, some form of play action in conjunction with the Over route is very helpful, because it influences those defenders you want to throw behind, and opens the lanes for the quarterback's potential throws. Using Over in this way is a very good method of attack on first down in a situation where you can reasonably be assured of some kind of zone. The first basic way we will do this is by faking away from the area we are ultimately attacking and bootlegging toward the crossing routes. The other basic type of play action is a straight fake to the crossing side, which really helps pull the linebackers up right where you're attacking. Examples of those versions are illustrated below:

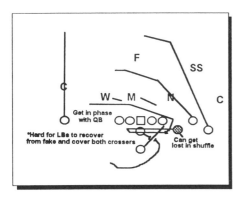

DIAGRAM 16-2
BOOT OVER VS. ZONE
SQUEEZE REX 6 H IDIOT 206 OVER

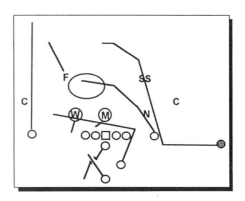

DIAGRAM 16-3
ATTACK SIDE RUN FAKE W/ OVER
SQUEEZE STRONG RAY Z10 307 OVER

In attacking man coverage, many times we will use our structural tags (see Appendix A) to create rubs either for the Shallow Cross or the Over. By switching assignments to allow a specific man to rub underneath another receiver on his way to the cross, we naturally impede a man defender and create separation.

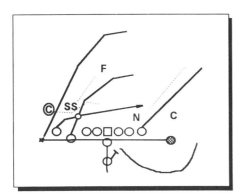

DIAGRAM 16-4
"SWITCH" CALL TO CREATE RUB
FOR SHALLOW CROSS
SQUEEZE RIP 9 Z11 150 OVER SWITCH

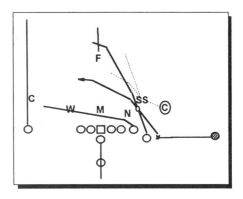

DIAGRAM 16-5
"WRAP" CALL TO CREATE RUB
FOR OVER ROUTE
RIP 6 Z6 50 OVER WRAP

One final tactic we can use with the Over route is to motion the Fullback wide to the one receiver side, getting him into his Flare route right away (automatically making him the "Q" receiver). This is a good approach in more than one setting. First of all, because of the coverages played, teams will often assign the Free Safety to handle any backfield motion adjustments in the Red Zone. This opens a hole for us to either throw the Climb or the Over cuts, which get to that area quicker out of Bunch sets A linebacker leaving to cover him creates a hole for the Shallow Cross. Secondly, against zones, a severe horizontal stretch is placed on that attack side area we're crossing into. Because the backfield is emptied out in this version, you have to pick your spots with it, but having the Fullback as the "Q" should keep you out of really bad plays.

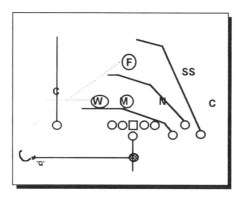

DIAGRAM 16-6
MOTION TO CREATE A HORIZONTAL STRETCH FOR OVER
SQUEEZE REX 6 F11 150 OVER

CHAPTER 17

The "Flood" Route

Introduction and basic attack concept

The three level Flood concept with a Go route deep, a Flat route short, and some sort of Corner/Sail route in the middle has long been a pass basic to many offenses, and, indeed, has been our "5" route for many seasons.

When we run this package from a Bunch set, we look to engage the outside-most deep coverage with the Go route so that we can bring the Corner ("Smash") route underneath and outside that defender into the open area. In any form of 2 deep coverage, for example, the hash safety almost has to move to shut off the Go—it is his most immediate threat. If we've looked to the Flat and the cornerback has widened with him, the Smash route will break wide open in the deep outside void. The tightened alignment really helps that particular throw because of all the additional space, and thus the additional leverage, created to the outside.

Technique and basic route mechanics

Diagram 17-1 shows the basic distribution of the Flood route in a bunched environment. It can function well using any kind of set with a three receiver side, including situations where #3 is aligned in the backfield. Having #3 in the backfield, in fact, may help the route time up better in many situations. A "Snug" call for the trio to split them eight yards is also applicable, as is the standard "Squeeze" adjustment that splits them four to five yards.

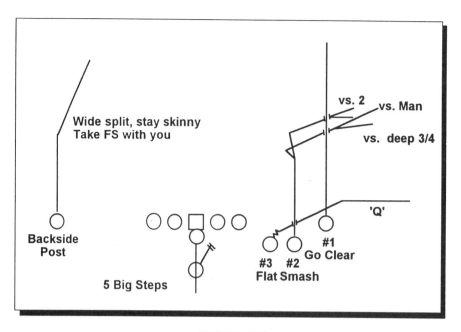

DIAGRAM 17-1
BASIC FLOOD ROUTE DISTRIBUTION

Frontside:

#1 wants to release clean and fast (he has to know his purpose again), sprint straight upfield. He has to be ready to use escape techniques at the line of scrimmage and/or on the move so that he does not get jammed inside *into* the route development. Again because of his purpose, we try and create situations where he aligns *on* the ball.

The technique for *#2* is a bit different than the one he would have for a normal 5 route. In a normal 5, he has a "Sail," in which his technique is more of a Comeback vs. man and almost a Slide vs. a 2 deep zone. In the case of a bunched 5 route his technique is for the most part the exact same as he would have on a "Smash" route, and so we use a "Smash" tag for him whenever calling it out of one of these sets (e.g., '55 Z Smash).

His release should be straight upfield for 10 yards, after which he pushes inside to 12, and accelerates all the way to the corner *underneath* the Go. If for some reason he is on the ball, he hesitates at the line of scrimmage to let the Go route get into the pattern ahead of him. His goal is to angle into the hole behind the first layer of coverage and out to the wide field, expecting to catch the ball between 18 and 22 yards deep. Because of the timing and the effect we're trying to create, he gets the inside push at 10 regardless of the coverage; we're trying to entice the man initially looking at the Go to stay with the Go.

If he feels a defender chasing him in Cover 1 or some other form of Man coverage, he'll accentuate that inside push and then look specifically to rub his man off on the Go route; the combination of having to turn his hips to recover over the top and then run around a rub to get to a receiver accelerating into wide space is very tough for a defensive back to handle.

Cover 2 technique is the same as it would be for any Smash, attacking the safety first, then looking to split the hole between him and the cornerback. Just as we have specific throws, like the bunched 8 route, that are tailor-made for 2 deep safeties who widen quickly off the hash, this particular route is perfect against safeties who basically stay on the hash and do not get fast width.

In the case of Cover 3 or Cover 4 where a deep ⅓ or ¼ cornerback gets wide and deep on his level, he flattens his Smash route in front of that man.

#3 has a normal 5 yard flat, releasing beneath the other two receivers. His *purpose* indicates to him that he should line up off the ball, where possible. If he feels man coverage, he has to make certain that he gets vertical push at some point during his route to turn the defender's hips, and also give a strong head and shoulder jab or nod right at the top of the route before accelerating away. He must not be in a hurry...if the defender wants to initiate contact, that often works to his advantage in this route because of the timing and the fact that sometimes the ensuing bounce he gets off that defender will create separation, shoving him further into his route with momentum and leaving the defender momentarily flat-footed.

As in other route packages, a "Late" call tells the flat-runner to delay just over a count into his pattern. This is excellent when cornerbacks try to sink underneath deep routes, especially Smashes and Fades, when they do not get an initial threat to the flat in Cover 2 "Match" situations. A huge vacancy will exist where the corner left, allowing the slower flat runner to get the ball in his hands and be making yards upfield before the cornerback can break up on him. "Late", then, becomes an excellent ball-control pass and third and medium distance call.

Backside:
Basic Post or Split route.

Quarterback:
The quarterback in this case is taking a drop of 5 BIG steps with a hitch step, because we're not interested in having the Flat come open as quickly as with the Mesh or other routes. His first look still has to be the Flat, though, because we cannot have underneath people retreating beneath the Smash. Our rule on this type of combination, again, is to never try and throw a Smash over the head of a retreating Cloud cornerback. The quarterback is geared to react to the Flat getting jumped,

however, so that he can step up and lay the ball out for the #2 receiver. Because this Smash will be running into so much open space if he becomes the read, "lay out" really becomes the operative phrase for this throw. He must allow the receiver to keep running to maximize the play, and not slow him up.

One opportunity that may exist against any type of two deep secondary relates to the possibility of a slow or mesmerized safety to the playside. If he does not work to get over the top of the Go route as he should because he's staring at #2—which very well could happen because so much is happening in front of him at once—then #1 will slip right by him for a chance at a quick score. This is a glance that we build in to each week's game plan based on safety play on film, and something we will watch for in the box during a game as well. Many times the best shot you will ever get at this option is the very first time it's run in the game. It is because of this possibility that the backside Post must split very wide and keep his course *skinny;* we cannot have the safety to his side collapsing back to help.

Flood variations for attacking coverage

Pass actions. One concern for coaches who either philosophically would prefer not to drop straight back or simply *can't* with great effectiveness because of the type of quarterback they have would be the distance of the throw for the Smash part of this route. Fortunately, this package marries up quite well with either half roll or full sprint protection which allow the passer to get closer to his receivers and shorten his throw. It marries well because of the *timing;* the routes are coming open in a rhythm that lends itself to being able to execute those actions and throw from a good position without rushing. In the case of any type of full sprint or "Dash" (drop 3-5 steps straight back and then break contain), the Smash should probably work for at least a full 12 yards on his break and not cut it short, and the Flat should adjust to a depth of 6 and get good vertical push initially so that he does not get width and run out of field before the passer can get him the ball. Examples follow:

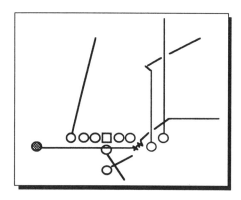

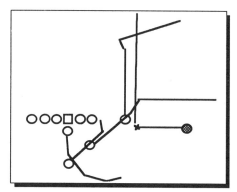

DIAGRAM 17-2
HALF-ROLL FLOOD

DIAGRAM 17-3
FULL SPRINT-OUT FLOOD

Because of its timing and the fact that it is designed to attack a flat defender, this route is very workable off of play-action, specifically off some sort of outside run action in which the secondary support defender has to step up to take it on, opening the Smash route even more behind him. One of our basic runs is the Stretch, or Outside Zone play, and a pass off of it fits this description very well:

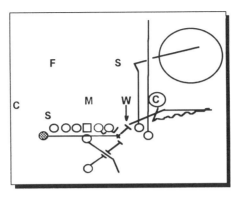

DIAGRAM 17-4
FLOOD ROUTE OFF OF A STRETCH PLAY FAKE
SQUEEZE RAY 7 H6 308 FLOOD X SMASH VS. 2 DEEP COVERAGE

Attacking basic coverages

This route is perhaps at its best against Man coverages, because of all the problems it presents for the defender initially over #2. As mentioned earlier, to effectively cover his man, he will have to react to a hard misdirection fake and then run through or over a rub in a very short amount of time. If there is some sort of Banjo or Switch technique built in between him and the cornerback, it will happen much later than normal switches do, and the receivers are in such close proximity of each other that the corner's job of breaking over the top of an accelerating Smash route in time is still a very difficult proposition. Because of these factors, we will generally hold the ball and wait for the Smash versus Cover 1 or 2 Man. It becomes, then, an outstanding Red Zone play because of the amount of man coverage played there, as well as a solid choice on third and very long where Cover 2 Man is predominant.

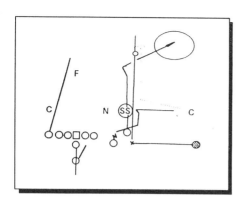

DIAGRAM 17-5
FLOOD IN THE RED ZONE VS. COVER 1
TIGHT RIP SLOT Z10 55 SMASH

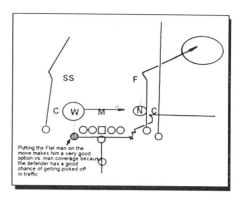

DIAGRAM 17-6
FLOOD VS. COVER 2 MAN
SQUEEZE LIZ 8 Y7 55 SMASH

The key against Cover 2 is the same as it is for the Mesh route—the Flat/Smash combination off the action of the cornerback. The Flood works just a bit differently because the Flat comes open a bit slower, and the route structure gears itself to anticipating a better chance that the Smash might be open. These are minor differences, however, because we still have to throw the Flat if it pops open first. A fundamental principle, vital to our pass offense, that we preach from day one of camp is: *"we will never pass up an open receiver to wait for another one."* As noted earlier, we're always looking, with this combination, for the hash safety who is flatfooted and lets the Go run right by him.

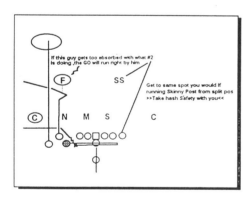

DIAGRAM 17-7
FLOOD VS. COVER 2
SQUEEZE LARRY 7 H IDIOT 155 SMASH

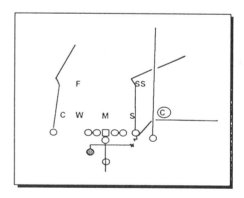

DIAGRAM 17-8
FLOOD VS. COVER 2
SQUEEZE WEAK RIP F6 55 SMASH

This is one of the best possible routes you could run against a **Cover 2 Robber** variation. Because of the defensive movement right at the snap often associated with this coverage (many teams try to give a Cover 3 or 1 look initially, then roll to it late), the stemming strong safety can get put into a real bind; he has to chase the Go running up the seam at the same time he's trying to get to the seam hole, and his momentum carries him directly away from the Smash. The cornerback rolling up is more likely to naturally sit on the Flat, and this becomes a real big play possibility.

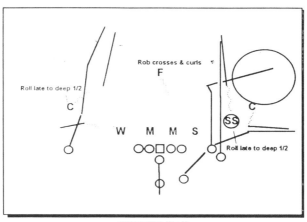

DIAGRAM 17-9
FLOOD VS. COVER 2 ROBBER
SQUEEZE BROWN REX 55 SMASH

The idea when throwing this route against Cover 3 is to take advantage of a cornerback who is undisciplined and, having been taught to defend the Go, gets sucked inside in an attempt to defend it, turning his hips in and allowing us to hit the Smash coming out into space behind him. If the quarterback cannot get a clear enough separation to throw the ball to him, he will come back down to the Flat as an outlet. If we're game planning a bunched 5 route against a Cover 3 team, we will slow the release of the Flat, to better time him up as an outlet. The same slowing principle can be used with the Smash man, especially by aligning him in the backfield, so that in developing this route later, we give the deep ⅓ corner more time to engage and run with the Go. This tactic makes it harder for that man to see any sort of Smash as a threat.

Whereas a bunched 5 route is a big play look against Cover 3, it turns into a ball-control pass against Cover 4. The two deep players within this coverage should naturally allow the defense to absorb our deep threats, but the person responsible for the flat is generally a slower linebacker who does not line up for width to begin with. Therefore, we feel like a good matchup exists to outrun him to the flat area in wide space. Keeping normal personnel in the game helps the matchup here, too, by making the defense less likely to substitute a nickel player for that linebacker. These principles of attack are shown in 17-10 and 17-11 on the next page.

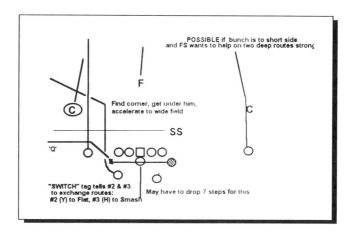

DIAGRAM 17-10
FLOOD VS. COVER 3
WITH LATER DEVELOPING SMASH
SQUEEZE SPLIT RIP Y7 155 SWITCH H SMASH

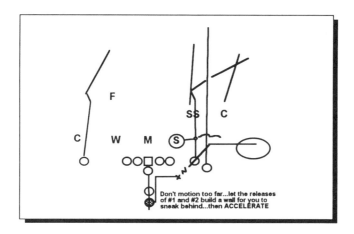

DIAGRAM 17-11
FLOOD VS. COVER 4
SQUEEZE REX H6 55 SMASH

CHAPTER 18

Creating "Packaged Sides" with the Bunch Principle

Introduction and definition

One tool that can be used with the "Bunch" principle is to create packages on either side of the ball designed to take advantage of specific defenses. In other words, you call a specific combination to the bunched side with the idea in mind that you are calling that route because you want it to attack a specific defense. You then "package" the side away from the Bunch, usually a single receiver, by tagging a specific route to attack another situation not exploited as well by the routes on the bunched side. This is simple for us to do because of the flexibility of our system. The quarterback has been trained throughout each particular week on what to look for, and before the snap he already knows which side to work. In doing this, you have accomplished a number of things:

- You have given yourself the chance to always be *right,* no matter what the defense does, and ensured that you will have a play called that has a chance of success.
- In turn, you build confidence in your players, having taught them that they have a specific place to go in any scenario. They also know, according to which side they're on, that they have a very specific *purpose,* related to defeating a specific defense. Therefore, they can be more focused on the very specified techniques needed to defeat that particular defense; *focus* is increased.
- The element of surprise, in large measure, has been taken away from the defense. You don't have to sit on the sidelines and guess what they'll be in and try to match your own calls with that guess. This is especially effective on downs where a defense has not shown particular coverage tendencies, or against a defense that mixes things up well. It's an insurance policy.

One particular experience exemplifies the value of having this sort of tool in your offense. We once played a team which played two basic defenses against us: a tight 4-4 with cover 3 behind it designed to handle the run, and a college 4-3 with cover 2, used primarily to shut off our quick passing game. About midway through the second series, we had seen that they were strongly favoring the 4-4 look on first down, and stuffing our running game. Just at the time we figured this out and called a Quick Hitch on first down to try to take advantage, they jumped into the cover 2 look and left us with a low-percentage play. This cat-and-mouse game continued throughout the first half, and we never really got untracked; we were being out-guessed, and our offense never got the chance to function at its fullest.

4.   You have gained this measure of effectiveness without adding any strain or complication for your most important player, the quarterback. The normal disciplines you have already built into your offense, i.e., his methodical scan of coverage with certain keys to look for, and coverage calls on the part of the receivers, pre-determine the side he's going with the ball before the snap. From there, everything is the same in his execution as any other play.

Following are some examples of how we might use this "packaged sides" tool out of the Bunch concept:

Packages to account for underneath structure

We feel that our basic Bunch routes should always be successful against a fairly normal distribution of underneath defenders. To account for the potential of a defensive overload—e.g., moving the weak linebacker to the strong side to use as an extra hook zone defender—we can tag the backside receiver on a route that brings him into the hole that is naturally created by that imbalance to our trips side. Diagrams 18-1 and 18-2 are examples (the underlined part of the call refers to the backside tag that packages the play).

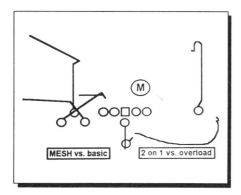

DIAGRAM 18-1
SQUEEZE LEX 7 157 X CURL

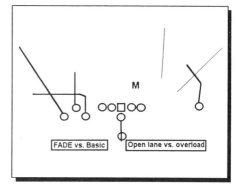

DIAGRAM 18-2
SQUEEZE LEX 7 190 FADE X SLANT

Packages to deal with Cover 2 and Cover 3

In a more general sense, we could use these packages to deal with either hard or *soft* corners to be more all-encompassing. In the examples given here, the frontsides have been programmed to defeat cover 2, while the backside is tagged to defeat a soft cover 3 player on the edge of the defense.

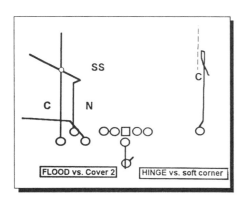

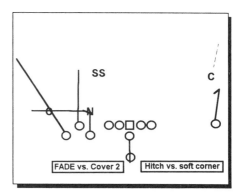

DIAGRAM 18-3
SQUEEZE LEX 7 155 X HINGE

DIAGRAM 18-4
SQUEEZE LEX 7 190 FADE X HITCH

Packages to account for Man and Zone

This ploy is especially valuable inside the Red Zone, where more and more teams are mixing zone concepts in with the traditional man coverages. We will use motion to reveal what the defense is doing, and through receiver coverage call and pre-snap recognition, the quarterback can know where he's going with the ball immediately.

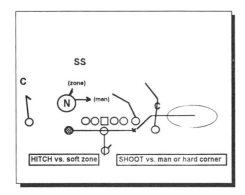

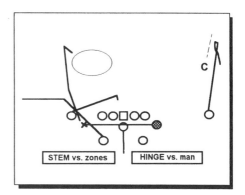

DIAGRAM 18-5
SQUEEZE RIP 9 H6 90 SLANT X HITCH

DIAGRAM 18-6
SQUEEZE SPLIT RIP Y7
157 STEM Z HINGE

Checking motion for #3 away from the strength of Cover 3

Versus teams who play cover 3 with a distinct rotation or strength to their call side, you can gain a numbers advantage through quickly motioning the remaining back away from their strength. It can be designated simply that an odd number in the quarterback's normal cadence tells the back to motion left, an even number sends him right. The motion must happen quickly, late in the count, so that the defense has no time to adjust. The receivers also know whether to function as frontside or backside by the number in the cadence.

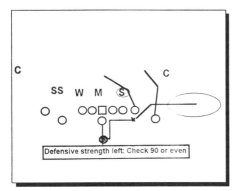

DIAGRAM 18-7
SQUEEZE RIP 9
MOTION CHECK 90 OR 190 SLANT

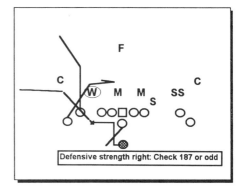

DIAGRAM 18-8
TWIN
MOTION CHECK 87 OR 187

CHAPTER 19

Scratching the Surface: Exploring Other Possibilities Offered by the Bunch Concept

While the focus of this book is the use of the Bunch principle in the passing game as it relates to certain route packages, its possibilities are certainly not limited to that. In this chapter, we scan some of the limitless other possibilities that are available within this principle of attack. This portion of the text is not intended to explore the ideas in detail, but rather survey some of the places Bunch can go, and serve as a catalyst for some of your own ideas.

Wing running game

If you use a wing running game, within systems such as the Wing-T or Flexbone, you can use basic Bunch sets for these same runs. Examples follow, using a Wing Counter and a Freeze Option. Because you are often working against fronts slid to the Bunch, these backside runs can be very effective.

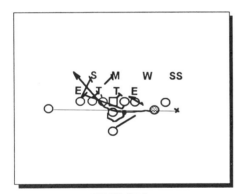

DIAGRAM 19-1
WING COUNTER FROM BUNCH

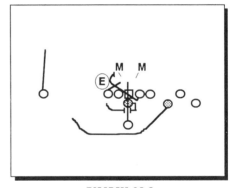

DIAGRAM 19-2
FREEZE OPTION FROM BUNCH

Counter with Tight End as a second puller

One recent development that has helped the traditional "Counter Trey" play be more efficient has been to use a tight end or fullback as the second puller instead of the backside tackle. This enables the backside tackle to squeeze to B gap initially and help slow down penetration before stepping back to block the end man on the line of scrimmage; plays become less apt to get destroyed from the backside. This also gets a better athlete leading the play up through the hole as a second puller. Such a scheme is easily adaptable to Bunch looks, putting Y as the #3 receiver off the ball to pull.

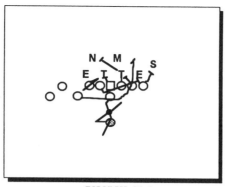

DIAGRAM 19-3
COUNTER "Y" FROM BUNCH

Attacking with wide runs to a shortened edge

This compressed receiver concept is especially advantageous if you have a speed player in your backfield, because it allows you to get him outside the entire defense and moving upfield very quickly on fast-attacking run actions such as Tosses and Speed Options. He can get to the all-important "corner" of the defense sooner because that "corner" has been moved in substantially by the alignment of the offense.

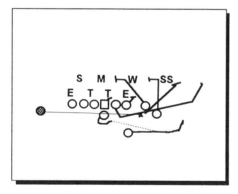

DIAGRAM 19-4
TOSS FROM BUNCH

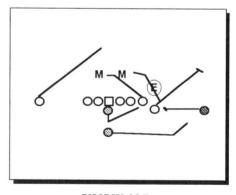

DIAGRAM 19-5
SPEED OPTION FROM BUNCH

Screens

We have found three basic ways in which we might use screens from Bunch: first, because of all the traffic involved in a compressed-split environment, it makes it easier for a screen receiver to get lost in the shuffle. Secondly, we can attack with backside screens as a way to exploit overloaded defenses. Third, Bunch principles can again be used to shorten the edge of the defense with the idea of getting someone quickly outside of it, in this case in a screen package.

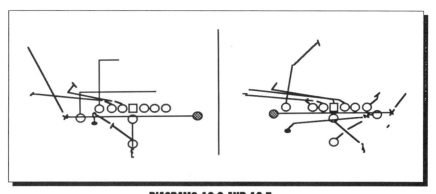

DIAGRAMS 19-6 AND 19-7
HIDING PEOPLE WITH BUNCH SCREENS
SLIP SCREEN OFF 9 ROUTE ACTION (LEFT)   DON CORYELL "BEHIND SCREEN" CONCEPT (RIGHT)

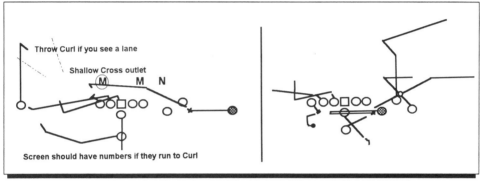

Throw Curl if you see a lane

Shallow Cross outlet

M   M   N

Screen should have numbers if they run to Curl

DIAGRAMS 19-8 AND 19-9 SCREENS TO EXPLOIT OVERLOADS TO BUNCH
BACKSIDE READ SCREEN (LEFT)   "SCREEN AWAY" OFF 80 ACTION (RIGHT)

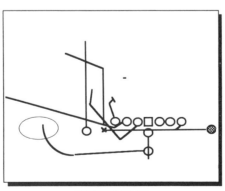

DIAGRAM 19-10
FAST SCREEN OFF FLOOD ROUTE DEVELOPMENT TO GET OUTSIDE QUICKLY

Gimmicks

Because of the close proximity of multiple receivers in a Bunch setting, the potential exists for multiple misdirections concepts using gimmick-type trick plays. Some possibilities are illustrated below.

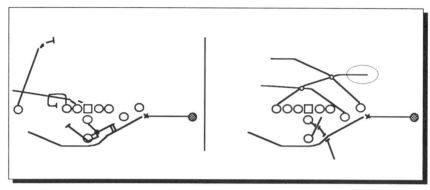

DIAGRAMS 19-11 AND 19-12
REVERSE SEQUENCE OUT OF BUNCH
REVERSE AGAINST DEFENSE THAT TIGHTENS DOWN TO BUNCH (LEFT)
"GAUNTLET" DOUBLE RUB PASS OFF REVERSE FAKE (RIGHT)

Other passes to attack the backside

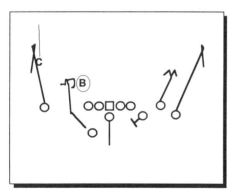

DIAGRAM 19-13
HINGE/CHOICE COMBINATION
SQUEEZE R 10 Y152 DOUBLE HINGE

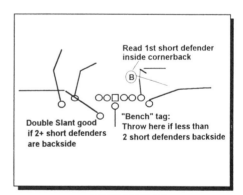

DIAGRAM 19-14
"BENCH" BACKSIDE PACKAGE
SQUEEZE B LARRY 6 190 SLANT BENCH

Frontside Hooking combinations

Because of the confused environment Bunch often causes underneath defenders to have to operate in, combinations of Hooking type patterns are very solid as an over-all concept within this principle. They allow a maneuvering, adjustable receiver to get into areas behind and between those defenders who may not know the exact right angles to take or may not be functioning within their pattern read as they should. Below are some different distributions for Hooking receivers that, while not fitting as neatly into our package as well as other things, have specific merit.

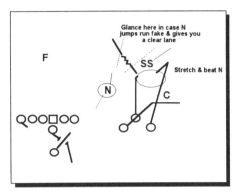

DIAGRAM 19-15
CURL/SEAM COMBINATION
OFF PLAY ACTION FROM SNUG

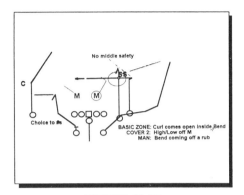

DIAGRAM 19-16
CURL BEHIND "BEND" ROUTE

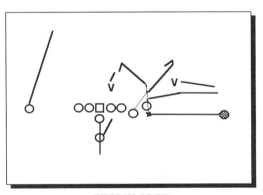

DIAGRAM 19-17
GREEN BAY PACKERS' STACKED RELEASE CONCEPT

Loop

This is a late-developing trail route concept that is particularly good if inside defenders work to wall off hooking routes. It also gives the appearance of a Bunch Fade release by #3, which can be very beneficial against loose man, because he will break right underneath a man who is running over the top and find open space inside. If you have established the Triangle route with the Option route coming from #1, the Loop becomes a doubly good route to sequence with that package out of the same formation; two of the three routes are giving the exact same sight picture to the defense upon initial release.

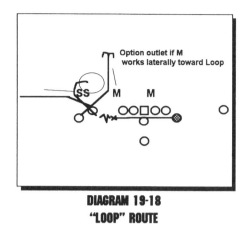

DIAGRAM 19-18
"LOOP" ROUTE

Deep combinations

A number of different ways exist to specifically target deep areas out of Bunch, using a seven step drop. Most of them have routes built-in to pry deep defenders apart, and bring someone deep into the void afterward. Two such examples follow:

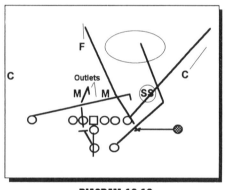

DIAGRAM 19-19
DEEP "DIVIDE" ROUTE

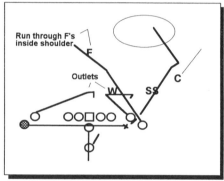

DIAGRAM 19-20
"POLE" ROUTE CONCEPT

"In" route

One route in our quick passing game that has developed through the years as an especially effective way to attack *man* coverages is a route we call "In." The basic premise of "In" is to release an outside receiver slightly to the outside, while an inside receiver runs to the inside leg of the outside defender. The outside receiver then breaks under the inside receiver, creating a natural pick on the outside defender. The ball is thrown on time as the rub occurs.

By using a "Cluster" set to do this, we get a potential additional rub from the #3 man, and we create space for the "In" receiver to run in once he has caught the ball.

We can also incorporate a ploy made very successful by Bill Walsh within this "In" concept. By putting our best receiver away from the Cluster and running him on a Slant, we force the defense to either provide inside help on him to the weakside or face the possibility of giving up a big run after catch after a quick completion to our best athlete. If they do provide inside help weak, no matter how they do it, they have likely opened up the "In" combination strong. In this way, we have created an excellent package that is particularly effective in the final two minutes of a half when you need big chunks of yardage, and the defense is often playing soft.

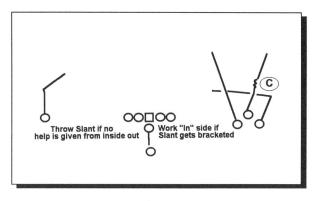

DIAGRAM 19-21
IN/SLANT PACKAGE CONCEPT
"CLUSTER REX 6 90 IN X SLANT"

CHAPTER 20

Down to Practicalities: Installing "Bunch" Principles Within the Overall Scope of an Offense

Implementing a new concept into an offense can be tricky; regardless of how good it looks on paper and how logical it seems, it must be PRACTICED and practiced **effectively** if it is to make a difference in your overall success. Thus, finding and allocating installation time for it in concert with the rest of your offense becomes the key question, because you only have a finite number of practice repetitions with which to work.

The first decision you have to make, of course, is on how large a scale you want to use Bunch principles in your offense. What percentage of practice time do you want to give it relative to the other phases of your offense? This question is best answered according to **situations**, because football is, in fact, largely a game of situations. If you only want Bunch to be a third and medium package for you, it will require substantially fewer practice snaps than if you want to use it on first down and in the Red Zone, because the latter two scenarios are more prevalent and therefore should occupy more of your practice space. The point is, no play or package should ever go into an offense just to go in. There must be definite, situational uses for it if you're to maximize your practice time. Once you have determined which Bunch combinations you want to use and when, you can begin to allow for how many practice repetitions each gets. Central to this decision process, of course, is give and take, weighing different options against each other in given situations, because each scenario demands only a certain number of plays.

In our case, we have had great success in our teaching using a "whole/part" approach. To establish a foundation from which to work, players are exposed on a surface level to the entire offense initially, tackling the whole thing and learning how its structures work. Through this process, we equip ourselves with a "toolbox" full of tools that we can employ in various ways and combinations. Then, bit by bit, we hone things down based on what they do best, using more specific combinations and detailed teaching. The parts of the whole not geared to each group's talents are deemphasized or discarded, and those that are get highlighted and repeated.

For our pre-season work, this translates into two distinct phases of camp for our players. The first is a *learning and fundamentals* phase, the second a *refining and situational* phase. Phrased differently, refer to the first portion as "building an arsenal," and the latter, "target practice." By presenting it to the players in this manner and showing them the end before they begin, you dramatically reduce anxiety, focus them on what is to be accomplished, and give each session a distinct *purpose*. This *purpose* helps you to stay productive and varied during a time where often drudgery and weariness overwhelm players, forcing them into a "survival" rather than "improvement" mode, which cuts down on learning.

During the *learning* phase, all of our basic route structures are put in from normal sets. The installation process begins with presentation on the chalkboard and video clips in the classroom, continues on the field where it is broken down into individual cuts and throws, primary reads are isolated and drilled, the whole route put together as a group against air, practiced against a skeletal pass defense, then finally run full speed against a total defense. This is done for all of our routes and concepts in the passing game, with the same points and details being stressed and restressed throughout each aspect.

In the *refining and situational* phase, or second practice week in our case, we take those same reads and cuts from select route packages and put them in a Bunch environment, talking about the subtle technique adjustments because of the reduced split. Generally, we will introduce only the "7", or Mesh route from Bunch at this point, teaching it as an all-purpose Bunch pass. Again, film is shown to reinforce teaching and provide a model for them to see. At the same time Bunch adaptations begin being installed, we will start using ten minute practice blocks during individual work for the receivers to work on the mechanics of their Bunch releases.

Following the initial Bunch teaching, additional routes from those that we have already installed will be incorporated into Bunch settings at a rate of one or two a day depending on the particular situation that is being practiced; the day's new Bunch route adaptations will be practiced within the confines of those situations. The basic release mechanics that have and are being drilled in those ten minute blocks will hold up for any new Bunch route adaptation that is installed.

By the end of camp, a foundation of learning and repetition will have been built that gives us the flexibility to be able to employ an almost limitless amount of combinations. More importantly, it is a foundation that dictates that our weekly preparation throughout the season will consist of REFINING and REAPPLYING things in the passing game that have already been practiced over and over instead of INVENTING new things that may only get practiced five to ten times. Teams that invent every week don't execute, and teams that don't execute get beaten. By merely refining what we already have instead, confidence and execution are maximized.

Following is an example of an installation schedule we might use for our pre-season work, showing the routes, techniques, reads, and situations that are being practiced or introduced each day. The schedule shown deals only with the teaching and implementation of the passing game; the running game would be broken down in a similar fashion. You will have your own schedule and your own routes, of course, but it serves as an illustration of how the Bunch principle can be practically incorporated, and how the "whole/part" dynamic works:

PHASE ONE: Learning & Fundamentals   "Building an Arsenal"

Day	Situations	Route Packages Installed	Individual Cuts Emphasized	QB Actions	QB Reads/ Techniques	Receiver Teaching
Fri		90 Hitch, 90 Fade	Hitch, Fade	3 step		6 second rule Hitch/Fade read
Sat		90 Slant, WR Quick Screen	Slant, Flat/Shoot		Uncovered receiver Basic coverage recognition	Uncovered principle Coverage rec. & calls
Mon		2 (Hinge), 3 (Curl), 4 (Seam)	Hinge, Curl, Choice	5 quick steps 5 big steps	Inside out read on flat coverage	Zone/Man settle/ separate principle
Tue		5 (Flood), 6 (Fin), 7 (Mesh)	Sail, Fin, Smash Whip Read		'Q' receiver drills Working Cover 2 cornerbk	Jam releases
Wed		8 (Switch)	Inside Vertical Outside Vertical	Play action: 306-307 336-337	Vertical reads: Working FS Working Hash saf Outlet receiver drills	Landmarks
Thu		Bootleg Rules, Over route	Over, Shallow Cross Slam Flat	Bootleg: 226-227 206-207	Scramble rules/throws	Scramble rules
Fri		1(Dig), 9 w/crosses Under tag	Middle Read, Dig Shallow Crs	7 controlled steps	High/low read	2 crosser technique
Sat	2 minute Goalline	Screens	Review	Screen footwork ½ Roll	Review	Screen rules

PHASE TWO: Situation and Refining Phase   "Target Practice"

Day	Situations	Route Packages Installed	Individual Cuts Emphasized	QB Actions	QB Reads/ Techniques	Receiver Teaching
Mon	1-10 Backed up	Bunched 7 vs. all coverages				Bunch release mechanics 10 min
Tue	2-Long 3-7 to 10 Blitz	Bunched 7 Stem vs. Cover 3 Bunched 5 vs. Cover 2 Man 3-12 plus	Stem			Bunch release mechanics 10 min
Wed	4 minute 3-3 3-4 to 6	Bunched 30 Slant vs. Cover 2 Bunched 6 vs. all coverages			Motion Flat v. Jam	Motion Flat v. Jam Bunch releases :05
Thu	Red Zn: +25 +15 +8	Bunched 9 vs. 1, 1 Blitz Bunched 7 Arrow vs. all cov	Arrow		GL scramble	Bunch releases :05 GL scramble
Fri	Goalline 3-1 2 pt play	Review & Scrimmage			GL scramble	GL scramble

CHAPTER 21

Closing Thoughts on the "Bunch" Principle

One of the most satisfying aspects of introducing a new concept within the framework of your offense, and then having success with that concept initially, is watching the excitement build in your players and seeing their confidence grow. We reached a point early in the development of our Bunch package where an ongoing dialogue was taking place between coaches, quarterbacks, and receivers, with them helping us refine our ideas and variations based on what they were experiencing on the field. A key touchdown in one game was even scored on specific Bunch combination that had been proposed and designed by one of our quarterbacks a number of weeks earlier. It fit easily in our package and was sound, so we used it.

It is our feeling that when your players have taken that much of a personal investment in understanding and being a part of your offense, you have enhanced your chances for success: they can now operate and make adjustments on their own with an understanding of the big picture once they're in the heat of battle, and they have strong confidence in your plan, because they feel like it's partially their plan, too. Of course, they would have never reached this point of confidence had you as a coach not earlier done your homework thoroughly, having understood the detailed teaching vital to the concept's success, and having gained a clear comprehension of how the concept fit in with the overall philosophy of your offense. Your ability to teach with this kind of thoroughness is where everything begins; we have endeavored to provide you here with a resource comprehensive enough to furnish you with that ability.

The Bunch principle, of course, is not an entire system in and of itself, but a distinct concept that can be used within anybody's systematic structure to complement the other things being done in the passing game. Likewise, it is doubtful that we would ever be able to fully explore all of the route concepts detailed here within one season, regardless of how much we employed Bunch. What we have tried to provide you in this book are two things: first, a solid basis of understanding in the specifics of why Bunch has been successful against defenses, and how you coach its principles in order to maximize your success; secondly, a "menu" from which you can extract whatever small or large an amount of particular route ideas that can have great effectiveness within the system you use, the abilities of the players you coach, and the types of defenses you face.

We are of the conviction that Bunch concepts are here to stay in offensive football. Since the beginning of its use as we know it in the 1980s and its rapid growth in popularity in the early and mid 1990s, defenses have begun to make large-scale adjustments against it. Bunch has, however, weathered that initial wave of adjustments and continued to thrive at the highest levels of the game. It is the adaptability of this package, in addition to its basic soundness, that provides us this conviction. In the long-term evolution of offensive approaches, ideas which come already equipped with the tools to adjust and grow are the ones that survive and have a lasting impact; those which do not have those tools go down as fads. Bunch has those tools. We hope that this text has proven to be a great value to you and your players.

Applying the Bunch Principle to Situational Football

Football has become more and more a game of specific situations for which an offense must specifically plan, teach, and practice in order to be successful. By pinpointing for you some exact game situations in which the ideas discussed here become viable, we hope to make this book even more useful for you. What follows is a reference guide that highlights some different concepts and combinations already illustrated in the book that could be applied to these crucial situations all of us face. Beneath each situation is a short list of things we generally anticipate from defenses, and basic points of emphasis that are stressed to the players as we practice those scenarios.

Of course, this is by no means an exhaustive list, and specific combinations themselves can be tailored specifically by formation, action, and tag to what you do well and what your opponents do, using your own terminology. It serves instead as a concept outline that organizes ideas already discussed at length into a situational approach, allowing you to refer quickly to detailed discussions of those thoughts earlier in the book.

First and 10

- Play action passes from familiar run actions and formations preferred
- Quick, high-percentage throws also a high priority; 3 steps or 5 quick
- Must not take a sack under any circumstances
- Option-style routes good to account for variations in coverage; this is often the down where defenses vary their looks the most
- Packaged sides also a viable idea to account for potential coverage variety

Refer to Diagram:	Formation	Play	Comments/Brief Summary
17-4	Squeeze Liz 7 H6	308 Flood X Smash	Flood off of a Stretch fake to pull outside run support and open Smash behind it
16-2	Squeeze Rex 6 H Idiot	206 Over	Bootleg to multiple crossing routes
16-3	Squeeze Strong Ray Z10	307 Over	Zone fake to pull LBs; Crosses behind them
8-3	Squeeze Brown Rex	90 Veer Slant	Freeze a run-playing LB; quick throw outside
8-2	Squeeze Rip 11 Y7	190 Slant	Quick, solid throw vs. all coverages to Flat or Slant
12-2	Squeeze Rip 9 Z11	156 Z Fin	Option-style route on the move to beat man or zone
18-2	Squeeze Lex 7	190 Fade X Slant	Packaged sides to guarantee high % play
18-4	Squeeze Lex 7	190 Fade X Hitch	Packaged sides to guarantee high % play
18-5	Squeeze Rip 9 H6	90 Slant X Hitch	Packaged sides to guarantee high % play
18-7	Squeeze Rip 9	Mo Chk 90/190 Slant	Packaged sides to guarantee high % play
10-5	Squeeze Split Rip Y7	341 Tringl H Fade	Good play-action deep shot w/ solid outlets underneath
13-9	Weak Lou Z6	336 Dig Special	Play-action to hold LBs for Dig behind; shallow outlets
7.21	Squeeze Ram X6	87	Good % cut vs. Cover 2 from strong run formation
7-25	Squeeze Brown Rex	336 Mesh H Slip	Play action shot down the middle with Whip outlet
7-35	Split Rip Z6	57	Basic Whip/Flat read off a quick drop
7-37	Squeeze Ram X Z Idiot	227 Mesh	Boot Mesh out of strong run formation
7-41	Squeeze Strong Rip Y Idt	336 Mesh Stem	Hi percentage hooking route off play action

Second and Long

- Above all, need some kind of completion to get to 3d and Medium or Short; favor high-percentage throws
- Rhythm throws off 5 quick steps preferred, with an option at the 2d level if shorter receivers get jumped
- Blitz down for many teams; be aware of 'Q' receiver
- Delays can be very effective, because zone defenders will naturally get into drops sooner and get more depth

Refer to Diagram:	Formation	Play	Comments/Brief Summary
15-7	Liz Slot Z11	152 Wrap Z Choice	Solid option-style route out of a Bunch
10-3	Twin X10	80 Triangle	Good, high % man-beaters frontside, Under as a backside guarantee against zones
10-7	Rip 6 Z6	80 Triangle Z Whip	Leverage for easy throw to Whip into open space
7.19	Rip Slot Z10	57	Solid gainer with Whip outlet
7-23	Squeeze Split Larry Z Ret	157 Late	Good R.A.C. when corner gets depth for Smash
7-29	Squeeze Rip 9 H6	57 Arrow	Good R.A.C. chance into cleared middle
7-39	Weak Larry Z6	57 Hide	Can hit "Q" Flat or Hide under loose coverage
7-44	Snug Brown Rex Z Idiot	57 Z Delay	Solid Delay route with option to throw quick Flat
7-46	Squeeze Larry 6 H7	157 Hi Y Delay	Excellent Delay if they overload to trips

Third and 3

- Coverage variety likely, with less emphasis on softer-type zones. *Accurate coverage calls by receivers at a premium.*
- Because coverage is likely to be tighter regardless of scheme, receivers must think in terms of hard upfield push and precise breaks and separation techniques
- Flat routes must flatten their break one yard beyond the first down marker
- High awareness needed of 'Q' receiver

Refer to Diagram:	Formation	Play	Comments/Brief Summary
6-2	Squeeze Rip 11 Y7	190 Slant	Quick throw off motion to a big target
11-8	Squeeze Ray 6 H Idiot	58 H Choice	Option-type route on the move—high % pass
10-8	Rip 6 Z6	80 Triangle Z Whip	Leverage for easy throw to Whip into open space
7-3	Squeeze Ram X	57 Under	Has a chance against zone, man, or full blitz
7-7	Squeeze Ray 6 H Idiot	57	Quick pop to Flat off Idiot motion; Whip outlet
7-22	Squ B Larry 6 F Return	Y157	Good chance to get Flat fast, especially vs. Cov 2
7-33	Squeeze Larry 6 H7	157 Arrow Flare	Rhythm Flare that is tough on man coverages
7-48	Squeeze Weak Rip F8	57 Switch	Basic Flat/Whip combination sped up
7-50	Squeeze Rip 11 Y7	187 Arrow F Flat	Another way to get 4 into frontside pattern quickly

Third and 4-6

- Coverage variety likely; many times teams will use their best or favorite coverage in this spot. Accurate coverage calls by receivers at a premium.
- Flat routes and Option-style cuts must flatten their break one yard beyond the first down marker.
- GET UPFIELD IMMEDIATELY AFTER THE CATCH—DO NOT DANCE.
- Often a blitz down; be 'Q' receiver aware.

Refer to Diagram:	Formation	Play	Comments/Brief Summary
7-4	Squeeze Blue Ray H6	87	Backfield motion can disrupt blitzes
7-6	Squeeze Brown Ray	157 H Late	Good vs. different kinds of coverages & key blitz
7-9	Rip 6 Z6	87	Good way to rub for Flat and get R.A.C.
7-12	Squeeze Larry 11 H7	157 Under	Solid, all-purpose crosses vs. man, zone, blitz
7-27	Squeeze Rip 9 H6	57	Fast motion Flat with Whip outlet
7-29	Squeeze Rip 9 H6	57 H Arrow	Good sequence with 7.27 on misdirection route
7-32	Squeeze Weak Rip F6	57 Hi	Rub for Shallow Cross as a man or zone-beater
7-40	Snug Larry 11 F11	157 Switch Hide	Wide stretch vs. zone/wall of rubs vs. man for Hide
8-4	Squeeze Rex H6	90 Slant	Quick percentage throw suited to Cover 2
10-8	Rip 6 Z6	80 Triangle Z Whip	Good Whip chance vs. banjoed man or zone
11-8	Squeeze Ray 6 H Idiot	58 H Choice	Option-style route good vs. any coverage
12-2	Squeeze Rip 9 Z11	156 Z Fin	Option-style route off motion
14-9	Squeeze Strong Larry 6	59 XH	Multiple crosses solid vs. man and zone
14-11	Squeeze Split Rip	59 X, H Arrow	Zones pried open for trail-type routes
14-12	Squeeze B Larry 6 Z6	59 H, Z Arrow	Misdirection route vs. Man
15-7	Liz Slot Z11	152 Wrap Z Choice	Hard for zone defenders to find Z

Third and 7 to 10

- Could be a blitz down, prefer maximum protection over Q receivers
- Emphasis on hooking patterns vs. zones, comeback-type routes on the edges vs. man coverage
- Shallow Crosses, Delays, and Hides good against certain teams to make a quick catch and get the first down on the run after catch
- Packaged sides a viable idea to account for potential coverage variety
- QB can hold the ball a little more, wait for receivers to get free; sack not as devastating

Refer to Diagram:	Formation	Play	Comments/Brief Summary
15-2	Twin	52 Double Hinge	Solid 12-14 yard outside combinations on both sides; QB can take his pick
15-8	Squeeze Split Larry	152 Wrap Z Flag	Max protection all-purpose man-beater
11-9	Squeeze Larry 6 H7	158 H Arrow	Good quick R.A.C. play when LBs get depth
13-8	Rip 6 Z6	51 Special X Lo	Crossing route through a wall of rubs; big R.A.C.
9-3 in a	Squeeze Empty	190 Fade	Rhythm throw vs. Blitz; two-deep coverage bind
12-6	Squeeze Rex H6	56 Change Z Mdl	Med distance zone or man-beater off crossed release
18-1	Squeeze Lex 7	157 X Curl	Packaged sides to account for Cover 2 or 3
10-7	Snug Ron 10 H10	80 Tringl H Optn	Option route working outside-in through traffic
7-14	Squeeze Ram Z9	187 Turn	Good chance vs. man or zones in 10-12 yard range
7-23	Tight Rip Slot Z10	57 Stem	Hooking route good if they react at all to shorter stuff
7-45	Nasty Rip 6 Z10	157 Hi X Curl	Good medium-range backside attack vs. overload

Third and 12 or More

- As a sweeping generality, Cover 2 Man and Cover 3 most often the ones to beat
- SMASH route the best percentage deep throw against most coverages
- OVER and DIG are also good combinations to get the yardage vs. most coverages
- Hooking-type routes have a good chance of completion and run afterward vs. soft zones
- Be aware of "Soft Blitzes", with LB rush to try and hurry your throw while DBs play off and tackle receiver in front of First Down Marker. Should favor keeping extra men in to block, should stay away from 'Q' receiver.

Refer to Diagram:	Formation	Play	Comments/Brief Summary
17-6	Squeeze Liz 8 Y7	55 Smash	Causes problems for Cover 2 Man trying to cover Smash route rubbing underneath Go
16-5	Rip 6 Z6	50 Over Wrap	Multiple crossing route levels, good chance vs. most coverages
11-3	Twin X6	58	Rub for an isolated outside vertical vs. 2 Man
12-4	Twin X6	86 Switch	Rub for Smash with Fin as a good R.A.C. outlet
9-5	Squeeze Strong Larry Z10	Max 90 Fade	Motion to leverage Cover 2 Man trail technique
18-3	Squeeze Lex 7	155 X Hinge	Packaged sides to account for Cover 2 or 3
18-6	Squeeze Split Rip Y7	157 Stem Z Hinge	Packaged sides to account for Man or Zone
7-30	Weak Lou Z6	57 Switch Z Spear	Chance to hit a man on the move 12-15 yds deep
7-34	Twin X6	87 Barrier Corner	Good all-purpose Corner route against man cov
7-51	Snug Larry 11 F11	157 Stem	Stretch defense and then find hole in 15 yd area

Red Zone: Plus 25

- Anticipate Man coverage, have an outlet vs. Zones
- Think in terms of routes with a touchdown shot built-in
- Free safety will often come out of middle to handle backfield motion
- Anticipate blitz

Refer to Diagram:	Formation	Play	Comments/Brief Summary
16-5	Rip 6 Z6	50 Over Wrap	Rub for a deep crossing route vs. Man
16-6	Squeeze Rex 6 F11	50 Over	Hole created by FS or LB motion adjustment
15-5	Squeeze Rex H6	72 Y Flag	Sprint-out with high-low on cornerback
11-5	Squeeze Ray 6 F10	58	Opening middle for Inside Vertical w/motion
11-7	Snug Lex 7	158 Split	3 deep threats; lots of pressure on FS
12-5	Snug Larry 6 H11	Y156 Twist	Deep rubs with crossing outlet; 7 man protection
13-6	Snug Ray	Max 51 Special	Max protection with rub for deep Post and Dig
13-7	Squeeze Weak Rip F6	51 Special F Up	Tough deep route through rubs vs. LB coverage
10-4	Squeeze Larry 11 H Idiot	180 Tringl H Fade	Multiple rubs for a quick Fade off motion
7-13	Cluster Rex H10	57 Hide	Hide a big R.A.C. play vs. loose man
7-15	Squeeze Strong Ray Z10	336 Mesh	Play action shot for Flat and Smash
7-24	Squeeze Larry 11 H Idt	157 X Shake	Good TD shot down middle when they play Smash
7-30	Weak Lou Z6	57 Switch Z Spear	Deeper crossing route off rub that attacks at 2 levels
7-31	Squeeze Brown Rex F10	57 H Arrow	If you catch them in 2 Man, this is a TD play
7-34	Twin X6	87 Barrier Corner	Good all-purpose Corner route against man cov

Red Zone: Plus 15

- Use crossing routes and outside leverage to the corner of the end zone; QB thinking in terms of leading receivers
- Anticipate blitz
- Free safety will often come out of middle to handle backfield motion
- Receivers stay alive if original pattern breaks down and work the back of the end zone, communicating with a demonstrative wave when you're behind and between people . . . practicing the scramble in this different environment is vital.
- Beware of switching, "lanes" coverage in anticipation of our rubs
- Receiver breaks must be distinct and pushed hard, because the reduced room will dictate tighter coverage technique.

Refer to Diagram:	Formation	Play	Comments/Brief Summary
17-5	Tight Rip Slot Z10	55 Smash	Tough for man coverage to handle Smash
16-4	Squeeze Rip 9 Z11	150 Over Switch	Rub created for a Shallow Cross
13-8	Rip 6 Z6	51 Special X Lo	Crossing route through a wall of rubs; big R.A.C.
9-6	Squeeze Larry 6 F10	90 Fade	Quick motion special to corner of End Zone vs. LB cov
7-10	Squeeze B Larry 6	157 F Arrow	Man-beater route into vacated middle; a proven Red Zone route
7-11	Squeeze Split Rip Y Idiot	57 Switch Hi	Rub for Shallow Cross
7-12	Squeeze Larry 11 H7	157 Under	2 crossers off motion; hard to banjo
7-15	Squeeze Strong Ray Z10	336 Mesh	Play action shot for Flat and Smash
7-21	Squeeze Ram X6	87	Smash behind quick motion Flat vs. Jam
7-26	Squeeze Split Larry Z Ret	157 Late	Late Flat solid against lazy man or zone
7-33	Squeeze Larry 6 H7	157 Arrow Flare	#4 Flare hard to handle in man coverage

Red Zone: Plus 5

- Flat and Option-style cuts must get one yard deep in the end zone.
- Heavy emphasis on crossing routes and play-action, for obvious reasons
- MUST NOT TAKE A SACK, must protect the football.
- If the quarterback is going to miss, he must miss outside and deep with his throws; Flat throws cannot be late or inside. Get your shoulders turned & step through the throw.
- Receivers stay alive if original pattern breaks down and work the back of the end zone, communicating with a demonstrative wave when you're behind and between people... practicing the scramble in this different environment is vital.
- Beware of switching, "lanes" coverage in anticipation of our rubs
- Receiver breaks must be distinct and pushed hard, because the reduced room will dictate tighter coverage technique.

Refer to Diagram:	Formation	Play	Comments/Brief Summary
7-8	Larry 6 Z Crazy	57	Special motion could be hard on man coverage
7-16	Squeeze Ray 6 F7	187	Special shift/motion Flat combination for goalline
7-17	Squeeze Larry 11 H Idiot	226 Mesh Under Late	Chargers' '94 goalline staple; man covering #3 often frozen by the counter fake
7-18	Squeeze Weak Rip F4	206 Mesh Under Sneak	Good sequence play with 7.17; Sneak is hard to find after boot fake
8-5	Squeeze Rex H6	90 Slant	Attack flat area quickly of fast backfield motion
10-2	Squeeze Ram X	80 Triangle	Basic, solid Triangle attack inside the 5
10-6	Squeeze Ram X6	80 Tringl Z Marke	Excellent complement to the Bunch Fade

Backed Up Offense

- Anticipate blitz with high awareness of 'Q' receiver
- Favor isolation routes to the edges of the field, accelerating away from people, out of traffic and potential interceptions
- More restrictive protection preferred

Refer to Diagram:	Formation	Play	Comments/Brief Summary
15-5	Squeeze Rex H6	72 Y Flag	Sprint-out pass to break contain; two legitimate outside route threats
15-8	Squeeze Split Larry	152 Wrap Z Flag	Max protection, Hinge route on outside
12-7	Squeeze Ray	Max 56 Wrap	Leverage for Smash with Max protection
7-4	Squeeze Blue Ray H6	87	Two threats on edge of field with 7 man protection

APPENDIX B

Structural Route Exchanges and Tags

"Switch" Adjustment

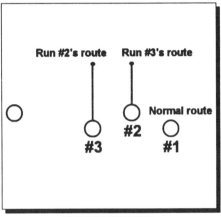

REGULAR RELEASES

"Inside" Designation

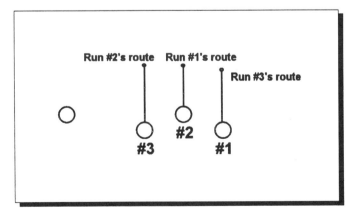

REGULAR RELEASES

"Wrap" Adjustment

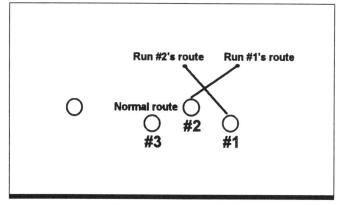

CROSSED RELEASES 4-5 YARDS DEEP OVER PLAYER'S ORIGINAL POSITION

* RECEIVER OFF THE BALL GOES UNDERNEATH

"Twist" Adjustment

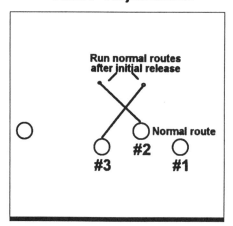

CROSSED RELEASES 4-5 YARDS DEEP OVER PLAYER'S ORIGINAL POSITION
*RECEIVER OFF THE BALL GOES UNDERNEATH

"Change" Adjustment

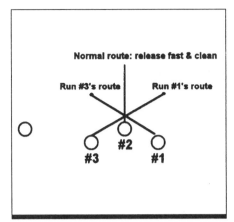

CROSSED RELEASES 4-5 YARDS DEEP OVER OTHER PLAYER'S ORIGINAL POSITION

*#3 GOES UNDERNEATH

"Swap" Adjustment

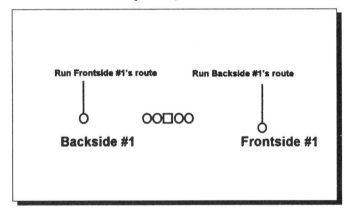

"Double" Designation

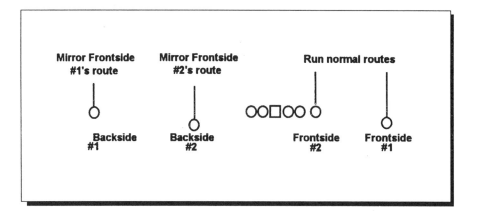

Basic Principles and Disciplines of Pass Offense

One of the great struggles we all have as coaches is taking ideas that look phenomenal on paper and translating them into success on field. One thing we have developed is a set of specific, spelled out principles upon which our pass offense is based as well as certain disciplines that are fundamental to what we do and critical to the success of any play or pattern. If our route structures and passing concepts are a high-performance engine that we've built, in analogous terms, these principles and disciplines serve as the fuel. They form the basis upon which people make decisions.

These things are taught and spelled out to the players over and over so that as they are taught specific things within the offense, it makes more sense to them because it fits within an overall, philosophical whole. An individual puzzle piece, for example, is much more clear in its definition and purpose when placed against a picture of a whole puzzle that has already been viewed.

This also has implications for us in practice, because it provides a finite, focused list of the things we must build into our players, and the specific things that have to be taught and drilled on the field.

Following, then, is our list, or "recipe", of the elements that we have found make for a successful passing game. These ideas, which are certainly nothing revolutionary, have been illustrated and embodied throughout this text on a specific aspect of our passing game. Elementary as some of them might seem, we feel that these are things that must be taught and instilled at the most basic level to players for us to have the kind of consistent execution we want.

1. *Multiplicity.* All plays can be run out of different formations.
   How: Small building blocks that speak to specific players are taught that can be assembled and fashioned in different combinations.

2. *Route Adjustment.* Routes are run differently against different types of coverage.
   How: Receivers understand their overall purpose within a route, so therefore adjustments that help them achieve that purpose follow logically.

3. *Route Conversion.* Some routes are totally changed against some coverages (e.g., an Out that converts to a Fade vs. a hard corner).
    Why: Some cuts simply will not work against some coverages.
    How: Pre-snap coverage calls, receivers and quarterback read on the move.

4. *Route Exchange.* Routes are run by players relative to their positions within each formation, generally numbered from the outside in (#1, #2, #3) on either side of the ball.
    Why: Different formations and motions put players in different positions, and this flexibility is key to creating positive matchups and being able to present a multiple look while keeping learning simple.
    How: Players learn the entire route package for each position when it is initially installed.

5. *Route packages with different elements that can be emphasized in different situations.* Any of our route packages can be used in multiple situations with the idea that if the basic read priority of a package does not fit a particular down and distance situation, another element of the package can be emphasized that does.
    How: Adding to the end of any call the name of the cut that should be preferred by the quarterback.

6. *Built-in Constants.* There are certain things built into the pass offense that do not change:
    *   If the free safety leaves the middle of the field, someone will be assigned to replace him and go deep down the middle.
    *   Against Cover 2, we will generally work to get three people deep.
    *   We will never throw the ball in the deep middle if a free safety is there.
    *   Crossing receivers never look back to make eye contact with the quarterback until they have identified coverage and are ready for the football. Quarterbacks never deliver the ball to any type of crossing receiver until they make eye contact.
    *   Versus zone coverages, receivers are to find holes and settle between pass defenders. Quarterbacks are to throw the ball into these holes and not lead receivers through them.
    *   Versus man coverages, receivers always work for separation, accelerating away from pressure, using misdirection moves. Quarterbacks are to lead receivers and allow them to keep running away from the defender, maintaining the separation.
    *   The quarterback will have a stationary outlet on most plays who is responsible for getting open and communicating to the quarterback if he is, in fact open. He does so by making eye contact with the quarterback if he feels he is free. If the quarterback sees eye contact, he throws to the outlet immediately, knowing he's open. No eye contact, throw the ball away.

- The quarterback will have built in to each route package a receiver designated to be open quickly if defensive pressure arrives quickly. This receiver is designated as the 'Q' receiver.

7. *The quarterback never passes up an open receiver to wait for another to get open.*
- If there is a Flat route in the initial read and down and distance does not warrant otherwise, the quarterback must *hit the Flat fast* to maximize the run after catch. We must make the defense cover the flat area first.

8. *Scramble Rules.* In the event of a scramble, receivers have definite breakoff responsibilities predicated on the type of route they're running and where they are on the field at the time of the scramble. The quarterback will never throw back into the middle of the field late on a scramble.

9. *Run after Catch.* All people involved in the passing game must be aware that over 50% of the yards gained in the passing game come after the catch. Receivers will be trained where to go after the catch based on coverage, and quarterbacks will be trained to provide the specific types of throws that enables receivers to maximize their R.A.C. gains.

10. *Protection first.* Protection is always the first consideration in any pass we call. If there is any doubt on the part of the quarterback, he should check to the fullest protection option.
    - We will train our backs and linemen with the general idea that we always want to protect inside-out, securing the pass rush threats that have the shortest route to the passer first.

11. *Pre-snap disciplines.* All backs and receivers will go through a programmed, methodical routine before each snap related to their assignment and purpose andwhat the defense is doing and can do in front of them.
    - The quarterback will scan the entire defense from right to left initially, looking specifically at the front structure, and scan it again from left back to right, looking at coverage.
    - Receivers will execute a pre-snap scan and make a call identifying coverage before each snap.

12. *Throwing the ball away.* Quarterbacks are to never take a sack on first or second down.

Route Package Reference Tables

This appendix has been provided to give you quick reference to the assignments we give receivers within each of our route packages. It is designed to help your understanding of the material presented in the book, not to prescribe for you how you should set up your passing game. It is a good illustration, however, of a systematic structure for the passing game that we feel has enabled us to communicate and teach a multiple pass offense with ease and efficiency over a number of years.

The first section is illustrative of our basic "Read" route packages, which can be employed with most any protection or action in our offense. In this way, you can teach one system and one set of routes to use with all your pass actions, and not have to limit yourself to specific routes with specific types of drops. Each of these route packages is given both a number and a name, and each has a basic set of assignments associated with it for frontside receivers. Backside receivers have the same rule for all of these routes, except for special cases or tags that dictate otherwise. This structure provides us with the base from which we can easily tailor-make adjustments and variations without changing everything or starting from scratch from week to week.

The second section shows our "Quick" route packages, which is set up slightly differently. These routes are used only with two step or three step actions, and always with 90 or 190 protection. With "Quick" packages, frontside and backside receivers operate using the same sets of rules, but the rules can change depending on whether two or three receivers are on a side.

I. "Read" Route Packages
Used with 50/150, 70/170, 80/180, 200, and 300 protections

Route #	Route Name	QB Basic* Drop*	Frontside #1	Frontside #2	Frontside #3	Backside Adjustments**
1	Dig	7 controlled steps	Dig	Cross	Flare/Flat	#2 Under
2	Hinge	5 big steps	Hinge	Choice	Flag	
3	Curl	5 big steps	Curl	Flat	Middle Read	
4	Seam	5 big steps	Hinge	Seam	Flat	
5	Flood	5 big steps	Go	Sail	Flat	
6	Smash	5 big steps	Fin	Smash	Middle Read	
7	Mesh	5 quick steps	Whip Read	Smash	Flat	
8	Switch	5 big steps	Inside Vertical	Outside Vertical	Choice	
9	Go/Cross	5 big steps	Numbers Go	Hash Go	Backside Hash	Special rules***
0***	Over	5 big steps	Climb	Over	Shallow Cross	Go
0***	Triangle	5 quick steps	Fade	Whip	Option	

*   QB drop can be changed through a change in receiver priority, special tags, or a different protection dictating a different action.

**   Unless otherwise specified, a backside receiver will run a Post if he's the only receiver backside. If there are two backside, #1 runs a Dig, #2 a clearing Go route.

***   In an untagged 9 route, all receivers work toward specified landmarks based on 1-2-3-4 receiver numbering across the formation.

II. "Quick" Route Packages
Used with 90/190 protection only, Quarterback uses 2 or 3 step drop.
Backside and frontside receivers use same rules.

Route Name	3 receiver sides			2 receiver sets	
	#1	#2	#3	#1	#2
Hitch	Hitch	Seam	Get Open	Hitch	Seam
Quick Out	Qk. Out	Seam	Get Open	Qk. Out	Seam
Slant	Slant	Slant	Shoot	Slant	Shoot
Fade	Fade	Seam	6yd Out	Fade	6yd Out
In	In	Fade Pick	Split	In	Fade Pick
Wheel	Hitch	Slant	Split	—	—
Bench	Go	Shoot	Bench	Shoot	Bench

GLOSSARY

Glossary of Terms

Backside - Side of the field away from the play call. Most often, it is the side opposite the one to which the quarterback initially looks in his read, and generally it is synonymous with the weak side of the formation.

Banjo - Defensive technique in which defenders in man coverage exchange responsibilities based on the initial releases of the receivers; i.e., the inside most defender covers the receiver who releases furthest inside.

Barrier - Offensive technique in which an outside or middle receiver takes a wide angle of release to create a "barrier" for the defender over the receiver inside of him to run around.

Bumped Man Coverage -A man-to-man defense in which defenders switch assignments when a receiver motions based on the relative position of the receiver; i.e., the outside most defender changes responsibilities when a new receiver becomes the outside most receiver instead of "locking" on the receiver he originally lined up over.

Bracket- Refers to a situation in which two defenders are naturally able to double team a receiver inside and out because of having been released from other responsibilities.

Bubble - Refers to the impeded, roundabout path a defender has to take in running around traffic to cover his assigned receiver.

Bunch - Concept of pass offense that entails compressing receivers in close proximity of each other to create certain advantages in attacking defenses.

Burst - Action of a pass receiver who, just before making a final, shorter break, drops his head and drives his arms quickly to convince a defender that he intends to go deep, thereby driving the defender backwards and away from the receiver's final break.

Change - Offensive term used to tell #1 and #3 receiver to exchange normal route assignments and cross each other upon release.

Cloud - Defensive term used to designate that the cornerback rotates up and has responsibility for the flat area.

Cluster - Offensive term used to set a group of receivers in tight proximity of each other approximately 12 yards outside the offensive tackle.

Crazy - Motion term in which a player starts in motion one way, turns to fake running motion back the opposite way, and then turns again to his final motion in the direction he originally started.

Curl - Refers to a "Cut" or individual pattern executed by a receiver in which he drives upfield for 10-14 yards as though he's going deep, then makes a tight turn to the inside and tries to work to holes in the defense.

Cut - Refers to the route or pattern of an individual receiver.

Dig - Refers to a "Cut" or individual pattern executed by a receiver in which he releases 10-12 yards, drives toward the middle as if he is running a Post route, and then flattens his route across the field at a depth of 15-16 yards.

Double - Offensive term that designates that backside receivers mirror the assignments of their counterparts on the frontside.

Fade - Refers to a "Cut" in which a receiver sprints deep and outside to a landmark 6 yards from the sideline and 20-25 yards deep.

Fin - Refers to a "Cut" or individual pattern executed by a receiver in which he makes an initial, lazy outside break at 6 yards, and then works to get open underneath based on coverage.

Flag - Refers to a "Cut" or individual pattern executed by a receiver in which he makes an especially deep, angled outside break at 12 yards in an attempt to get over the top of a deep outside defender.

Flat - 1. Refers to the short, outside area of defensive coverage.

2. Refers to a "Cut" or individual pattern executed by a receiver in which he works upfield 4-5 yards before breaking "Flat" into the short, outside area of a defense.

Free - Designation given a pure man-to-man coverage scheme with a free safety responsible for the deep middle $1/_3$ of the field.

Frontside - Side of the field, as designated by the play call, given as a reference point to determine route assignments and direct protection. Most often, it is the side to which the quarterback initially looks in his read, and generally it is synonymous with the strong side of the formation.

Hard Corner - Term used to describe a defensive cornerback who aligns and/or plays closer than six yards from the receiver he's over.

Hash Player or Hash Safety - Term used to refer to a defender who often aligns on the hashmark and is responsible for a deep $1/_2$ of the field, generally in a 2-deep defensive scheme.

Hi - 1. Offensive term for a crossing receiver telling him to cross over the top of another crosser.

2. Route package designation changing the receiver is who is "lo."

High-Low - A type of read in which a certain defender is isolated against a short receiver and a deeper receiver. If the defender works for depth, the quarterback throws to the shorter of the two receivers; if he doesn't he throws to the deeper receiver.

Hinge - Refers to a "Cut" or individual pattern executed by a receiver in which he drives at the defender for 13-15 yards, trying to threaten him deep, and them opens to the inside, accelerating back toward the quarterback and outside. A variation of the traditional "Comeback" pattern.

Hitch - Refers to a "Cut" or individual pattern executed by a receiver in which he drives straight at the defender over him for 5-6 yards stops, turning to the inside.

Idiot - Refers to a type of receiver motion in which he sprints hard in motion one direction, passing the center, and then returns in motion the other direction before the snap.

Landmark - A specific spot on the field which to a receiver is to run his route.

Lanes - Refers to a goalline coverage technique similar to a Banjo in which defenders cover vertical lanes of the field, using man-to-man techniques within those lanes, switching receivers when a receiver leaves their lane.

Late - Adjustment to a Flat cut that tells a receiver to hesitate $1\frac{1}{2}$ counts before running his pattern.

Lo - 1. Offensive term for a crossing receiver telling him to cross beneath another crosser.

2. Route package designation changing the receiver who is "lo."

Locked Man Coverage - Form of man-to-man coverage in which defenders remain assigned to whichever receiver they aligned on initially, regardless of offensive motion or alignment change.

Marker - An individual cut in which a receiver pushes to the deep corner of the end zone, plants, and accelerates toward the front corner, or "Marker" of the end zone.

Match - Coverage term that designates that a defense is going to use pattern-read principles and play man-to-man techniques within a zone.

Mesh - 1. A specific route package, i.e. the "7" route, in our offense.

2. Can also refer to the point at which two receivers cross closely.

Middle Read - An individual cut by a receiver in which he releases 10 to 12 yards and hooks, crosses, or splits the deep middle depending on coverage.

Misdirection Route - A type of individual cut in which a player releases and fakes as though he is running a certain route, and then breaks opposite that route.

Near-stack - Refers to a bunched alignment that, through a receiver's motion into it, has become almost indistinguishable at the snap in terms of who the outside, inside and middle receivers in the alignment are.

Nod - A brief change of direction by a receiver designed to gain separation from a defender; it is done without losing speed.

Option-style Route - Any of a series of individual cuts which have designated that the receiver has his choice of paths based on the reaction of the defense. Most often, these types of routes are at a depth of eight yards or less.

Outlet - Refers to a receiver to whom the quarterback can go if his initial reads do not get open; often this is a stationary receiver, preferably coming into as opposed to going away from the passer's line of vision. Generally it is this man's responsibility to determine whether he is open and communicate this to the quarterback.

Packaged Side - Side of a route that has been set up or tagged to attack a specific defense.

Pattern -An overall distribution of individual cuts designed to work together in attacking defenses.

Pattern Read - Defensive technique in which zone defenders react specific ways to specific releases and routes by the offense, often employing man-to-man principles within a zone instead of just dropping to pre-determined spots on the field.

Phony Acceleration - Technique by a receiver in which he uses exaggerated arm drive to convince a defender that he is gaining speed when he's not.

Post - Refers to a "Cut" or individual pattern executed by a receiver in which he releases for 11 to 13 yards and makes a deep, angled break toward the middle of the field, attempting to get open in the deep middle portion of the defense.

Q - Designates a receiver within a route package who is a quick-developing option for the quarterback should he get immediate pressure from a pass rush.

R.A.C. - Refers to a receiver's yardage or opportunities to make yardage on the Run After the Catch.

Red Zone - Term used to describe the area of the field from the defense's 25 yard line to the defense's goal line.

Robber - Refers to a coverage technique in which a player (usually a safety) who is expected to be in deep coverage moves to a short or intermediate area late in an attempt to disrupt normal offensive reads and "rob" certain pass routes.

Route - Refers to either an individual route by a receiver, or a series of routes within a package that work together.

Route Package - An overall passing attack concept that begins with a basic distribution of routes and can be varied by tags. In our system, packages are generally numbered 1-9 (e.g., "Mesh" package is "7").

Rub - Offensive term used to describe two receivers running routes in close proximity of each other in hopes of defenders colliding or being otherwise impeded.

Safety Slot Zone - Defensive adjustment in which flat area defender exchanges responsibilities with second short zone defender upon the snap of the ball.

Shallow Cross - Refers to a "Cut" or individual pattern executed by a receiver in which he crosses underneath the coverage at a depth of five to six yards and makes adjustments based on coverage.

Shoot - Refers to a "Cut" or individual pattern executed by a receiver in which he sprints to the flat area at a depth of two to three yards.

Six Second Rule - Pre-snap discipline used by receivers in which they go through a specific mental checklist between the break of the huddle and the snap to get properly aligned, recognize coverage, and properly prepare mentally for the upcoming play.

Skinny - Descriptive technique term used to tell a inside-breaking receiver not to bring his route very far into the interior area of the defense; a "skinny" angle would be 60-70 degrees as opposed to 45 degrees.

Sky - Defensive term used to designate that the strong safety rotates up and has responsibility for the flat area.

Slant - Refers to a "Cut" or individual pattern executed by a receiver in which he pushes up the field for five to six yards before making a distinct, angled break in.

Slot - Offensive designation that puts the "H" receiver just inside the "Y" receiver, who has split out.

Smash - 1. Refers to a "Cut" or individual pattern executed by a receiver in which he releases for 10-12 yards and makes some kind of break to the corner of the field based on coverage.

2. Offensive term used to describe the "6" route package in which the #3 receiver is assigned a "Middle Read", #2 a "Smash", and #1 a "Fin".

Snug - Offensive term used to set a group of receivers in tight proximity of each other approximately 8 yards outside the offensive tackle.

Soft Corner - Term used to describe a defensive cornerback who aligns and/or plays deeper than six yards from the receiver he's over.

Speed Out - Refers to a timed "Cut" or individual pattern executed by a receiver in which he releases for 10 yards, executes a rolling, full-speed break outside and flattens his course at a depth of 12 yards, looking for the ball.

Split - 1. The distance a wide receiver aligns outside of the offensive tackle or tight end on his side.

2. An offensive term used to designate that both backs (H and F) align between the offensive guard and tackle to their designated side at a depth of four to five yards behind the center.

3. Specific pass route in which a receiver is told to "split" the defense and get open anywhere beyond 20 yards deep on the other side of the guard on his side.

Squeeze - Offensive term used to set a group of receivers in tight proximity of each other approximately 4-5 yards outside the offensive tackle.

Stacked Releases - Release technique within the Bunch principle in which receivers release in a particular order in as close a horizontal proximity as possible—for a moment nearly one behind another—to confuse defensive recognition and coverage.

Stem - 1. Refers to the initial upfield release of a receiver before he makes his break; he should be trained to make this portion of the route look identical every time.

2. A specific, Curl-type route given to an inside receiver in which he executes an outside weave before making his inside, hooking break.

Swap - Offensive term telling frontside and backside #1 receivers to trade route assignments.

Switch - 1. An exchange of assignments by pass defenders when offensive receivers cross, often within a "Banjo" technique.

2. Offensive term used to tell #2 and #3 receivers to trade route assignments.

3. Offensive term used to describe a route in which two vertical receivers exchange route paths using crossed releases.

Tag - Word or words added to the end of a play call to change one or more people's routes within a route package.

Trail Technique - Technique used by man-to-man defenders in which they play tightly inside the receiver, "trailing" him by one half to one full step wherever he breaks.

Trail-type route - A type of individual cut designed to get into an area vacated by defenders who chased receivers who ran through the same area earlier in the play.

Triangle - 1. A defensive technique played by three players in which the outside defender has the first receiver to release outside, the middle defender has the first receiver to release deep, and the inside defender has the first receiver to release inside.

2. A type of route design in which three receivers' patterns are spaced so that they form a "triangle" that is difficult to defend.

3. A specific route package used in our system, described in Chapter 10.

Trips - Any formation with three receivers on a side.

Turn - Refers to a "Cut" or individual pattern executed by an inside receiver in which he releases upfield for 10-12 yards and then breaks outside, accelerating away from man coverage, or "turning" into the first available hole in a zone coverage.

Twist - Offensive term that tells the #2 and #3 receivers that they are to cross each other's releases, after which they execute their normal assignments.

Under - Tag given to a backside receiver telling him to run a Shallow Cross pattern.

Weave - Refers to the initial angle of release taken by a receiver.

Whip Read - Route in which a receiver angles inside as if he is going to cross at a depth of 5 to 6 yards, then spins back and runs the opposite way with certain adjustments against various types of coverage.

Wrap - Offensive term that tells the #1 and #2 receiver that they are to cross each other's initial release and change normal assignments.

About the Authors

Andrew Coverdale

Andrew Coverdale joined Taylor University staff as quarterbacks and tight end coach this past spring after three years' coaching at the high school level. While at Northwestern High School in Kokomo, Indiana in 1994, he was promoted to Offensive Coordinator and gave clinic presentations on Tigers' "Bunch" passing game, and has also been published on the same topic in the coaches' association's quarterly manual. In his first year at Noblesville High School in 1995, a receiver under his direction earned AAAAA all-state honors and set a school record for receptions. Coverdale has also worked as a receiver instructor at the Bishop-Dullaghan Passing Clinic in Franklin, IN. He is a member of both the Indiana and American Football Coaches' Associations.

Dan Robinson

Dan Robinson will begin his 2nd season as Offensive Coordinator at Taylor University this fall, after being a high school head coach for 13 years at Northwestern High School. Prior to assuming his duties at Northwestern, he was Offensive Coordinator at East Central High School for 9 years. During his tenure at Northwestern, the Tigers became known for their pro passing attack and explosive offense, which helped produce two undefeated regular seasons, 4 Mid Indiana Conference titles, two sectional championships, and a trip to the Indiana AAA State Championship Game. The Tigers were among the state's top ten passing teams several times in his tenure, leading the state in 1983. Six quarterbacks under Coach Robinson's tutelage earned all-state honors. He has worked various summer camps for many years, including the Bishop-Dullaghan Passing Clinic, where he wrote the camp's Receiver Manual. He also lectured at clinics throughout Indiana on Northwestern's offense, and published several articles on different aspects of the Tiger attack. Robinson is a member of the IFCA and AFCA.

ADDITIONAL FOOTBALL RESOURCES FROM

■ *COACHING LINEBACKERS*
by Jerry Sandusky and Cedric Byrant
1995 ▪Paper▪ 136 pp
ISBN 1-5716-059-9 ▪ $15.00

■ *COACHING OFFENSIVE BACKS*
by Steve Axman
1996 ▪Paper▪ 230 pp
ISBN 1-57167-088-2 ▪ $19.00

■ *DEVELOPING AN OFFENSIVE GAME PLAN*
by Brian Billick
1996 ▪Paper▪ 102 pp
ISBN 1-57167-046-7 ▪ $15.00

■ *101 DEFENSIVE FOOTBALL DRILLS*
(3 VOLUMES)
by Bill Arnsparger and James A. Peterson
1996 ▪Paper▪ 128 pp▪ $15.00 each
Vol #1, ISBN 1-57167-084-x
Vol #2, ISBN 1-57167-085-8
Vol #3, ISBN 1-57167-086-6